A Compact Study of Numbers

A Compact Study of Numbers

William T. Miller

WIPF & STOCK · Eugene, Oregon

A COMPACT STUDY OF NUMBERS

Copyright © 2013 William T. Miller. All rights reserved. Except for brief quotations in critical publications or reviews, no part of this book may be reproduced in any manner without prior written permission from the publisher. Write: Permissions, Wipf and Stock Publishers, 199 W. 8th Ave., Suite 3, Eugene, OR 97401.

Wipf & Stock
An Imprint of Wipf and Stock Publishers
199 W. 8th Ave., Suite 3
Eugene, OR 97401

www.wipfandstock.com

ISBN 13: 978-1-62032-770-8

Manufactured in the U.S.A.

Unless otherwise indicated, all biblical quotations are taken from the New Revised Standard Version Bible, copyright © 1989, Division of Christian Education of the National Council of the Churches of Christ in the United States of America. Used by permission. All rights reserved.

For three close friends:
Owen Cummings, professor, deacon, author; Myles McDonald, whose life can be summed up in one word—caregiver; and my nephew, Christopher Kyriakakos, now entering the medical profession.

Contents

General Introduction to Numbers   ix
Instructions for Study Groups   xv

Numbers 1:1—10:28

Section One: 1:1–54   3
Section Two: 2:1–34   7
Section Three: 3:1–51   9
Section Four: 4:1–18   13
Section Five: 5:1–31   20
Section Six: 6:1–21   25
Section Seven: 6:22—8:4   29
Section Eight: 8:5–26   34
Section Nine: 9:1—10:28   41

Numbers 10:29—21:35

Section Ten: 10:29—11:35   47
Section Eleven: 12:1–16   54
Section Twelve: 13:1—14:45   59
Section Thirteen: 15:1–41   67
Section Fourteen: 16:1—17:13   72
Section Fifteen: 18:1–32   80
Section Sixteen: 19:1–22   85
Section Seventeen: 20:1–22   90
Section Eighteen: 21:1–35   95

Numbers 22:1—24:25

Section Nineteen: 22:1–41   105
Section Twenty: 23:1–30   109
Section Twenty-One: 24:1–25   114
Review of the Balaam Traditions   118

Contents

Numbers 25:1—36:13

Section Twenty-Two: 25:1–18   127
Section Twenty-Three: 26:1–65   132
Section Twenty-Four: 27:1–23   138
Section Twenty-Five: 28:1—29:40   142
Section Twenty-Six: 30:1–16   153
Section Twenty-Seven: 31:1–54   157
Section Twenty-Eight: 32:1–42   162
Section Twenty-Nine: 33:1–56   170
Section Thirty: 34:1–29   173
Section Thirty-One: 35:1–34   176
Section Thirty-Two: 36:1–13   182
Author's Retrospective of Numbers   186

Answers   193

Bibliography   239

General Introduction to Numbers

In this study guide I will focus on the book of Numbers. Numbers continues the narrative from Exodus about the spiritual and physical travails of the forty years in the wilderness. The book also profiles many tribal and liturgical structures of these pioneers that seem to contribute to their stability. Some of these structures might be idealistic or anachronistic by our standards, but the faith behind the accounts must be taken seriously.

Of course Numbers builds upon the foundations of Genesis and Exodus. For many of the details in the book of Numbers I rely on Baruch A. Levine's two volumes on *Numbers* in the Anchor Bible commentary series. Levine sheds light on what otherwise would have been numbing cascades of details of long discontinued ordination and worship ceremonies, fragmentary areas of jurisprudence, archaeology, geography, and history. It is an honor to try to make some of his insights more available, especially to average Christian readers. Since I do make extensive use of Levine's insights, mainly in summary or in paraphrase and in individual verses, I am grateful to Yale University Press, the current owner of the Anchor Bible series, for permission to use Levine's work in this way specifically for this study guide. I am, of course, responsible for any mistakes in presentation.

Most Bible study group members or individual readers probably began their Old Testament studies with Genesis or Exodus or perhaps one of the prophets. With the guidance of a commentary or two, it is relatively easy to get a sense of the flow and inner structure of some biblical books.

To study Numbers one may need more assistance, since there isn't as much support for modern readers forthcoming from the authors and editors of this story of the wandering in the wilderness. The authors project back to the time of Moses as many things as possible. The people all march and share duties by tribes and clans; dozens of liturgical regulations are itemized, as well as property rights and some basics of criminal law. The different sacramental and ceremonial duties of priests and Levites are carefully defined. We are told of some battles won and lost, and of several incidents where the people rebel against Moses and God. God himself gets upset at times and hurls down stern punishments. Amidst all this, the pagan prophet Balaam speaks in majestic tones of the high religious destiny of the LORD's chosen people.

The overall effect of the book is to credit God (working with Moses, the lawgiver) for as much guidance as possible as far back as possible. God remains the source of Israel's national and religious identity. This occurs despite vivid incidents of discontent and rebellion by God's own people.

One could divide the book into four or five blocks, using simple modern patterns of analysis. 1:1—10:10 provides a large amount of basic information: camping and marching systems, the ordination ceremonies and subordinate duties of Levites, Nazirite vows, review of Passover rules, and so on. At 10:11 the people begin the journey from Mt. Sinai (about eleven months after arriving there in Exod 19:1, and about nineteen days after the events of Num 1:1). From this point in chapter 10 to the end of chapter 21 the main focus is on the many travails of the journey: the people complain about the food provided, Aaron and Miriam challenge Moses' sole authority, some Levites rebel at their subordinate status, many disagree about going to war, and so on. The oracles by Balaam (chs. 22–24) provide welcome relief from all the wrangling. Finally, in chapters 25–36, we return to a block of information and events that is less dominated by travails. Yet along with the mention of the annual major holydays, the agreement for some tribes to live across the Jordan, and other matters of vows and property rights, the great idolatry of chapter 25 and the gruesome war of chapter 31 are sobering accounts for the modern reader.

Levine sees a natural break in the book at the end of chapter 20, with the deaths of Miriam and Aaron and the start of important battles to the north.

Another way of reacting to this book is to see it as a combination of events that continue the storyline begun in Exodus (e.g., the need for manna, Aaron and Miriam rebelling, the episodes of spying out the land of Canaan), along with timeless regulations (e.g., ch. 6, Nazirite vows; ch. 19, red heifer sacrifice; chs. 28–29, the liturgical calendar). Admittedly, many chapters seem of little use now (censuses, lists of donations, support systems for priests and Levites). Such a quick form of triage by chapters may simply reflect our own impatience, and could lead us to miss some worthwhile insights of the biblical authors and editors. Let us just take the chapters in order.

I have divided the thirty-six chapters of Numbers into thirty-two Sections of varying length. Each section starts with an Introduction, containing basic information that might be useful to have at the start of each assignment. Composing these introductions is more of an art than a science; there is always the danger of overloading the reader with too much information too soon. I have an interest in mentioning specific biblical Hebrew vocabulary, at times with cross references. Pease do not let these notes slow you down. Biblical Hebrew is quite different from English, and uses fewer synonyms. I hope any reader who knows the language will allow for my oversimplification in transcribing Hebrew words into English letters.

The heart of this study guide is found in the Questions at the end of each Section. These should be studied and answered by individuals or members of a group before referencing the Answers section at the back of the book. Some of the answers are quite long, while others are brief. They all should help bring everyone closer to the text itself, rather than just keeping one awash in commentary. About two-thirds of the sections will end with a Conclusion. This is the place to tie up loose ends, or to note larger theological topics.

The plan is that working steadily through each Section will contribute to a cohesive guided tour or virtual classroom experience. I hope that my own interest in providing so much information for general readers does not prove daunting or counterproductive. Readers should provisionally scan anything too technical (except for the Questions), so as not to lose a sense of progress through the book.

The book of Numbers furthers the narrative of Exodus and precedes the complex retelling and continuation of the narrative in Deuteronomy. In some ways Numbers paints the darkest parts of the picture: the frustrations with Moses' leadership (and God's by implication), the anger over limitations of food and water, the cumulative stress of the years of marching, and the lures of idolatry. These darker events are interwoven with serene descriptions of priestly duties and the yearly liturgical feasts. Beginners might not be aware of the hundreds of significant cross references in Exodus, Leviticus, Deuteronomy, Joshua, Judges, 1–2 Samuel,

General Introduction to Numbers

etc., but we will note some of these as we go along. The book of Numbers does not stand alone; its traditions cover many centuries and find their counterparts in the historical books and even in the prophets.

Beginners need to be aware of some of the research about the complex editorial layers within the different books of the Pentateuch. Theories about the main editorial layers are still useful, although scholars are more careful now about absolute claims for these working models.

One can still look for the Yahwist (J) and Elohist (E) layers, generally taken as older traditions from the Southern and Northern Kingdoms respectively. Many commentators simply refer to a combined JE level, without trying to isolate E verses by themselves. In his two Anchor Bible volumes on Exodus, William Propp argues for many E passages in that book. In Numbers the JE passages carry much of the narrative and dramatize the struggles, the dark pictures mentioned above. Baruch Levine, the scholar upon whom I rely for much in this profile of Numbers, considers the Balaam Cycle (chs. 22–24) and parts of chapter 21 to be a special collection of Transjordanian Jewish traditions, and groups it with the E traditions.

The Deuteronomist level (D) enriched not only the Pentateuch but also the historical and prophetic books. Some Deuteronomic theology is clearly pre-exilic. Their focus is on sin and repentance, law, covenant, and land. They are in agreement with David's establishment of the temple in Jerusalem as the primary official shrine for the whole nation, and they argue that this was the plan from the time of Moses.

Priestly traditions (P) probably were assembled during and after the exile. Priestly traditions in Exodus (chs. 15–17, 24–31, 35–40) fit in very well with the bulk of Priestly concerns in Numbers. These Priestly traditions and layers of editing focus on the corporate dimensions of God's relationship to the whole world and to the nation of Israel. They also preserve details of genealogies, censuses, itineraries, and liturgical directives. They made efforts to arrange traditions in chronological order, although they did not have all the evidence needed to be completely successful in this.

Scholars are more cautious now in picturing Priestly editors as always being the final editors of our biblical books. Sometimes the final editors are simply unknown to us.

There are two items in Numbers that I think I should mention here, just to show that we need to take each chapter on its own literary merit.

General Introduction to Numbers

First, while Numbers tells us much about the subordinate status of Levites as assistants to the priests of Aaron's line, older traditions in Exodus, Leviticus, and Deuteronomy consider all Levites as priests. There is no way to reconcile this disparity, except to assume that the subordinate status of Levites as priestly assistants must have taken time to develop.

Second, as Levine carefully demonstrates, the various traditions in Numbers do not agree on all the details of how and where the people spent the majority of the forty years wandering in the wilderness. In the JE tradition in Num 13, Moses sent scouts to find out more about the land of Canaan, and after forty days the scouts returned to Moses and the people at Kadesh (13:26), which readers would assume was where the scouting mission began (see Num 32:8). As a result of rebellion after the scouting mission, God sentenced the people to wander for forty years, until the older generation passed away. Num 21:4–12 covers most of that period of wandering. The account by Moses in Deut 2:13–15 also notes that the wandering lasted thirty-eight years after the rebellion at Kadesh, thus agreeing with the JE tradition in Numbers that the arrival at Kadesh came relatively early after the exodus from Egypt. Deut 2:1–16 is another passage that covers the thirty-eight years, and it simply focuses on the very last steps before the people came to cross the Jordan.

By contrast, the P tradition in Numbers is that most of the forty years was spent in southern regions closer to Sinai. Priestly writers used unusual detours and broader geographic terms such as the *wilderness of Sinai* or the *wilderness of Paran* (to the north). They put Kadesh within the wilderness of Paran (13:26), when Kadesh was actually much further north.

In both JE and P traditions Num 21:4–12 represents most of that thirty-eight years of wandering, regardless of where and when it took place. This passage is as brief and unenlightening for us as the few verses in Deut 2:1–16. As with the status of the Levites, there is no way to reconcile this disparity about where the many years of wandering actually took place. Later editors of Numbers tried to save as many traditions as they could, even when they were contradictory or unclear.

But we cannot allow our penchant for accurate detail to distract us from what the book of Numbers does achieve. The JE traditions, enriched by the Balaam oracles, describe real crises of faith, and may well explain ethnic tensions with Israel's neighbors closer to the time of the writers than to the time of Moses.

The Priestly traditions describe laws and worship ceremonies as gifts from God himself, gifts that still make sense even though neither Jews nor Christians sacrifice animals or birds or grain. In the P tradition, having the majority of the forty years spent closer to Sinai enhances the religious content of the period of the exodus and the wilderness. It might also have helped to downplay the era of Transjordanian settlements; those conquests to the east of the Jordan were not an important topic for Priestly writers.

Instructions for Study Groups

1. This book is designed for individuals or study groups, more than for students in a traditional classroom. Students in class can rely on the teacher for explanations, assignments, and instructions. Individuals or groups have to shepherd themselves along. Groups have to decide many practical details—when, where, and how often to meet, which members can lead in prayer, in providing refreshments, and in keeping the meeting place free of distractions. Experience suggests that groups should have about eight members; they should be willing to read some texts aloud, pray in common, and suggest ways to apply Scripture to daily life.

2. A group leader will have to read far enough ahead in this study guide to estimate how many biblical chapters can best be covered during each meeting. The leader should not tip everyone off about the answers beforehand.

3. The Answers in this book should be examined for the first time at the group meeting, after everyone has shared their own answers (the leader holding back). Those who tend to be shy about speaking should be given a second personal invitation to participate before the group moves on. Should some answers or lines of analysis seem unsettling or untraditional, it may be best to revisit these at the start of the next session, after everyone has had time to think them over.

4. It will be easier for individuals or for a whole group to use a clear academic biblical translation, such as the New Revised Standard Version (NRSV). The NRSV is used in this study guide except where I mention other translations or provide one of my own for a specific verse or phrase. Some English versions of the Bible intended for a wider audience contain too many paraphrases to be useful in this task.

Numbers 1:1—10:28

Section One

NUMBERS 1:1–54

Introduction

The first four chapters of Numbers present Priestly traditions of the Israelites in the desert as a tribal alliance of troops on the march; there is little mention of their families, livestock, daily chores, and the like. God begins by ordering the census of men of military age. The date in Num 1:1 is a month after the dedication of the tabernacle in Exod 40:17. Let us assume that the intervening body of laws in Leviticus does not affect the time line of the main story of the journey in the desert.

We can subdivide this chapter into three parts (following Levine, *Numbers*, 1:125)

Num 1:1–19	Census procedures, including the twelve tribal leaders
Num 1:20–47	Census data; the final total is close to that in Exod 12:37
Num 1:48–54	Levites not being counted, because of their role

In both Num 1:1 and 1:19 we are reminded that these things occurred in the *wilderness of Sinai*. God speaks to Moses at the *tent of meeting* (*ohel moed*). This is usually equated with the tabernacle, the movable large shrine, but it originally meant the smaller prayer tent found in Exod 33:6–11. There is an echo of this older tent in Num 7:89. Generally, Priestly editors combined terms and images like this to show the continuity in God's purposes and self-revelation.

In Num 1:2 we find another common Priestly word, *adah* (*congregation*). Some translators prefer to use the word *community*. The word for *clan* (*mispah*) represents extended family, including cousins. The phrase for *ancestral house* (*house of the fathers*) seems to refer to something larger than a clan but less numerous than a tribe. Priestly editors favored the word *matteh* for tribe, rather than the more common word, *sebet*. At times the mention of a clan can represent a whole tribe, or even all of Israel (see Jer 8:3; Amos 3:1).

Another term for a leader, *head*, appears in 1:4. In 1:16 these heads are called *nasi* (*leaders* or *princes*) of their tribes. In 7:2 both words, *princes* and *heads*, are used in the plural to refer to the same group. In 3:32 Aaron's son Eleazar will be called *the prince of the princes* of Levi. Levine suggests that these examples imply that a tribe could have more than one highly placed leader at a time. As time went by tribes broke into more and more subdivisions because of population growth. This growth is assumed in the story of Abraham in Gen 15:16, where God speaks of the fourth generation after Moses returning to the Promised Land.

In 1:3 Moses and Aaron *enroll* (*pqd*) the men. The verb in Hebrew can mean *to count*, but also *to assign* to duties. Thus in 1:50, "you shall *appoint* [*hpqd*] the Levites." Levine prefers the word *muster*, which combines both meanings in English. In 1:49 the Levites are not to be *enrolled* (*tpqd*), a play on the use of the same verb.

In Num 1:10 Joseph's two sons, Ephraim and Manasseh, count as separate tribes, thus keeping the number at twelve without the tribe of Levi (see Gen 48:5).

In Num 1:3 and several more times in this chapter, the phrase *to go to war* uses the noun *sba*, which really means *service* (or *warriors*). Related forms in Exod 38:8 and 1 Sam 2:22 refer to women sanctuary workers, and in Num 4:23 and 8:24 combinations of the verb and noun refer to Levites performing cultic service. The plural of the noun, *sabaoth*, also found in Num 1:3 and 1:52, refers to the *companies* or *divisions* of the soldiers, and is used in Exod 6:26; 12:41, 51 in the same way. In many places in the Bible the term *Yahweh sabaoth* is a title—*Lord of hosts* (*hosts* perhaps meaning angelic armies rather than human armies).

The late Hebrew word *degel* is used in 1:52. The word has traditionally been taken as meaning *banner* or *standard*, hence in context *tribal subdivision*. Here the NRSV paraphrases it as *regimental camp*. Levine argues that the word is so late that we should take it in the Persian meaning of a *fighting force*. Persian references using this word often indicate stationary border fortress patrols, who would have been able to have their families with them.

Most of the leaders of the census are known only from this list. The names are common enough that they do not by themselves prove their antiquity. In 1:16 the word for *divisions* (*alpi*) has traditionally been related to the Hebrew word for *thousands*. Levine argues against this derivation, and suggests that it is instead a very generic term for troop strength.

All the census numbers are multiples of 6. In Exod 12:37 and Num 11:21 the total is simply 600,000.

In 1:50 there is reference to the *tabernacle of the covenant* (*mishkan haedut*). The word *edut* means *reminder* or *relic*; other translations use *witness* or *testimony*.

We do not know what exactly was preserved within the ark itself, but those objects did serve as the main memorial of the great event at Sinai. The objects in the ark would have been left undisturbed, and not used as master documents for research or legislation.

In the same v. 50 the Levites are to *tend* (*shrt*) the tabernacle. The same verb is found in 3:6; 8:26; 16:9; 18:2. It's primary meaning is of *assisting* at religious rites, but not of *officiating* at them.

The reference to the death penalty in 1:51 may sound harsh; it refers to any unauthorized Israelite or non-Israelite. In 1:53 the *wrath* spoken of would be divine wrath. Both warnings are ways of emphasizing the gravity associated with places of worship. Similar warnings of death were found in Exod 19, as God prepared to come close to his people on Mt. Sinai.

1:53 refers to the Levites *performing guard duty* (*shmr mshmrt*). While that is a valid translation of the verb and noun in some instances, such as Exod 12:16; 16:23–24; 2 Kgs 11:5–7, in other contexts it refers more broadly to duties or service in general (see Lev 8:35; Num 3:28–32; 8:6; 18:3, 7). In Num 18:8 it seems to mean *control* or *jurisdiction*.

Questions

1. Numbers begins just one month after Exod 40:16–34, when Moses set up the tabernacle and the LORD blessed it with his presence. Judging just from Num 1:1–19, how are the authors depicting these same people of the exodus, who met God at Sinai

(Exod 19–24), who failed so quickly (Exod 32), and upon whom God showed great mercy (Exod 33–34)?

2. Could there have been additional advantages to taking this census, other than as a system for having the larger and smaller tribes share military duties equitably?

3. In Num 1:47–59 the men of the tribe of Levi have special duties and are excused from the military census. In this one paragraph, what duties are set down for them?

Section Two

NUMBERS 2:1–34

Introduction

The focus on camping and marching in this chapter was initiated in 1:50–53, with its many references to the Levites camping near the tabernacle, and striking and pitching it again when it is being moved. One word for *camping* and *pitching*, *hnh*, is used five times in those four verses.

The late Priestly word *degel*, for *ensigns* in 2:2, was also used in 1:52, there translated as part of the idiomatic phrase for *regimental camps* (literally, *each one with his own tent and each with his own banner*). This same word *degel* can be found in 2:3, 10, 17, 18, 25, 31, 34. The Priestly style can be ponderous at times; in 2:17 perhaps the intention was to strike a note of solemnity, but the overuse of so many words and phrases can be dull.

Levine's preference to take the word *degel* in its Persian sense to mean a fighting force leads him to assume that Priestly editors of that period (fifth century BCE) added this word to their vocabulary to be up to date, and to imply that ancient Israelite tribes had the same system of military organization. We could look on this as a deliberate anachronism.

Each group of three tribes is described as *setting out* (*nsy*) in a strict order. The verb is used in 2:9, 16, 17 (twice), 24, 31, 34. In 2:34 the parallel *so they camped . . . so they set out* can certainly complete the overall impression that the camping and setting out is being thought of as a military procedure.

NUMBERS 1:1—10:28

Question

4. What sort of map or floor plan could you draw, using the instructions of Num 2?

Section Three

NUMBERS 3:1–51

Introduction

In Num 3 Aaron and his descendents are identified as priests (3:1–4, 6, 10, 38, 48, 51). The link between Aaron and the tribe of Levi is the Kohathite clan and Amram (3:19), who was the father of Moses and Aaron, according to Exod 6:20. Aaron functioned as the first priest during the Exodus stories, and the first ordination account is found in Exod 28:1–5 and in all of Exod 29.

This chapter has several subdivisions (Levine, 1:154–62):

Num 3:1–4	Mention of Aaron's sons
Num 3:5–10	Aaron's line will be priests; the rest of the tribe of Levi (Levites) will assist
Num 3:11–13	These Levites will represent Jewish firstborn males (8:16–19)
Num 3:14–37	Census of all Levites by clans, including their several specific ceremonial duties and camping order in the inner square around the tabernacle
Num 3:38–39	Priests camp on the east side, closest to the tabernacle entrance
Num 3:40–43	Census of all Israelite firstborn males
Num 3:44–51	Extra numbers of firstborn, above the number of Levites, need to pay a special redemption tax to the priests

Several words in 3:3 refer to priests alone. *Cohen*, the participial form, and *chn*, the verb, refer to this office. (Even today among Jewish people the last name Cohen [with many variant spellings] is assumed to indicate priestly lineage. The custom of noting this name now is honorary, since there are no longer any temple duties to perform.) The priests are identified as *anointed* (*mshh*), the same term forming the basis for the word *messiah* in later theology. In Lev 8 and 21:10–15 only the high priest seems to get anointed, but in other places (Exod 30:22–23; 40:1–38; Lev 7:34–38) the anointing is for all priests.

Aaron's actual act of ordaining his sons is that *he filled their hands to act as priests*. The image of *filling hands* may mean putting some of the sacred objects into the hands of priests at the time of ordination. One small example of this is found in Lev 8:27–29.

In 3:4 mention is made of the striking deaths of two of Aaron's sons, Nadab and Abihu, who had committed sacrilege earlier. The account is in Lev 10:1–7.

In 3:6 the other Levites will *assist* (*shrt*) Aaron and his sons. The verb *shmr* and related noun *mshmrt*, found in 3:7, 8, 38 and elsewhere, refers to *duties* or *tasks* in general, not simply guard duty, as was explained above regarding 1:53. Another verb (*ybd*) and noun (*ybdt*) pair in Num 3:7–8 is even more general; they are *to do* whatever needs *to be done*. The Hebrew word for *give* (*ntn*) is used three times in 3:9; the last phrase, literally *given, given they are*, is translated *they are unreservedly given* in the NSRV. This firmly emphasizes the subordinate rank of the Levites.

The word *consecrated* in 3:13 is from *qdsh*, a very broad verb that can indicate divine approval or special designation.

The number 8,600 in 3:28 is an error; it should read 8,300, as in some ancient manuscripts. In 3:31 *the priests minister* (*shrt*) using the vessels; the Hebrew simply has *they minister*, but we take this to refer to the priests in context.

In 3:32 Eleazar the priest is also *the prince of the princes* of the Levites. This is another way to emphasize priestly high rank.

The word for *redeeming* and *redemption* in the last several verses of Num 3 is from *pdh*, and is the standard word for such financial dealings. The context does not have to do with sin or forgiveness. Levine considers the references to firstborn cattle in Num 3:41, 45 as interpolations not otherwise developed here.

There are brief references to redeeming firstborn animals and humans in Exod 13:1–2, 11–16; 22:29–30; 34:19–20. The custom of offering firstfruits and firstling animals in worship was common in the ancient Near East, and in nomadic cultures the oldest son usually (but not automatically) inherited leadership and elementary priestly roles. In Exodus the logic calls for substitute sacrifices for the firstborn of humans and for those of unclean animals such as donkeys. Scholars dispute the actual practice of these customs. They note Lev 27:27 along with Num 3:47–51, where small fees can replace substitute sacrifices, and Num 18:15–16, where killing a firstborn unclean animal is not even considered. It seems consecrating or dedicating firstborn males often involved blessings, prayers, and small donations rather than sacrifices.

In discussing the logic of offering firstborn animals and dedicating firstborn humans, Priestly writers described these as already owned or claimed by God. Thus humans have to be redeemed, or purchased back, from that owner. A modern technical term is *desacralized*. Propp suggests that one old form of redeeming might have been to have young men perform temporary religious duties at shrines. Propp examined another theory, that in ancient Near Eastern cultures infant sacrifice might have been practiced. He firmly labels what references we have to this custom to be urban legends (my term), rarely or never carried out. The dedicating of firstborn animals for (eventual or periodic) sacrifice might have been practical when local shrines prevailed, but would not be possible when long pilgrimages to Jerusalem were involved. Moving a grazing animal such a long distance could too easily result in injury, rendering it unfit for sacrifice.

The matter of Levites representing all the firstborn lies behind Num 1:48–54; 3:11–13, 40–51; 8:16–19, and parallel sites in Leviticus and Deuteronomy. Levine raises the topic of the "dynamics of substitution." He asks

> what does it mean to have Levites serve most of their productive life in the Tabernacle in repayment of God's claim on the firstborn of Israel? From an institutional perspective, we could say that priestly tradition rationalizes the service of the Levites after the fact, by basing their compulsory service on an unsatisfied divine claim. (1:177)

He mentions 1 Sam 1–2, where Hannah dedicated Samuel to votive service as a child, and Lev 27:1–8, where people of various ages seem to be vowed to similar service. Anyone vowing self or someone else to the

LORD incurred a debt to God, payable in some manner to the temple and the priests. Levine assumes that, while some people like Samuel actually served at shrines, most such vows were able to be renegotiated, so to speak, and be settled by payments. He further assumes that some of those who actually served at shrines may have come from needy families. Levine concludes that in the Priestly and Deuteronomic traditions about Levites, "the Levites were trading off this form of support and sponsorship for the more normal economies of the Israelite tribes who possessed productive lands" (1:178).

This is a compex subject, and I am not sure that Levine has enough evidence to talk about needy families or poorer classes providing Levitical service over the centuries.

Questions

5. How would you describe the style of 3:11–13? Read these verses out loud, using your best soap opera voice, as a way to find the answer.

6. The priestly clan of Aaron and his sons are from the tribe of Levi, and in this chapter we see that many other descendents of Levi will serve as assistants to the priests, but not be classified as priests themselves. How do the authors of Num 3 explain the origin or development of these assistants to the line of Aaron?

Section Four

NUMBERS 4:1–18

Introduction

In this chapter we learn of some of the priestly duties in wrapping and packing (and presumably unpacking and unwrapping) the most sacred objects associated with the tabernacle. The three clans of Levites who assist the priests are assigned various duties, and Aaron's two sons, Eleazar and Ithamar, are to oversee these procedures personally, making individual assignments as needed (4:19, 28, 33). There is no mention of individual leaders or marshals within the three clans. Eleazar himself is to have charge of the oils and incense supplies (4:16).

The most important Levitical clan, the Kohathites, are to carry the most sacred objects personally, and they are warned in detail (4:15, 17–20) not to touch anything before it is fully wrapped, nor to give even a passing glance at any item not yet properly prepared or fully wrapped for the moving.

The text is a bit confusing in 4:18, where the Kohathites are called a *tribe* of clans.

In the second half of the chapter (4:21–48) the duties of the other two clans are mentioned, the eligible men of all three clans are counted, and the total sum is mentioned.

In 4:2 the *sons of Kohath* are *from among the sons of Levi*. By speaking of this clan first, and by using this last phrase only here (and not in 4:22, 29), The Kohathite clan is given the highest honor. In 4:3 the adult men of the clan are described as those who can enter *the service* (*zba*) to do the *tasks* (*mlach*). We have seen the first noun before at 1:3 and elsewhere, and the second term is a very common noun. Elsewhere (4:15, 19, 23, 47) the work is called a *burden* (*msa*), or described with the common verb *to lift* (*nsa*), as in 4:25.

The *most holy things* (4:4, 19) is the same term used elsewhere to describe the innermost room of the tabernacle itself, the *Holy of Holies*. The *fine leather* in 4:6 might be dolphin skin, but the meaning is uncertain.

The solemn repetitions of Priestly authors build up in this chapter. Note the ponderous style in 4:47, *everyone who qualified to do the work of service and the work of bearing burdens*.

Questions

7. In Num 4 the duties of both priests and Levitical assistants are described with regard to moving the entire tabernacle as often as needed during the many years of wandering in the desert. How great is the difference between the duties assigned to the two classes?

8. Would it be fair to say that the emphasis on the priests wrapping and concealing all the sacred objects from the view of laity, and even from the Levites, could lead to some sort of clericalism in the long run, a way of narrowing the ordinary person's access to God?

Conclusion

When biblical scholars study the tabernacle traditions in Exodus, Numbers, and elsewhere they have two tasks to perform. First, they must search for the inner logic of this ancient liturgical system, and that of the shrines and then the temple in the following centuries. Seeking this inner logic is essential to understanding the foundations of Jewish belief and theology, and of components of Christian belief also. This task is complicated by the fact that many biblical writers describe ceremonies and procedures under the assumption that later readers are (or will be) fellow believers. Given this, the reasons behind the details of the ceremonies are not usually explained.

For readers or study groups wishing to start to learn more about Jewish liturgical theology, I strongly recommend the following. The section on cult in Walter Brueggemann's *Theology of the Old Testament* (650–79) does an excellent job of analyzing Old Testament worship systems. E. P. Sanders' *Judaism: Practice and Belief, 63 BCE—66CE* explains the workings of the temple and the faith of ordinary people in the century around the time of Jesus. Chaim Raphael's *Festival Days: A History of Jewish Celebration* catches the emotions and the mutual support found in the yearly cycle of current synagogue services, and explains those well for non-Jewish readers.

The second task for scholars is to attend to the historical part of historical-literary criticism. They do need to look for exaggerations and inconsistencies in the accounts, as part of their faithful search for the literary and theological genres under study. In the tabernacle traditions in Exod 25–31 and 35–40 the authors were not concerned just to describe an ancient set of items used only in the wilderness period; they were thinking of the tabernacle as representative of the ideal way to worship God for the indefinite future. They would have been content to have this assemblage of poles, curtains, tent and ark, lamps and incense serve the people forever.

Many scholars, however, are of the opinion that this complex worship space, with its corps of priests and Levites, was an imaginative ideal, projected back into a period centuries before the authors lived. Nomadic groups would have been hard put to spare the manpower and resources to move all these things each leg of a journey, even with carts and oxen. Then too, a nomadic group could never have been as large as this one was claimed to be to start with. The entire tabenacle image could have been engendered by the destruction of Jerusalem and the exile in Babylon. If the exiles thought of themselves as the unfortunate new refugees from Egypt with Moses, their imagining of a tabernacle could sustain their hopes of a new temple and a restoration of their homeland that depended entirely of God's help. Within any religious system liturgy is its own justification. It is not the main instrument of evangelization, but rather the main instrument of communal worship and an incentive to communal and individual prayer. We can say that the tabernacle is for God for the sake of Israel.

Levine takes a very careful approach to the whole subject, and tries to cover all the relevant biblical sources. He notes the very large number of adult male Levites eligible for service (8,580) and the number of Levite males from infancy on mentioned in the earlier census (22,000). Another anomaly is that one could serve as a soldier at the age of 20, but Levites had to be 30 years old to begin their active service. He assumes that in this wilderness tradition there were more Levites than actually needed, and that this makes the burden on the rest of the tribes all the more unrealistic. He notes that "it would be difficult to pinpoint any historical period in which such regulations would have made the most sense" (1:172).

Levine argues that cult sites were traditionally stationary, and in the historical books of the Old Testament several shrine sites are mentioned by name. They served the people well, even beyond the point where David centralized much worship in Jerusalem. The occasional references to the tabernacle in the Holy Land, such as Josh 18:1 or 2 Sam 6:17; 7:2, are clearly Priestly additions or undeveloped allusions.

Levine suggests that references to a portable ark, and perhaps to a small menorah and presentation table, might have more historical merit. So in Num 10: 33–36 the two ancient poetic sayings may reflect the actual carrying of an ark. It is featured in the well-known stories of 1 Sam 4–7.

In many of these earlier references the ark is carried by priests, since all Levites were considered to be priests in those older sources. The JE and Deuteronomic traditions in the Pentateuch kept to this priestly status for all the men of the tribe of Levi. In Deut 17:9, 18; 18:1; 21:5; 24:8; 31:9 compound phrases such *as levitical priests* or *the priests, the sons of Levi* are used. Deut 18:1 refers to *the levitical priests, the whole tribe of Levi*. Priestly traditions in Exodus and Leviticus maintain the same.

The story of the priests with the ark who wish to accompany David in his retreat (2 Sam 15:24–29) refers to the same people also as Levites. Levine suggests that the account in Ezek 44:4–14, an exilic or early post-exilic passage, could be an indicator of how the rank of assistants to the priests actually began (as a disciplinary action). Given Ezekiel's respect for the Zadokite priestly clan, perhaps the rise of the Aaronide clan came somewhat later. Thus the focus on Aaron in Exodus, Leviticus, and Numbers could be firmly post-exilic.

Throughout the Old Testament there are indirect references to serious competition among priestly families or lines. Since the office was customarily inherited, one way to compete would be to question another's genealogy, or to bring up the misdeeds of another's ancestors. Kings at times promoted or demoted individual high priests, thus adding to the mix of information we now have.

Section Four

As Levine reviews the history, our best reconstruction now is that early on men called *Levites* (possibly from a verb meaning *attached* or *hired*) were hired to perform priestly functions at various shrines. These were men from certain villages or small clans where priestly manners and ritual style were taught and handed down. In later traditions these individuals became sons of Jacob's son Levi. There are various traditions as to why the Levites were selected for priesthood by God. The scene in Exod 32:25–29 is one such story.

When King David planned to have a major temple in Jerusalem, he forced some local shrines to close, but offered those Levites duties (perhaps part-time) in Jerusalem as compensation. When David installed the ark in Jerusalem he appointed Abiathar (a northerner) and Zadok (a southerner) as co-high priests. Solomon later dismissed Abiathar and so Zadok's line led the priests. Some prophets, like Jeremiah, were anti-Zadokite, and others, like Ezekiel, were pro-Zadokite. As mentioned above, in Ezek 44:9–14 the non-Zadokite priestly families were imaged as being demoted for all time to serving only as assistants to the Zadokite line because of their recent lapses into idolatry. As time went by the Aaronide line of priests came to the fore. The genealogy in Exod 6 is one indicator of this change.

Priestly editors in the Pentateuch generally favored the Aaron traditions. Other Pentateuch sources seem less favorable to Aaron. Deut 9:20 even mentions God thinking about destroying Aaron for his making of the golden calf. JE traditions, such as Exod 18:12, show Aaron attending a ceremony presided over by Jethro, rather than Aaron being in charge. The final editors learned to live with all these conflicting claims. They accepted the Aaronide supremacy, but retained as many favorable traditions about the older Levitical families as possible. They felt no need to exalt Aaron entirely, despite his high status. Even in Exod 32 the Levites earn God's approval for stopping the festival, while Aaron appears to be a whining, awkward figure.

Even so, respect for priestly duties remains dominant. In the early chapters of Numbers, where late Priestly editors separated the Levites and their duties from those of the priests, the Levites can only carry the most sacred objects after they have been wrapped by the priests with no one else present.

Levine notes some interesting details of ark stories in the books of Samuel and Kings. In 1 Sam 6:14–16 the ark was returned to Israel. First

Sam 6:15 refers only to Levites, but Levine suggests that this could be a shortened reference to the *levitical priest* compound phrase used regularly in Deuteronomy. He does point out that 6:15 is very likely a later Priestly addition to the story; it rephrases 6:14 more than anything else. In 1 Sam 7:1 the ark is brought to the house of Abinadab, whose son is then consecrated to take care of it. This consecration is ordination to priesthood. In 1 Sam 14:19 a priest accompanies the ark. The long account in 2 Sam 6 about David moving the ark to Jerusalem mentions two more sons of Abinadab caring for the ark, although they are not described as having been ordained. In 1 Kgs 8:1-6, 10-11 Solomon has priests carry the ark into the newly built temple. A Priestly layer of comment is interpolated in 8:4-5, mentioning *priests and Levites*. Levine suggests that the mention of Levites here could simply indicate the post-exilic thinking of the Priestly editors or that it could have been another mistaken alteration in the compound phrase *levitical priest* from Deuteronomy. Levine concludes that no early biblical source would have had non-priests touching the Ark under any circumstances.

Levine goes on to compare these two stories (1 Sam 6 and 1 Kgs 8) with passages in Chronicles that recount the same incidents. Keeping in mind that the Chronicles passages are from a much later period, the changes are interesting. In 1 Chr 15-16 we again have the story of David moving the ark to Jerusalem. But here priests and Levites from all their clans seem to share almost equally in the various duties. Many groups and individuals are named, and emphasis is put on the effectiveness of all the ceremonies, singing, and music. The authors are not interested in making clear who touches what and when.

In 2 Chr 5 the ark is brought into Solomon's new temple. Again priests and Levites share many duties and much is made of all the singing and music.

Levine considers the Chronicles examples as realistic for the period of David and Solomon. Music and singing roles had become important, and whatever duties Levites perform seem to be settled between them and the priests on an *ad hoc* basis. For example, in 2 Chr 17:7-9 several Levites along with a few priests and other high officials taught the law to subjects of king Jehoshaphat, and in 2 Chr 24:4-11 Levites and priests served as fundraisers for repairs to the temple.

So Levine concludes that Numbers, with Samuel and Kings and many layers of Pentateuch traditions, stands in the middle, on one side, with Chronicles on the other. We can see a spectrum going from all Levites as priests, to Levites as very restricted assistants for the tabernacle, to an *ad hoc* combined corps of priests and Levites performing complex and beautiful ceremonies as well as important administrative duties in the major national temple.

The Numbers tradition about the tabernacle never refers to music, and rarely to verbal texts for prayer or ceremony. It focused on the simpler needs of those refugees on a long journey.

I appreciate Levine's broad study of the roles of priests and Levites over many centuries. Obviously it is hard to pin down the details since so much of the tradition was assembled so many years after the fact. More importantly, we get a feel for the authors and editors of Numbers; they are presenting their own insights, even as they attribute everything to God's meticulous intent.

Section Five

NUMBERS 5:1–31

Introduction

The Priestly editors of Numbers make a sudden switch here, moving from technical ceremonial regulations to some special cases involving physical abnormalities or sinfulness. In many points of these cases there are cross references found in the book of Leviticus.

To start with, three groups of people need to be isolated outside the camp, perhaps for short periods of observation while things may change.

Those called *leprous* (*zrwy*) most likely did not have what we call leprosy (more precisely, Hansen's disease) but other troublesome skin ailments such as vitiligo or severe psoriasis. The subject is treated at great length in Lev 13–14. The priests had to examine people with these conditions and declare whether and when the ailment subsided. Jewish people with these same problems still had to be examined by their priests in some stories in the New Testament.

Secondly, those with *discharges* may have experienced abnormal secretions from the genitals. The root meaning of the verb *zwb* is *to flow*, often used in positive contexts, such as the phrase *a land flowing with milk and honey*. In Lev 15, where such cases are discussed in detail (perhaps uncomfortable detail, for many modern readers), the sufferers may not have to stay outside the camp; here in Num 5 the isolation outside seems more strict.

Thirdly, those *unclean* (*tma*) by virtue of contact with a corpse had to follow certain steps to no longer be unclean. One such ceremony can be found in Num 19.

Section Five

The presence of any person with skin or discharge problems, or recent contact with a corpse, was considered to impact the entire camp. These conditions, ranging from long term to short term, are handled by isolation, but there is no moral condemnation or judgment being made about the individuals themselves. The only reason given for their isolation is that God *dwells* (*shkn*) in the camp.

In 5:5–10 the basic sin of doing some wrong to another person is also thought of as an offense against God (*breaking faith* [*myl*] with God). In Lev 5:14–16 the topic is *breaking faith* by misappropriation of sacred property, presumably unintentional to some extent. In these unintentional cases one could make restitution plus 20 percent, and offer a guilt sacrifice, as here. In Lev 6:1–7 these procedures were extended to civil cases where an oath of innocence or guilt was all the proof one could find. So someone could admit that he or she had originally made an oath of innocence about a crime, but later admit that he or she had lied. So one could then make restitution and a guilt sacrifice in order to make things right.

Assuming that the situations in Num 5 are similar to those mentioned in Leviticus, the restitution should be to the injured party or to the heirs of that estate. In the unlikely case that there were no heirs at all, restitution should be made to a priest at the tabernacle. All this restitution and expiation in Num 5 seems to be more lenient than what we find in Num 15:30–31.

In Num 5:11–31 the description of a trial by ordeal for possible adultery by a married woman probably strikes most modern readers as superstitious and oppressive. One could even call this trial procedure as useless for us now as a rusted blunderbuss or a gruesome pile of damaged dinosaur bones.

Still, I think it is worth a few minutes of our time to learn the precise purpose and logic of the original ceremony. While ancient Rabbinical commentary on the passage is extensive, the use of such a trial was outlawed by Mishnaic custom as far back at the third century CE. One could imagine that the ceremony was not often requested even in its era.

In the case in 5:12 the wife may have *gone astray* (*sth*). The verb always connotes immoral activity. She may have been *unfaithful* (*myl*). This is the same verb used in 5:6 about someone *breaking faith* with God. So here in 5:12 the woman in her infidelity betrays her husband and God just as the sinners in 5:6 betray not only their fellow humans but also

God. The Hebrew at the start of 5:13 is *if a man lies with her with a lying of semen*. Then the wife has *defiled herself* (*tma*). This is the same verb used in 5:2–3, referring to some being *unclean* or *defiling* the camp. In that paragraph there were no moral judgments being made; here the possible sin of the woman is clearly being condemned.

Levine notes that we should assume that the woman in the case is currently pregnant, and that her husband suspects that he is not the father, but cannot prove that for certain. Levine argues for this by working backward from the content of the ceremony itself, which focuses on the woman's uterus and reproductive health. Commentators do not agree among themselves about this assumption of pregnancy.

In 5:14 the man experiences a spirit of *jealousy*. A similar case is mentioned in Prov 6:34. Levine translates the phrase as a fit of *envious possessiveness*. The root verb *qna* can mean *eagerness* or *ardor* as well as *envy* or *jealousy*. It is even used in the solemn phrases about the Second Commandment in Exod 20:5, where God refers to himself as a *jealous God*. The phrase from Exodus may sound odd to us, but it is a vivid anthropomorphic way to depict monotheism.

When the husband brings his wife to the priest, he may be preparing his divorce case. Levine argues that the priests limited divorce to reasons of adultery or serious sexual misconduct, based on the law in Deut 24:1, which speaks of some *indecent* or *improper matter* or *situation* caused by the wife. The NRSV phrase *something objectionable* is perhaps too vague a translation. Levine assumes that the woman would only agree to undergo this ordeal in order to prove that she had not been unfaithful, and therefore to save her marriage and retain her property rights.

The husband brings the required grain offering, which the woman will hold until the priest uses it. Here it is simple barley, the lesser grain (not wheat), and no oil or incense is added to it. It is a deliberately austere offering, perhaps reflecting the purpose of the ceremony. The phrases *grain offering of jealousy* and *grain offering of remembrance* (*zcr*) are stark titles, but do not imply that every woman undergoing the ceremony is guilty from the start.

In 5:18 the phrase the *water of bitterness* (*mr*) *that brings the curse* (*arr*) is another stark title stressing the ceremonial power of the water. Levine suggests we think of the fluid as a litmus test. The priest *makes her take* an oath. We could also say he *administers* an oath. The oath has two parts. In 5:19 the priest recites the negative claim that she had not sinned,

Section Five

and the oath says that then she shall be *immune* (*nqh*). That is, she shall not be punished.

In the second part (5:19–22) the details of the curse are spelled out, not just alluded to by some general phrase like *be not immune* or *be punished*. The priest recites the claim that she had committed adultery, calling it the *oath of the curse* (*sbyt halh*). This is another solemn title, and the language is similar to the curses of the great oath in Deut 29:12, 21. The same two words are repeated in 5:21, *the LORD make you an execration (alh) and an oath (sbyh) among your people.*

The graphic nature of the oath continues, referring to God making her *groin area* to *fall*, and her *abdomen* to *swell* (*zbh*). The water shall enter her *bowels* (*myh*) and cause all this. The several words do not always mean the *uterus*, but they most likely do in this context. The *falling* and *swelling* are also general words, but here they must refer to disasters with the woman's reproductive system. Such disasters might include dropsy, pelvic prolapse, or miscarriage.

The woman replies *Amen* twice, once to each part of the oath.

In 5:23 we find out that the curse is also to be written down on parchment or leather, and the ink of the written curse scratched or washed off into the bowl of water the woman will drink. The expectation in 5:24 is that the fluid will cause *bitter pain*. The Hebrew has *for bitter things* or *for bitterness*.

The account goes on to describe what disasters will affect a guilty wife, and in 5:28 an innocent wife will be *clean* (*thr*), will be *immune* (*nqh*), and will be *able to conceive children*. This last phrase in Hebrew is *to be sown with seed*, but context certainly indicates that successfully bearing children is the topic.

Whatever the outcome of the trial, the man shall be *free* from *iniquity*. The word for *free* (*nqh*) is what we have been using for *immune* in 5:19, 28. The word *iniquity* (*ywn*) can also mean *guilt from iniquity*, as it does here. In the somewhat chopped style at the end, the focus is on a guilty wife, who shall *bear her guilt from iniquity*. How she will bear this or be punished is not spelled out in detail, and there is no mention of what happens to an innocent wife, who should suffer no ill effects to her organs. Nor is there any mention of how the couple could repair their marriage.

Questions

9. Given that the persons with skin or secretion problems, or those who by accident or necessity have had recent contact with a corpse, have not committed any sins, by what logic can God be depicted as saying that these people defile the camp and the tabernacle area?

10. In 5: 5–10 injustices or crimes require restitution, as one would find in any civil society. What else do we learn about the injustices and restitution in this paragraph?

11. 5:11–16 introduces a striking ritual ceremony, a type of trial by ordeal for some troubled marriages. Staying with just these five verses, why would any husband risk the publicity of bringing forward his marital problems? Why would any wife freely participate in such a ceremony? Did either party have any other alternative?

12. In 5:16–22 the priest prepares the bitter water and administers the two-part oath to the accused wife. She swears to the two-part oath by saying *Amen, amen.* Why is the priest so sure that God will guarantee one of the two outcomes of the oath?

13. In 5:23–31 the ceremony is concluded, with one or the other result expected or promised (no deadline is mentioned). In v. 31 what is the meaning of the phrase that the husband *shall be free from iniquity*?

Section Six

Numbers 6:1–21

Introduction

Numbers 6 describes in detail special temporary vows that men or women may take. During the time of the vow those involved (Nazirites) must avoid all grape products and leave their hair unshorn. They must also avoid any contact with a corpse for any reason. Should any such contact occur, the Nazirite had to undergo an eight-day expiation ceremony and then repeat the entire time vowed, from the very beginning. Custom indicates that the minimum vow period may have been for one month, but many of them may have been for longer periods.

After this basic outline in Num 6:1–12, the next set of verses goes on at length to describe the closing ceremonies. At the end of the vow period the Nazirite had to provide several animal sacrifices, shave his or her head and burn some of the hair in the final sacrificial fire, and donate some of the sacrifice to the priest as usual, and then host a party for his or her own supporters.

Finally, 6:22–27 records a special blessing prayer given by God to Aaron and his sons to use in their priestly ministries. It is a famous blessing, but does not seem to be related to the previous information about the Nazirite vows. We will examine this blessing in the next section.

There are relatively few details about particular vows in the Old Testament. Deut 23:21–23 and Eccl (also called Qohelet) 5:4–6 warn us that taking vows is a voluntary but very serious self-imposed obligation, and not fulfilling them would be an offense against God. Better not to take one in the first place. Later we will come to Num 30, wherein fathers or husbands are obligated to confirm or nullify some vows their daughters or wives have made.

Some of the Hebrew vocabulary in this chapter is difficult. In 6:2 someone *makes* or *vows* (*pla*) a *special vow* (*lndr ndr*). The verb *pla* usually means *to be difficult* or *marvelous*, and in causative form means *to do something marvelous*. The second phrase (*lndr ndr*) simply means *to vow a vow*. In one case, Lev 22:21, the verb *pla* is used with *ndr* to mean *to fulfill a vow*.

Levine (1:218) argues that we should look at another verb close in spelling, *plh*, which means *to treat differently, to be distinguished*, or *to treat with distinction*. So Levine translates "when anyone, man or woman, sets [*himself or herself*] apart by pronouncing a vow."

In Num 6:2 the word for *Nazirite* (*nzir*) is related to the verb *nzr*, both meaning *to abstain from certain things* or *to accept certain deprivations*. Here the abstentions are *for God*, so NSRV has "the vow of a nazirite, to separate themselves [*lhzir*] to the LORD. " So in this verse the verbs *pla/plh* and *nzr* are nearly synonyms. This vow will involve isolation or deprivation.

Levine suggests that the verb *nadar* and noun *neder* (about vowing), and the verb *nazar* and noun *nezer* (about abstaining) developed from a common root. He argues that *ndr* forms are more positive in their range of meanings, while the *nzr* forms accentuate the restrictions. Even though Levine's suggestion about the relationship of the two verbs is only a theory, it does remind us of the main topic of this passage.

In 6:5, 7, 9, 12 the noun *nezer* will be used in the phrases *for which they* separate *themselves*, consecration, and consecrated *head*. Translating from Hebrew to English involves much paraphrasing and use of synonyms; the two languages are more different than alike.

In Num 6:3 the strong drink is presumably another grape-based mixture rather than beer. Levine suggests new wine, used immediately after production. He notes that raisins were a mainstay in Middle Eastern diets, and that grapes had many uses besides making wine.

In Num 19 there are many rules about purification for touching a corpse. The sanctions for Nazirites are almost as strict as those for high priests, as found in Lev 21:11. The topic of *defilement*, mentioned in 6:7, 9, was used about sins and adultery in Num 5. In 6:9 the defiling contact would have been entirely accidental, but must still lead to cleansing ceremonies.

In Lev 14:8–13; 15:28–30 we find somewhat parallel eight-day ceremonies for the cure of lepers and women who had had longstanding discharge problems. In Num 6:11 the sin offering and burnt offering constitute the expiation needed. This is also found in Num 8:12, as part of the purification and ordination ceremonies for Levites.

The *sanctifying* of the head in 6:11 is really a *reconsecrating*.

In 6:12 another animal, a lamb, must serve as a *guilt offering* (*asham*). In other cases, such as Lev 5:14—6:7 and Num 5:8, actual property was stolen, necessitating sacrifices of guilt or atonement. The logic in 6:12 may be that the Nazirite has been *stolen from God* by the matter of the corpse, or the time lost to fulfilling the vow has also been lost as a sacred gift to God.

The closing ceremonies for a successful end to a Nazirite vow period are elaborate. The one finishing the vow offers a burnt sacrifice, a sin offering, and an offering of *well-being* (*shelamim*), along with bread, grain and wine offerings. The priest gets certain parts of the offering of well-being; the rest is for the Nazirite and his or her guests. Levine prefers to translate *peace* offerings or offerings of *well-being* as *sacred gifts of greeting*. His logic is that this offering is one of tribute or a way to initiate a diplomatic meeting. No one term will suffice in every case; in general we will stay with *well-being*, the usual NRSV term.

Num 6:21 seems to indicate that well-off Nazirites should go beyond the minimum sacrifices. The Hebrew speaks of quantities *beyond that which his hand may hold* (*nsg*). Levine paraphrases the entire verse as follows: "This is the prescribed instruction for the Nazirite. But one who pledges his offering to YHWH in excess of his required restriction, in accordance with what his means allow, must fulfill the vow he has pledged in excess of the instruction prescribed for his restriction."

Questions

14. In 6:1–5 what do you learn about people who wish to be Nazirites for a certain period of time? What do the authors fail to explain in these same five verses?

15. In 6:6–12 the third obligation of Nazirites is mentioned, along with the possible complication that any one Nazirite might

suddenly wind up in the presence of someone who had just died. What do the authors fail to explain in this passage?

16. In 6:13–20 we read of the normal end-of-vow-period ceremonies for a Nazirite. While we may not know every significance of the components of the ritual, how would you describe the logic of the whole ceremony? What is the point of the appended verse (6:21)?

Conclusion

According to Levine, the description of Nazirite customs may include some truly ancient Near Eastern elements of ritual. The first item we shall look at is the matter of leaving one's hair unshorn, and then having it shaved at the end and putting some hair into the sacrificial fire. If we consider hair to be a natural part of human vitality, avoiding haircuts could help one's health and strength. Offering some of one's own cut hair in fire could then be a way to offer that vitality back to God.

One may think of Samson, called a Nazirite, whose hair must not be cut (Judg 13:5, 7). But in that case his mother was the one told to avoid wine and unclean foods. Levine speculates that the Samson story may originally have been about a hero, and only later were Nazirite customs added. Since Samson himself was not very devout, perhaps the avoidance of wine and unclean foods were shifted to the mother. In 1 Sam 1:11 the infant Samuel was dedicated as a Nazirite by his mother, Hannah.

Nazirites were described as hounded in Amos 2:11–12, and Joseph was called a *nezer* in Gen 49:26 (also in Deut 33:16). The meaning there might be that he was *separated* from his brothers, or that his hair was *dedicated* or *unshorn*. The translation is difficult.

In Judg 5:2 there is mention of people with *long* or *unbraided* hair (*pry*); the same word is used in Num 6:5. The context in Judges might refer to soldiers. In Deut 32:42 enemy soldiers have long hair. In Lev 25:11 *unpruned vines* are mentioned. The Hebrew phrase is that the vines were *Nazirite-like*. This unusual idiom would have only made sense to those who knew that Nazirites did not cut their hair.

Levine concludes that what we have in Num 6 may be an amalgamation of several old practices originally followed by soldiers, ascetics, or devout laity. The vows were usually voluntary, but there may have been some parental dedications of infants.

Section Seven

NUMBERS 6:22—8:4

Introduction

Many suggest that this blessing in 6:22–27 would logically fit in better at Lev 9:22–24, when Moses and Aaron dedicated the tabernacle, following the basic story of Exod 40. In Num 7:1—8:4 and especially in 7:1–2, 88, we have another account of that same dedication ceremony. Perhaps this is why the blessing was located just prior to Num 7:1.

Levine mentions two seventh-century-BCE silver amulets with an almost identical blessing as this etched on them. They were found near Jerusalem in burial caves.

The blessing at the end of Num 6 has a solemn introduction. Moses is to pass on to Aaron the exact words given by God. In the formula of Num 6:24–26 the addresses are in the second-person singular, but clearly the intention is to treat the people as a unity. The six verbs of the formula are wishes or requests for God's cooperation.

Levine argues that this blessing is not an abstraction, state of mind or spiritual condition; it is a plea for real physical gifts or material benefits, such as progeny, prosperity, well-being, or peace in the land. He suggests that the verb *to bless* (*brk*) may simply have been generated by the noun *berakah* (*blessing* or *gift*); whereas in most cases in Hebrew a verb generates related nouns. So *to keep* should mean *to guard or protect from danger or defeat*. When God's face *shines* and he becomes *gracious*; gifts follow. When God *lifts up his countenance* and gives his *peace*, things change for the better. The word *peace* (*shalom*) also includes *health* and *prosperity* in its range of Hebrew meanings.

Since the priest will use God's name in this blessing, God promises to hear and to respond favorably. This liberal self-obligation on God's part parallels that of Exod 20:24, where God promises to come to every altar of sacrifice and bless the people gathered there.

At the start of Num 7 we return to details about the beginning of tabernacle ritual, as in Exod 40 and Lev 8–9. The subdivision of the Levites by clans, and their specific duties as assistants to the priests, are based on the new categories of Num 3–4.

The various references to anointing, consecrating, and presenting offerings use the regular priestly vocabulary. The phrase for *covered wagon* (*yglt zb*) in 7:3 is quite rare. The *tent of meeting* is equated with the *tabernacle* in 7:5, as often in Priestly sources.

In Num 7:10–11, 84, 88 the ceremony is called the *dedication* (*hnch*), from which comes the modern Hebrew term *Hannukah*. Some such prayers and sacrifices are essential in beginning ceremonies. The verb *to dedicate* (*hnc*) is also used when Solomon inaugurated the temple in 1 Kgs 8:63, and it appears in Deut 20:5 concerning husbands starting to use new homes.

The bowls, basins, and dishes mentioned will have several functions in the ongoing rituals. They were not simply one-time containers for flour and incense at this dedication.

The freewill offerings in the closing chapters of Exodus for the construction of the tabernacle seem surprising, given that we had been reading about desperate shepherding peasants fleeing from Egypt. There seemed to be no end to donations of gold, silver, fine wool and linen, fine leather, spices, oils, and precious gems. In Exod 36:2–7 Moses had to stop the gathering of these materials because of the great surpluses already turned in! Here too, in Numbers, the wagons, gold, silver, incense, and livestock for sacrifices seem to be readily available. There is room for exaggeration in all these accounts.

The final verse, Num 7:89, has another reference to the *tent of meeting*, one of the older images now combined with the tabernacle image. In both Exod 25:22 (where God will speak to Moses in the holy of holies), and in Exod 33:6–11 (where God speaks to Moses in the small tent of meeting outside the camp) the emphasis is on lawgiving, and not on worship ceremonies at which the high priest presided. In Exod 33 this small tent of meeting for prayer was available for others to use, although Moses probably used it the most.

In 7:89 the Hebrew says that Moses heard the voice of God coming from above the *mercy seat* (the ornate superstructure of the ark of the covenant). The verse concludes with *thus he spoke to him*. Context would indicate that this means that God spoke to Moses. The NRSV has *it spoke*, apparently referring to the voice (God's voice) speaking to Moses. Technically the original phrase *he spoke to him* could also mean that Moses spoke to God. The ambiguity could be deliberate.

The word for *mercy seat* (*kprt*) derives from the verb *kpr*, which means *to cover*, and more broadly, *to reconcile, forgive*, and *atone*. Levine remarks that, given the broad meanings of the word, we should stay with the traditional phrase *mercy seat*, or with other phrases that recall forgiveness or atonement, rather than less rich words such as *covering slab* or *lid*.

Questions

17. In 6:22–27 we find one of the most well-known blessings in the Old Testament. The priests can say this blessing at any ceremony; it does not pertain exclusively to the topic of the Nazirites. Imagine that you are the one giving the blessing; recite it out loud a few times. What is there about the style of 6:24–26 that is so effective? How does this blessing work? Why does it work? Have you ever heard this blessing used in Christian ceremonies?
18. In 7:1–11 we find another story of the generosity of the Israelite tribes for the support of the tabernacle ceremonies. What does the author stress in 7:4–5, 11? He will do the same in 8:1–2.
19. Read 7:84—8:4 as a unit. Given the focus of these verses, how does 7:89 fit into the larger picture?

Conclusion

Levine suggests that this detailed tally in Num 7 is a prose rendition of a spreadsheet, a type of account list quite common in the ancient world. The written style of the tally is very wooden, as though the scribes were reading a large tablet of clearly labeled rows and columns of entries and subtotals.

The Hebrew mentions some of the animals first and then the corresponding numbers. The NRSV polishes this by putting the numerical quantity first each time, since English style demands that. In many of the individual sentences in the Old Testament where numbers of people or things are mentioned, the Hebrew numerical adjectives also precede their nouns.

But in extensive lists the style changes to the more wooden format. Levine notes Num 29 and Josh 12:9–24; 15:32; 18:28 as examples. He cites research that notes that spreadsheets tend to highlight bigger or more important items by where they place them in the main rows or columns, whereas in rituals the exact order of sacrifices or use of incense, oils, or the like may follow a much different sequence.

To end on a point of prayer, let us return to the blessing at the end of Num 6. Levine cites similar ancient Near Eastern expressions about gods' faces shining on or looking at petitioners, and about gods offering protection and well-being. He notes biblical greetings offered by ordinary lay people or civic leaders. In Ruth 2:4 Boaz and his workmen greet each other in the LORD's name. In Gen 43:29 Joseph blesses his brother Benjamin with a simple prayer for God's graciousness to Benjamin.

In Gen 24:1 we are told that God blessed Abraham in all things, referring to his prosperity. In Gen 33:11 Jacob attributes his own success to God's graciousness.

Levine sees these religious ideas as underlying the more formal prayers and blessings developed for ceremonies over the years.

Looking for other roots of liturgical prayer, Levine returns to the two silver amulets with blessings similar to that in Num 6. After analyzing them in great detail, he suggests that they may have been purchased from priests at a shrine or received by the donors in thanks for votive offerings. At times they may have been buried with loved ones, as protection for existence in Sheol.

This blessing from Num 6 is referred to in Sir 50:18–24, during another important temple event centuries closer to our time. Priests at Qumran said something close to this every day. Mishnahs refer to how it was said in the temple and in early synagogues. Levine comments, "we are warranted in regarding the priestly benediction as multifunctional, surely in the exilic and postexilic periods. In its extraliturgical utilization, it may well have connoted the wish for well-being in the afterlife, as it did in later periods of Jewish religious experience" (1:244).

Section Seven

Levine's interest in this blessing is understandable. It is a beloved text for both Jews and Christians, and is often used in Christian burial services. It expresses our common faith that only the LORD can truly keep us and give us peace.

Section Eight

NUMBERS 8:5–26

Introduction

In this chapter we learn about the ordination rite for Levites, which is different from that for priests. The differences stem in part from Num 3–4, which is where the Levites' status as assistants to the priests was clearly defined for the first time.

Preparations include sprinkling them with the *water of purification* (*mi hatat*), the cutting and shaving of hair, and the washing of their clothing. Levine explains that while *mi hatat* literally means *the water of sin offering*, the sense is *water for the removal of sinfulness*. Two young bulls are brought forward for sacrifice, one by the Levites and one by Aaron. He is to *assemble* (*qhl*) the whole *community* (*eduth*), who are then to lay their hands on the Levites.

Then Aaron presents the Levites before the LORD and figuratively *elevates* them (*nwp*) as an *elevation offering* (*tenupah*) from the Israelites, so that the Levites may *assist* in *ritual service* (*ybd ybdt*). The verb *nwp* is found in 5:25 and elsewhere. Levine prefers to translate the verb and noun as *make a presentation* and *presentation offering*, avoiding older translations using *raise*, *elevate*, *wave*, or *heave*. The Levites then lay their hands on the bulls, and Aaron in turn offers one of them as a sin offering and one as a whole-burnt offering. In 8:12 these sacrifices *atone* (*cpr*) for the Levites. Levine argues that translations like *ransom* or *protect* more accurately reflect the context, relying to some extent on 8:19, where the Levites serve as *atonement* (*protection*) for the rest of the Israelites. Num 8:13 essentially repeats 8:11, although the LORD and the Israelites are featured in v.11, while the LORD and the priests are featured in v.13.

The explanations offered by God in 8:14–19 repeat some of the themes in 3:5–13, 40–41, 44–51. The language is dramatic. The Levites are *separated* (*bdl*); they are *unreservedly given* (*ntunim ntunim*) to God, and *taken* by him for himself and *consecrated* by him. The climax in 8:19 is that God now designates the Levites as *gifts* (*ntunim*) to Aaron and his sons. In current English we might say that someone designated as a gift is someone *assigned to a role*. The main role of the Levites is to assist at the rites and thus protect ordinary Israelites from coming too close to the holy places. Levine notes the subordinate status of the Levites in this passage. They may be dedicated to God, and regifted by him to the priests, but they don't seem to have much say in the matter.

The next few verses (8:20–22) indicate that every instruction was carried out. In summarizing, the Levites are described as *purifying themselves from sin* (*hta*); then Aaron made of them a *presentation offering* (*tenupah*) and *made atonement* (*kpr*) for them.

In 8:26 retired Levites may *help* (*shrt*) other Levites at ceremonies, but the context clearly indicates that they are not to undertake official duties such as they had before retiring.

We can compare this Levite ordination ceremony with that of the priests as found in Exod 29 and Lev 8–9. Recall that in these two books all Levites were priests. In Exod 29 several sacrifices are made, special vestments are worn, anointing is done with oil and blood, and the newly ordained alone eat sacred portions of the sacrifices for seven days.

In Lev 8–9 the details are a bit more elaborate and there is more emphasis on the first round of public sacrifices at the newly erected tabernacle, but the ordination ceremony is quite similar to that in Exodus.

In Numbers the Levites (non-priests) were ordained after the consecration of the tabernacle, not as part of the inaugural services. Numbers will stress their subservience to the priests to a great extent. The Levites are sprinkled with purifying water, but not anointed with oil nor smeared with blood. The images of Levites as a presentation offering, or as ransom for the first born, or as clans given to God, focus on their precise status as assistants rather than on the religious value of their duties. One verb for their *purification* (*thr*) in 8:6 is not used for the priests in Leviticus; other terms are used to get across the same idea. In the Old Testament the term *thr* is often used of offerings, so the Levites are being likened to an offering here.

The sequence of a sin offering and then a burnt offering is similar in the priestly (Lev 8:14–21) and Levitical (Num 8:12) ceremonies. The first was to make the officiants worthy, and the second was their first act of worship in their new roles (see also Lev 16:3).

If we think of sin offerings for a moment, rather than presentation offerings, Levine reminds us that there were two types of sin offerings. Some were for the entire community, and involved whole-burnt offerings; others, such as we find in Lev 4:22—5:13, were for specific expiations, and were not entirely destroyed. The sin offering for the Levites in Num 8 is more like those of Lev 4:22—5:13.

Questions

20. Most of Num 8 outlines God's explicit instructions for the ordination rites and duties of the Levites, even though we were introduced to some of the same ideas in 1:48–53; 3. Looking at the first part of the ceremony (8:5–11), what religious concepts do all these ceremonial instructions illustrate?
21. The ceremony continues in 8:12–15. What additional religious concepts are highlighted here?
22. In 8:16–19 God continues to explain his own thinking about Levites and their roles. If you were to play God for a moment, saying these four verses aloud with conviction, what would you learn about God?

Conclusion

Although I discussed some of the current thinking on priestly lineages and the origins of the Levitical rank in the conclusion to Section Four, I would like to summarize more of Levine's comments here, at the risk of some repetition. Levine (1:279–90) examines some passages in greater detail at this point, and that can help us to catch on to the thinking of the editors of the book of Numbers.

Just as Lev 1–7 provides background information before we come to chapters about priestly ordination and ministry in Lev 8–10, so also in Num 1–4 and 7 we are given background that helps us appreciate the ordination ceremony for Levites in Num 8.

But the subordinate duties of the Levites is a major innovation of this very book of Numbers. Levine asks two questions at this point. First, was there originally a tribe of Levi, or did a liturgical guild eventually take on the image of a tribe? Second, how can we learn anything more of the internal workings within that guild or tribe?

Many Pentateuch sources speak of the tribe of Levi, descendants of one of Jacob's sons. But outside the Pentateuch no pre-exilic biblical sources ever name Levites as one of the tribes. Levine thinks that this gap between the Penteteuch and the other pre-exilic sources is so sharp that we need to examine it seriously.

Regarding the question of origins, let us start with the pre-exilic passage in Judg 17–18. In 17:7–13 we read of an itinerant Levite who was hired to be a priest. He is described as being of the clan of Judah from Bethlehem. The word *Levite*, used five times in this short passage, seems to refer to a profession rather than to a tribe, especially since the man described himself as being a descendent of Judah. Judg 18 recounts the conquests of the tribe of Dan. In taking land for themselves the Danites hired away that same Levite (Judg 18:3–4, 15–20, 24, 27, 30). In this entire episode the man is consistently described as a priest, except for the term *Levite* in 18:3. The focus is on the man's profession, not his tribal roots.

Judg 19–20 tells a grim story of a Levite living in the territory of Ephraim, whose minor wife was from Bethlehem. As that passage describes a civil war by all the tribes against the tribe of Benjamin, the Levite whose protests started the war seems to be just one individual; there is no specific mention of the tribe of Levi.

Second Sam 8:17–18 indicates that King David appointed Zadok and Ahimelech as chief priests, and that some of David's own sons were priests. In 2 Sam 15:24 the two chief priests, with all the Levites, bring the ark to David. Here the reference seems to be to a small group of clergy, not an entire tribe.

Returning to Pentateuch passages, the tribe is mentioned in Gen 29:34 (J). Genealogies mentioning Levi are also found in Gen 35:23–26 and 46:8–27 (both P).

These brief mentions by P could be late.

In Deut 10:8–9, a pre-exilic passage, the tribe of Levi is set apart. In Deut 17:9, 18; 24:8 they are called *Levitical priests* (in Hebrew order, *the priests, the Levites*). In Deut 18:1 these same Levitical priests are called *the whole tribe of Levi* (*kl sbt lwi*); so all Levites are priests, and all legitimate priests are Levites. In Deut 21:5 the reference is to *the priests, the sons of Levi*.

Levine admits that all these Deuteronomy texts have their complexities, but that we can say in general that Deuteronomy does not stratify within the ranks of Levites as we have in Numbers. Deuteronomy does refer to the Levites at times as having tribal roots.

Levine now goes to Gen 49:5–7, where we find the stern words of Jacob against Simeon and Levi. Jacob alludes to Gen 34 (P), where these two sons avenge their sister Dinah. Levine argues that the story of Dinah is late; it features circumcision and mentions *getting property* (*ahz*) in Gen 34:10. This topic of property comes up in Lev 25 and in other P passages in the Pentateuch. In Gen 49:7 the punishment for the descendents of Simeon and Levi is that they shall be dispersed and scattered throughout Israel. This is what we find in Deuteronomy; the Levites are a group without land, living in various towns, as in Deut 14:29; 18:6; Josh 13:33. So Gen 49:5–7 could be an etiological reference, a retrojection rather than solid evidence of an ancient tribe.

If we look at Deut 33:8–11, Moses blesses the descendents of Levi for being faithful to God at Massah and Meribah; so they shall act as priests and offer incense and animals on the altars. In Exod 32:26–29 we have another tradition that the faithfulness of the Levites occurred at the time of the golden calf incident. The blessing in Deut 33 says that the Levites will also teach and instruct. This matches what we read of in Deut 17:2–13, where priests and judges settle important cases. So the blessing in Deut 33 may also be etiological, rather than firmly historical.

We are on more solid ground when we look at the ancient shrines throughout the Promised Land. Scholars speculate that there were families or small clans that gradually formed a priestly guild. At times outsiders could join the guild, as we read in 1 Sam 1–3, where Samuel eventually replaces Eli at Shiloh. Samuel, an outsider, was more worthy than Eli's own sons.

Such men with priestly skills could have lived near shrines in villages of their own (see Lev 25:32–34; Josh 21; 1 Sam 22:19; 1 Chr 6). Then too, later generations of Israelites might have thought of such priests as a tribe, and traditions about them and their shrines were then put back into the Mosaic or patriarchal eras. This is a normal traditioning process. Levine (1:286) concludes that theorizing about skilled families of priests eventually being thought to have roots in one tribe is more convincing than to accept a questionable genealogical tradition about an ancient tribe, within a league of tribes, dedicated en masse to cultic service. The entire question of the origins and growth of all twelve tribes is beyond the scope of this study, but for the founding ancestors to have been twelve siblings is unlikely.

Moving on to the second question about internal distinctions among the priestly clans, we have very little information outside of Numbers about the Levites being subdivided into priests and lower ranking assistants. Deuteronomy usually thinks of all Levites as priests. In Lev 25:32–34 we find legislation about houses in the cities of the Levites. It might be possible to imagine that this group did not have the same status as priests, but the text sheds no light on our question. This passage is the only place in Leviticus where the term *Levites* is used by itself.

Levine (1:287–89) looks for changes within the historical priesthood that may be behind some of the ideas in Numbers. He examines Ezek 44:4–16 and 2 Kgs 22–23.

There is reason to argue that in Ezek 44:4–16 the text originally passed directly from v. 8 to v. 15. We can call this the outer passage. The additional inner passage, vv. 9–14, shows some priests (and their descendents) being permanently demoted to lesser duties for grave misconduct.

Several arguments support the distinction between the inner and outer passages:

- In the outer text the term *Levitical priest* is used in 43:19 and 44:15. This term is not used in the inner passage.

- In 44:6–8 foreigners illicitly acted as priests, and in 44:15–16 the Zadokites will have exclusive priestly responsibilities. In 43:19 and 44:15–16 the priests are said *to minister* (*srt*) in the temple, a common verb in Deuteronomy for their most sacred service. In the inner passage at 44:11–12 the same verb is used to describe the lesser duties of Levites, and their previous illicit co-ministries with foreign priests. The same verb is found in Num 8:26 referring to retired Levites helping out. Obviously the verb is general enough to apply to either group.

- Another phrase used deliberately in both outer and inner passages is *keeping charge* (*shmr mshmrt*). In 44:8 and 15–16 it refers to priestly duties. But in 44:14 the same phrase refers to the lesser work and duties of Levites.

- In 44:15 the Israelites (but not the Zadokites) had *gone astray* (*tyh*). But in 44:10 it was the Levites who had also *gone astray* along with Israel.
- Finally, in 44:7 and 15 the fat and blood of priestly sacrifices are mentioned. The phrase is not used in the inner passage.
- The crafting of the inner passage in Ezek 44:9–14 enfolds it within the larger message of Ezekiel. It very likely originated after Ezekiel's lifetime.

Levine notes that in 2 Kgs 23:8–9 King Josiah had to punish some priests who had done improper or idolatrous services at the illegitimate high places throughout the country. In 23:9 we are told that those disgraced priests could not serve in Jerusalem, but *ate unleavened bread among their kindred*. This may be a reference to their being unemployed, or getting some support from temple revenues.

Levine (1:289) concludes that the notion of subservient Levites in Numbers may have stemmed from the disgraced priests of the time of Josiah, and that their permanent demotion was endorsed in the post-exilic interpolation of Ezek 44:9–14. So the Numbers understanding of Levitical roles is likely also post-exilic.

Readers should not be surprised that post-exilic authors and editors would push matters of theology, law, or ritual back to the time of Moses. The intent was not to deceive later generations (or modern readers), but to give God credit for all his revelations and for all his help.

Section Nine

NUMBERS 9:1—10:28

Introduction

Before describing the pillar and cloud that accompanied the tabernacle, the system of trumpet calls, and the initial move of the camp after Sinai, the Priestly editors added some fine points regarding the Passover rite.

Num 9:1 refers to the first month of the second year of freedom from Egypt. Num 1:1 speaks of the first day of the second month of the second year. Perhaps 9:1, relying on Exod 40:2, was already fixed in its text before 1:1 was put at the head of the book.

The word for *appointed time* (*moed*) in 9:3, 7 is the same word used for *meeting* or *assembly*, as in *tent of meeting*. The word for *unclean* (*tma*) in 9:6, 7 is also translated *defiled* in other places, and refers to being ineligible to attend communal worship. The question *why must we be kept?* in 9:7 comes from *gry*, a forceful word that means *why must we be diminished?*

By the end of the passage the writers are looking centuries ahead to people being away on *journeys*, or people at home deliberately *failing* (*hdl*) to observe the holy day. The laws of participation must cover *resident aliens* as well as *natives* (or *citizens*). These two civil categories will only make sense after the followers of Moses have settled down in their own land. In the Old Testament earlier occupants of the Holy Land are never referred to as *resident aliens* or *natives*.

It sounds odd that some would complain about restrictions that apply to Passover. The next one, coming in a few weeks, will be just the second Passover ever held, and corpse-related ineligibility for other holy days is not mentioned here. Levine notes that the early system of shrines in the Holy Land was flexible; someone on a short journey could be close enough to one of the shrines not to miss the celebration. On the other hand, after the temple was established in Jerusalem and the other shrines closed, the problem of travel could have become more pressing for some. The solution of having an alternate feast day a month later makes sense, but we do not know how often such cases arose. One might wonder if later generations of believers would find the need so imperative to go to Jerusalem a month later, with fewer relatives and friends. Would they have enjoyed the spiritual force of the event under those circumstances?

In 2 Chr 29–30 there is an interesting description of temple reforms under King Hezekiah. At that time the entire nation delayed Passover for one month due to problems of scheduling and purification.

In Num 9:15–23 the writers remind us of the guidance offered by God using the pillar of cloud by day and of fire by night. A cloud of protection is mentioned in Exod 14:19–24, and the cloud for journeying in the wilderness in 40:34–37.

In Num 9 the Priestly style is quite repetitive, assuring us that God had them move by his own schedule, without consultation. In 9:19, 23 the obedience of the people is called *keeping the charge of the LORD* (*shmr mshmrt*). The same term has been used in Numbers about priestly or Levitical ceremonial duties. Here all the people are involved in this larger liturgy of procession.

The closing phrase in Num 9:23, *at the hand of Moses*, reminds us of Moses' ongoing role as co-leader; God works with Moses consistently all through the book of Numbers.

The rules about using trumpets seem reasonable, and a *shofar* (a simple instrument made from a ram's horn) is still used at certain Jewish holy days even now. The first verb for *blowing* the instruments (*tqy*) is a basic word, here meaning *using* the trumpets. The *sound* (*trwyh*) in 10:5 can mean *signal* or *alarm*. It becomes harder to translate 10:7, where the writer distinguishes the blowing for assembly from the blowing of the signal for breaking camp. In 10:9 the trumpets are for use in wartime, and the verb for *sounding an alarm* (*rwy*) is the root for the noun used in 10:5, 7. So translators need to use different words for *blowing* one or two trumpets for assembly, sending *signals* about breaking camp, and sounding an *alarm* in time of war. Levine talks of *short blasts* and *prolonged blasts*, following synagogue customs.

Section Nine

Having described so much about the civil and religious structures of the chosen people at Sinai with Moses, the Priestly writers finally focus on the first leg of the long journey ahead.

One major disagreement between the P and JE traditions occurs at Num 10:12, where the next site on the journey is called the *wilderness of Paran*. While the extent of what is called Paran is uncertain, it is generally thought to cover much of the north central region between the Gulf of Suez and the Red Sea, and thus is directly north of the wilderness of Sinai and Mt. Sinai (Jebel Musa). It can also be said to end southwest of Kadesh. Priestly writers generally tended to exaggerate the size of the Paran range. In Num 13:3, 26 the early spying mission went from Paran, through some of Canaan, and ended back at Kadesh. For the Priestly traditions, most of the time of the wandering will be within the Paran range. The JE tradition is quite different, as we shall see.

Num 10:13, much like 9:23, mentions the role of Moses as co-leader, the close partner relaying all of the LORD's commands.

Questions

23. 9:1–5 indicates the importance of the annual ritual of Passover. God reminds Moses about this, and Moses supervises the procedures. Is the request in 9:6–7 an odd or unusual one?

24. God's reply to the request obviously looks centuries ahead, to the temple in Jerusalem. What does God's reply tell us about this holy day?

25. Note 9:14. In the future, why should Israelites in the Holy Land allow resident aliens to participate in Passover ceremonies, when most such resident aliens would not be Jewish?

26. In 9:15–23 the pillar of cloud and fire is used by God as the indicator for the actual path of travel and for the duration of traveling or remaining in camp. What is the emphasis and style of these nine verses? Why does God use this unusual visual aid rather than just giving clear directions and times to Moses and Aaron?

27. In 10:1–10 trumpets are designated for what we might call practical or secular reasons as well as for use at certain religious ceremonies. Note the second-person references to *your God* in 10:9–10 and the closing *I am the LORD your God*. How does 10:8–10 contribute to the religious style of the whole passage?

Conclusion

By Num 10:28 the average person who has never read Numbers before might be forgiven for being lulled by the serenity of all these events. The only unpleasant topic so far has been the procedures for trials by ordeal for suspect wives (Num 5).

The new journey into the wilderness now begins from Sinai, where the people first arrived in Exod 19. One could hardly call the two covenants and the disaster of the golden calf serene events (Exod 19–34), but since Exod 35 we have been shown the details of the construction of the tabernacle, the massive body of ritual and moral guidelines in Leviticus, and these further ritual points made in Num 1–10.

The purpose of these sections of Exodus and Numbers, along with Leviticus sandwiched in between, is to create an ideal profile of ritual, morality, and justice. A golden age is laid out, a time when this people was given guidelines as they needed them, and when Moses served God mainly as the great giver of laws.

Numbers 10:29—21:35

Section Ten

NUMBERS 10:29—11:35

Introduction

In the next large block of Numbers, 10:29—21:35, most of the stories are from the older JE traditions, and they paint a much more melodramatic profile of the stress everyone was under during the years in the desert. There will be no fussing about holy days or trumpets here.

For convenience we will look at 10:29–11:35 as one section, although the two small units in ch. 10 are not directly related to the crisis in ch. 11.

In 10:29 we are introduced to Moses' father-in-law, Hobab. In Exod 18 Moses' father-in-law was called Jethro. The Exodus tradition is from E, and the reference here in Numbers is from J. Small differences such as two different names for the same person were usually retained in biblical stories, even if that seems confusing to modern readers. The name *Hobab* may mean something like *loved one* or *loved by [some specific god]*. In Deut 33:3 a similar form from the same verb, *hbb*, refers to God as *lover of peoples* or, as the NRSV prefers, *favorite among peoples*.

The saying from God *I will give it to you* is stronger in Hebrew than in English, because the word *it* comes first. Moses promises Hobab that they would *treat him well*. The verb root is *twb*, the basic word for *good*. The same noun is also in the next phrase, that the LORD has promised *good* to Israel.

While Hobab is reluctant to remain away from his own Midianite people any longer, Moses politely pleads for his assistance, saying that Hobab knows *how* (or *where*) they should camp, and that he could serve *as their eyes*. This last is a unique idiom in the Hebrew, but the meaning is obvious. In 10:32 the verb for *treating well* or *doing good* is used twice, along with one use of the noun. The text says *the good with which the LORD does good to us, we will also do good to you*. Clearly Moses is optimistic about the future, as he has just emphasized in both 10:29 and 32. Most commentators assume that Moses' invitation to Hobab and his family includes the right to settle in the Promised Land.

In 10:33 the *mountain of the LORD* is clearly Mount Sinai; elsewhere the phrase usually refers to Mount Zion and Jerusalem. The *ark of the covenant of the LORD* is also mentioned in Num 14:44, in a military context. In many of the older sources the contents of the ark are not precisely identified. But it is not only a chest or reliquary; it also serves as a throne or sign for God's presence, thus the mention of the cloud.

In saying that the ark goes *to seek* (*twr*) a resting place for them, the writer is, of course, describing God's providence. The *resting place* will be a temporary campsite, although the word can mean *permanent location* at times. See Deut 1:30–33 for a very similar profile of God accompanying the people. Levine argues that Num 10:33–34 are from the Priestly editors, mainly because of vocabulary.

The sayings by Moses in 10:35–36 are durative or standard phrases, meant to be used whenever the ark moved or rested. The command *arise* can also mean *advance* or *attack*, which might fit in better with the mention of *your enemies* and *your foes* (in Hebrew, *those hating you*). Levine suggests that the verb forms are not wishes, which call for the style *let them be scattered* and *let them flee*. He argues that we can better translate them as facts: *Attack, YHWH! Your enemies disperse; your foes flee your presence*. He cites Ps 68:1 for a parallel that focuses on God's power.

In 10:36 there is no preposition relating the command *return* with the noun phrase *ten thousand thousands of Israel*. The NRSV connects the noun phrase with YHWH himself—*Return, O LORD of the ten thousand*—but that is a conjecture. Levine prefers to make the noun phrase the direct object of the command, so he translates, *Bring back, O YHWH, the myriads of Israel's militias*. Levine is also conjecturing, in that he pushes the idea that this verb in this form can take a direct object. The conjecture is based on the idea that good commanders bring back most of their troops alive.

In any case, Levine suggests that the use in 10:33–34 of the ark and cloud on a three-day journey now precede and dampen the more militant image of God leading in battle in 10:35–36. In 10:33 the people *set out* (*nsy*) and the ark *sets out* (*nsy*); the ark *seeks* the *resting place*. In 10:35

the ark *sets out*, and in v. 36 it *rests*. In these ways the ark is personified; the ark is the subject of the verbs. No one speaks of people carrying the ark or of people deciding to put it down. The two ancient sayings in 10:35–36 portray God himself attacking enemies and bringing back his own soldiers unharmed. The two images, 10:33–34 and 10:35–36, are not identical. Levine finds the Priestly editor highlighting the ark in such a way that it takes our focus away from the older image of God himself as the great warrior.

In Num 11:1–3 and 11:4–34 we are called up short by two instances of the Israelites complaining. It is not only the complaints themselves that come up suddenly; the punishments God sends down upon them are also severe and immediate. The images of rebellion and punishment in Exod 32–33 come to mind.

In 11:1 we read of the *people* (*ha'am*). This is from JE; the Priestly writers in Numbers usually refer to the *community* or *congregation* or *the sons of Israel*. The word for *complained* (*ann*) is rare; elsewhere it is only found in Lam 3:39. The use of the word *misfortunes* may be an attempt to smooth over the word *rey*, which might mean the people were *evil* or that the complaining was *about something evil*. God's immediate reaction was a *kindled* or *burning* anger; his *fire* then *burned* (*byr*) among them and *devoured* some of them. The standard vocabulary about God's anger explains little here. We have no idea of how faithless or blasphemous the complaints were.

The crisis ends just as quickly as it began. The people *cried out* (*zyq*), Moses *prayed* for them (*pll*), and the fire *sank down* (*shqy*). The place name *Taberah* (*tbyrh*) is based on the verb *byr*, *to burn*. Levine remarks that *crying out* to God is usually understood to be a sincere reaction, and the *praying* done by Moses can mean that he submitted the people to God for judgment, with the hope of God's mercy. The link between *praying* and *judging* can be found in 1 Sam 2:25, where *pll* is best translated *intercede*.

However dramatic that event may have been, it did not serve as much of a deterrent to further complaining. The people soon became unhappy with the daily gift of manna. In 11:4 two groups are mentioned, the *rabble* (*aspsp*) and the *sons of Israel*. The rabble may have been non-Israelite mercenaries or, more likely, fellow refugees. The mixed crowds in Exod 12:38 are usually considered to be non-Israelites serfs who threw in their lot with Moses and his people. The rabble had a *strong craving* (*hitawah tawah*, literally *they desired a desire*), and the sons of Israel *also turned* and *wept* or *wept again*. The verb *to desire* (*awh*) is found in the Ten Commandments in Deut 5:21 about *not coveting* a neighbor's property.

The complaint of both groups was "Who will serve us meat?" They describe their lives and strength as *drying up* (*bshh*); this is a statement of emotion and self-pity, since the manna is life sustaining. They say the fish in Egypt had *cost nothing* (*hnm*).

Whatever the merit of this grousing, both God and Moses reacted immediately. In 11:10 the Hebrew says that *in Moses' eyes it was evil*. But Moses finds the burden of everyone's complaints to be too much for him, and he lashes out at God unexpectedly in 11:11–15, 21–22. This shifts the focus away from the question of manna and meat for the moment.

In 11:11 the phrase *why have you treated your servant so badly?* is from the verb *ryy*, meaning *to do something evil*. The word *nurse* (*hamn*) in 11:12 can mean *keeper* or *guardian*. In 11:11 Moses speaks of *not finding favor with God*; in 11:15 he begs for God to kill him at once *if he has found favor with God*. His plea is almost incoherent in its sadness. He ends by begging not to see any more *misery* (*rey*, the basic word for *evil*).

God's first reaction to this overwrought plea from Moses is not one of disapproval or argument. Instead he moves quickly to get Moses the help he needs. In 11:16–17 instructions are given for Moses to choose seventy elders to assist him in governing. God himself will empower them, transferring some of the spirit he has already put upon Moses.

Shifting back to the irate crowds, God orders Moses to call an assembly and relate God's words about how much meat he will provide. The phrase in 11:8 about their wailing *in the hearing* [*ears*] *of the LORD* echoes the complaining *in the hearing* [*ears*] *of the LORD* in 11:1. In 11:20 the quantity of meat will become something *upsetting* or *loathsome* (*zra*) because they have *rejected* (*mas*) God himself. The word for loathsome is possibly related to the verb *zwr*, referring to terrible smells.

Moses' reaction to God's promise of a large supply of meat is befuddlement.

Once before Moses had worn himself to exhaustion, in Exod 18:13–27. In that case Jethro had to intervene and suggest setting up seventy elders as judges.

Now Moses thinks he is responsible to acquire the meat or fish. In the Hebrew of 11:22 the phrase *for them* is used four times; the repetition is an obvious way to highlight the stress on Moses, even if it is self-imposed.

In 11:23 God responds cryptically, assuring Moses that soon he will see whether or not God's *arm is too short*.

Moving to the next scene, Moses makes the two announcements: to gather the seventy and to have everyone else assemble the next day. The seventy leaders gathered at the tent of meeting, the small prayer tent outside the camp. God *took* (*nzl*) some of the spiritual power within Moses and put it within each one of them. The vivid Hebrew verb *nzl* can also mean *snatch away* or *rescue*. The new power within them led to prophecy for a few minutes, but they are called to be judges and advisors, not prophets.

The incident involving Eldad and Medad is puzzling. Although they stayed behind in the camp, for some reason they were found worthy of getting some of Moses' spiritual power. The plea of Joshua that Moses *stop them* (*cla*) need not imply punishment or condemnation for them. Moses' reply seems to be good-natured; he doesn't want anyone to be *jealous* (*qna*) for his own status. The word *qna* can also mean *zealous*, as of Phineas in Num 25:13 or Elijah in 1 Kgs 19:10–14. A few commentators imagine Moses as depressed or listless, rather than jocular, as he wishes that everyone could be spirit-filled.

The shift to the final scene of mass landings of quail and the festive gathering and eating of the meat is so brief that the reader is all the more shocked by the scene of stern judgment and death at the end of 11:33. The immediate mention of the mass burials, the renaming of the location, and the moving on to Hazeroth afford the reader no comfort whatsoever. Hazeroth is a few days' journey northeast of Mt. Sinai.

Note that the same verb, *nsy*, is used for the wind *going out* from the LORD in 11:31 and for the people *journeying* in 11:35. Using the same word for two very different situations can create irony.

Levine notes that Mediterranean quail still migrate south from Europe to Africa, and on the longer legs of the journey they virtually collapse at the end of the day into protective bushes and shore areas. Local hunters usually let them be, but set up traps to the south side of the resting areas to catch the birds as they take off. Trapped birds are often caged and fattened up before being eaten. In our story the people apparently dried some of the meat in the sun, another way of preserving meat.

Questions

28. Why would any author or editor preserve the information and conversation found in 10:29–32?

29. As you compare 10:33–34 to 10:35–36, all of which depicts the importance of the ark in their journeys, what is the main difference between the two passages?

30. 11:1–3 contains a brief story about complaint and punishment, which would be incomprehensible without the many other stories of murmuring in Exodus and Numbers. Why is God so stern? How sincere is the repentance of the people?

31. Compare and contrast the level of detail in 11:1–2 and 11:4–10.

32. Identify the various concerns and emotions of Moses in 11:11–15.

33. 11:16–17 shows God aiding the elders who will help Moses. At this point in the story, what would be their working roles?

34. Does the harsh style of 11:18–20 remind you of any of the divine speeches in the book of Exodus?

35. Why does Moses say 11:21–22? Comment on God's reply in 11:23.

36. In 11:26–30 what details are unclear?

37. Why does God hold onto his anger throughout 11:10–34?

Conclusion

The identification of Hobab (called Jethro in Exod 18; also called Reuel in Exod 2:18) as a cooperative Midianite is significant. Other mentions of the Midianites outside of Exod 2:16–22; 18 and Num 11 usually cast them as enemies; so they are in Judg 6:1–6 and 1 Kgs 11:18. The battle in Judg 6–8 seems to have involved the northern Israelite tribes in the main.

However, in several important passages there seems to be a change in names; the people we expect to be identified as Midianites are called Kenites instead. As far as we know, Kenites were a small subgroup of Canaanites. In Judg 1:16; 4:11 Kenites are mentioned specifically as descendants of Moses' father-in-law, and Jael, the wife of Heber the Kenite, sided with Israel when she was in danger (Judg 4:21–22). See also 1 Sam

27:10 and 30:29, wherein Kenites seem to be allies of David and the tribe of Judah. In 1 Sam 15:6, when Saul spared some Kenites, he made a clear reference to their ancestors' kindnesses to Moses and his people when they left Egypt.

If some Kenites were allies at the time of the conquest of Canaan and the early monarchy, stories about them could have been projected back to the time of Moses. The traditional solution to this blending of references to Kenites and Midianites in the Pentateuch was to assume that the Kenites were a Midianite clan. But that solution may have simply been circular reasoning.

Instead, Levine argues that the Priestly editors consciously used the term Midianite for other reasons, substituting and inserting the name in several places in Numbers. At times they used Midianites to represent all Canaanites. One example might be Num 22:4, 7, where Midianites are included by Priestly editors in the Balaam story, which has to do mainly with Moabites. At the end of that account, the JE story continues by mentioning Moabite temptresses (25:1–5). Once again, Priestly editors (25:6–18) shift the story back to the Midianites, focusing on one woman, Cozbi, in particular.

Various peoples and kingdoms opposed the Israelites during the conquest period. Saul battled Amalekites (1 Sam 15), descendants of those who opposed Moses in Exod 17. Ammonites and Edomites were hostile, but conflicts with them were avoided in the main storyline of Numbers. The Moabites were in some sense neutralized by Balaam's oracles. Midianites were slaughtered by Moses in Num 31, a Priestly chapter. Levine suggests that JE editors paid less attention to Midianites, but that P included them to make up for JE omissions.

As we jump back and forth between Numbers and the later histories in Joshua, Judges, Samuel, and Kings, the various Pentateuch traditions, J, E, and P, push ethnic and regional feuds back to the time of Moses whenever possible. This pattern helps anyone to justify conquering the descendents of his ancestors' enemies. On the other hand, remembering the cooperative Kenites (or the few non-hostile Midianites) is important. The descendents of an ancestor's allies (even an ancestor's in-laws) represent the allies in Judges and 1 Samuel, and remind readers that Canaanites eventually made peace in various ways with their conquerors. They were not all put to the sword, despite the huffing of Priestly and Deuteronomic editors.

Section Eleven

NUMBERS 12:1–16

Introduction

The disputes of Num 11 do not prepare us for the sudden outburst from Aaron and Miriam in Num 12. The brief introduction (12:1–3) leads to firm praise from God for Moses' unique role and relationship with God (12:4–9). The panic of Aaron and Moses that follows the skin disease that afflicts Miriam is met by God's merciful limiting of her punishment to seven days, but the force of 12:14 is still troubling for many readers. Another worthwhile question is why Aaron does not receive any punishment at all for his complicity in the original complaint. The final verse is from P, and seems to be an attempt to fine-tune an independent JE tradition.

The verb and preposition *to speak against* (*dbr b*) Moses in 12:1, 8 is also used for the phrases *has the LORD spoken only through Moses* and not *spoken through us* (both in 12:2), and *with him I speak* (12:8). English needs many more prepositions than Hebrew does. *Speaking against* someone can certainly signify true rebellion (see Num 21:5–7 and Ps 78:19, a direct allusion to Num 11).

The reference to a Cushite wife is somewhat unclear. Moses' wife Zipporah, in Exod 2:16–22, is a Midianite. The land of Cush traditionally covers regions of Sudan, Nubia, and Ethiopia, all south of Egypt. Hab 3:7 puts the lands of Cush and Midian in poetic parallel.

Levine assumes that the Cushite wife was not Zipporah, but another woman he married after divorcing Zipporah—a possible, but not definite, interpretation of Exod 18:1–6. Other commentators simply take Zipporah as the reference.

Levine agrees that most Cushites were probably black (as in Jer 13:23), but he denies any interracial implications in Num 12:1. He suggests instead that the underlying issue might have been alimony or property rights for Zipporah and her children, or some similar social issue relevant at the time of the early monarchy, when the story may have been composed. Our solitary verse, 12:1, sheds no light on any of this.

In 12:2 Aaron and Miriam consider themselves worthy of the same status as Moses. Moses stays out of the line of fire here; God intervenes directly to debate their claim. In 12:3 Moses is called *humble* (*anw*). The plural form is *anawim*, an important theological term describing one's spiritual relationship to God. In context, the humbleness of Moses might be mainly his obedience to all of God's directives.

The first half of 12:6 is difficult. The literal translation is *if there is your prophet [who is of] YHWH, by an appearance to him I will reveal myself; in a dream I will speak with him*. There have been many attempts to reconstruct the original text; the NRSV is adequate for our purposes. In 12:7, as God calls Moses *my servant* (*ybd*), one *entrusted* (*amn*) with all my *house* (or *household* or *court business*), he bestows the highest possible praise. The key virtue of a servant is loyalty. Levine notes that this is the only biblical reference where God is described as having a *household*.

The words for *vision* in 12:6 and for *clear vision* in 12:8 (translated as *clearly* in NRSV) are from the same root. *Clear vision* is presumably more powerful.

In Num 12:11 Aaron begins by saying to Moses, *On me, my lord*. The NRSV may give a pale translation here. Levine has *by my life, master*. He also suggests that the phrase *on me* might be short for a phrase such as *the guilt should be on me* or *I am willing to substitute my life for Miriam's*. So Aaron seems to be truly repentant for both himself and Miriam.

In Num 12:11 Aaron admits to *acting foolishly* (*yal*). This is a rare Hebrew verb (see Isa 19:13 or Jer 5:4).

When Moses *cries out* (*zyk*) he calls God by the older name of *El*. The text quotes Moses as saying *El na rpa na lah*, literally *God, I beg you, heal, I beg you, her*. Levine suggests that *El na* was originally *Al na*, as in Aaron's request in 12:11, *do not, I beg you*. He polishes his translation of Moses' words to "No more, I beseech you! Heal her, I beseech you!" The double use of *na* in such a short quote indicates strong emotions.

Spitting is obviously an act of shaming, as in Deut 25:9 or in the well-known saying in Isa 50:6. In Lev 13:4 the smallest new skin discoloration demands a seven-day quarantine before reexamination.

Levine takes 12:14–15 as a JE tradition, rather than Priestly, even though the notion of quarantine is dominant.

On the other hand, Num 12:16 could be a Priestly insert, an attempt to reaffirm the P tradition in Num 10:12, where they had gone directly to Paran, with the JE tradition in Num 11:35, where they had just arrived at Hazeroth, an area likely outside of Paran.

Questions

38. For whatever reason Moses' marriage to a Cushite could be questioned or challenged, how central to Num 12 is the marriage?

39. How does God deal with Aaron and Miriam in 12:4–9?

40. In 12:10–15 Miriam is publicly punished for her complaints against Moses. This comes after Aaron's confession that he was equally guilty, and after Moses' heartfelt plea for mercy. Why was Aaron not punished in some commensurate way? Why such a dramatic finale to the story? How does this passage enhance the lessons of the chapter?

Conclusion

At the end of commenting on Num 11–12, Levine (1:338–43) offers an overview of the role of Moses, in light of Exodus passages and some depictions of King David. I think his remarks are worth summarizing here.

In Exod 18, at Jethro's suggestion, Moses appointed skilled people (not necessarily elders) to be minor judges. In 18:21 they are called *able men from among all the people*. In 1 Sam 8:12 all kings are described as appointing competent commanders as needed. In Num 11:16 Moses chose some of the elders to be given spiritual power to help him rule. So Moses makes his own choices, and God supports him in those choices by empowering those people.

In Exod 24:1–2, 9–11 elders go with Moses and Aaron to higher places on Mt. Sinai. In 24:11 the elders are called *chief men* (*azilim*). This is the only use of this word in the Bible. The apparently related verb *azl* was used in Num 11:17, 25 to mean *to take some* of the spirit.

The cloud that covers the tent of meeting in Exod 33:7–11 is the same cloud that came down in Num 11:25.

Parallels of this sort recall Exodus chapters and so put the events of Numbers in context.

When the spirit came upon the seventy chosen elders, they *prophesied* for a short time. This form of the verb *nba* focuses on the result of being empowered; one speaks in ecstatic tongues or delivers a specific message. Prophetic speech is often portrayed as a temporary effect.

In Num 11:25 the spirit *rested* (*nwh*) on the seventy men. This verb does not focus on speech, but on the very conferring of the spirit. We assume that this conferral permanently endowed these elders with the ability to help Moses govern.

In biblical stories about heroes, the spirit empowers them to specific feats of strength or military victory, but the authors never speak of that spirit *resting* on them. The only exception is David. In 1 Sam 16:13 David was empowered by the spirit at his anointing *from that day forward*. The great passage in Isa 11:1–9 describes the unending rule of a great king upon whom the spirit *shall rest* (*nwh*, in 11:2).

In Num 11:29 Moses wishes that everyone could be prophets. But Num 12:6–8 reminds us that Moses' role and power is way beyond that given to any prophet at any time. God says in Num 11:8 that he speaks *face to face* with Moses. Similar phrases occur in Exod 33:11 and Deut 34:10. The phrase must refer to having unfiltered or crystal-clear communication between Moses and God. This does not annul the more doctrinal remark in Exod 33:20 that no one can see God and still remain living on earth.

So Exod 18 and Num 11–12 profile Moses not only as a prophet but also as a king, and as the model for future kings, such as David. Look again at Num 12:7, *my servant Moses is entrusted* [*amn*] *with all my house*. A strong parallel can be found in 1 Sam 22:14, where Ahimelech says to Saul about David, "Who among your *servants* is so *faithful* [*amn*] as David . . . he is honored in your *house*." So the Pentateuch pushes back terms used of King David to honor Moses, thus legitimizing David's later rule. It also compares Moses to prophets, to honor him all the more.

In summary, Levine (1:343) points out that any right-minded king will rely partially on elders according to the ancient tribal system, appoint other highly skilled people as needed, yet submit himself to the power of the prophetic spirit of which we read in Isa 9:1–11. He should rule with justice and equity, promoting peace, prosperity, and security for all, and always seeking to have more of the proper fear/awe of the LORD.

Section Twelve

NUMBERS 13:1—14:45

Introduction

In the next two chapters the people have another important task: scouting out parts of the land of Canaan and planning an initial attack from the southwest, the direct route from their journey from Egypt. This story is also summarized in Deut 1:19-45.

Levine lists the complex interweaving of P and JE sources in these two chapters. Putting the sources in two columns will shed light on the editing process for this emotionally packed episode. It can be quite helpful to outline the sections of biblical text with different colored pens to better follow the interweaving of the variant traditions.

P Verses		JE Verses	
13:1-17a	scouts chosen in Paran	13:17b-20	tasks specified for Negeb
13:21	variant tradition about sites	13:22-24	Negeb visited
13:25-26	scouts return to Kadesh	13:27-31	extensive report given, Caleb urges battle
13:32	very negative report given	13:33	Nephilim mentioned
14:1a, 5-7a, 10	people panic	14:1b, 2-4, 7b-9	Moses, leaders trust
		14:11-25	Moses pleads with angry God
14:26-38	God speaks of punishment, most of the scouts die in a plague	14:39-45	people choose to battle without God's approval

59

Taking 13:1–17a as a Priestly introduction, God wants *leaders* or *princes* (*nsi*) from among the ruling classes of each tribe to *spy* or *scout out* (*twr*) the Promised Land. P uses this verb *twr*; JE will use the ordinary word for *see* or *observe* in 13:18, and Deuteronomists use *hpr*, meaning *to uncover* or *explore*. The term *land of Canaan* is used mainly by P, but other sources use it also. God speaks of *giving* them the land, which is normal covenantal language. P mentions the *land of Paran* in 13:3.

Several of the names of the scouts are not found elsewhere; perhaps the list was known only to Priestly editors. Caleb from Judah and Hoshea from Ephraim are well known, of course. Note the change of name from Hoshea to Joshua in the gloss in 13:16.

In the JE tradition, starting in 13:17b Moses sends the spies north or northeast and then has them *go up* into the central mountain range of Canaan. The verb *go up* often means *go north* in regions where rivers run to the south.

The commission in 13:18–20 to gather information about the land is picturesque. The word for *unwalled towns* is the word normally used for *campsites*. The season of the first ripe grapes is our late summer.

Levine notes that in Canaan there was always a mix of unwalled and walled towns, and some marginally fertile sloped areas were at times occupied and at times abandoned. Some of these marginal areas were in hilly upper Galillee, Ephraim, and Judea. Others include the semi-arid regions of the Negeb highlands, some of the Beersheba valley, and Judean hills around Hebron. The last three areas, all in south-central Canaan, are mentioned in these two chapters.

The P addition in 13:21 adds mention of the wilderness of Zin, Rehob, and Lebo-hamath. Levine locates these places in the far north of Canaan.

Returning to JE in 13:22–24, the remark that Hebron was built seven years before Zoan (Tanis) in Egypt is quite wrong. Apparently many ancient traditions claimed that Zoan (Tanis) was much older than it was in fact. Scholars estimate that it was founded about 1100 BCE.

As we return to another P section in 13:25–26, the editor links the city of Kadesh with the wilderness of Paran. This is an artificial linking; Kadesh is too far north and east for anyone but the Priestly editors to consider it to be within the wilderness of Paran.

At the start of the next JE section, 13:27–31, Levine suggests that the *honey* in the compound phrase *land of milk and honey* might well be a generic reference to the sap of fruit trees. We can think of agricultural and grazing riches, rather than primarily of beehives. On many of these mountain slopes vines and orchards vied with grazing grounds.

The reference to Amalekites (13:29) might be a retrojection from the time of David, but they are mentioned in the Negeb in 1 Sam 15:5; 30:1, 18. Jebusites are mentioned in the central range in Judg 19:10–11 and Sam 5:6. Others suggest that the mention of Amorites (westerners) and Hittites (possibly Syrians) seem to be anachronisms here. In any case, the tone of 13:29 is to point to powerful enemies all around.

In 13:30 Caleb *quiets* (*hsh*) the people; this is a very rare verb. When he suggests that they are *able to occupy* (*rshh*) the land, he is referring to taking it by force. The spies' responses in 13:31, 33 indicate their fear or misgivings about such a battle. In 13:33 they compared the Anakites to the Nephilim, the semi-divine legendary beings elsewhere mentioned only in the primeval legend of Gen 6:4. The reference to *grasshoppers* is melodramatic. The scouts felt tiny in comparison to the walled cities and the Anakites, and they imagined that the Anakites had exactly the same impression of them as tiny scouts.

The P editorial insert in 13:32 goes beyond the legitimate misgivings of the scouts. It speaks of them *choosing to issue* (*iza*) an *unfavorable* or *bad report*, a *calumny* (*dbh*) about the land itself. These charges are repeated later in 14:36–37. In 14:37 it is even called an *evil calumny* (*dbh ryh*). To describe a land as *devouring its inhabitants* is to use the language of cursing, as in Lev 26:38 or Ezek 36:13–14. Such curses may mean that the people of the land slay invaders, or that they offer their own children in ritual sacrifice. A striking blessing, the exact opposite of the image in Num 13:32, is found in Ezek 36:8–12.

The Priestly editors took this deliberately distorted report by the scouts as a very serious sin, and not just an exaggeration made in panic.

Levine suggests that while the Priestly editors assembled 14:1–10, they borrowed several notes from the JE account. So the P editing sections are 14:1a, 5–7a, 10.

The JE phrases, in 14:1b, 2–4, 7b–9, focus on the fear of battle, and on their leaders trying to quell that fear. The people could consider returning to Egypt instead of fighting.

Within the same passage Priestly editors use the term *congregation* consistently, and describe the intense attitude of prayer of Moses, Aaron, Caleb, and Joshua. The final image, in 14:10, is that the whole congregation *threatened to stone* the four leaders. This sinful anger rouses the LORD in his glory, who comes to the tent of meeting immediately.

The effect of the Priestly editing of these ten verses is to dramatize all the more the fear noted at the end of Num 13, and to turn it into sinful rebellion.

In 14:2 the people *complained* (*lwn*) or *murmured*. Levine suggests that this complaining is a formal procedure in 14:36 and 16:41. In several other citations the murmuring is instigated by others (see 14:27; 16:11; 17:5). In all these cases we should see that murmuring is not simply individuals grousing over the back fence or at the water cooler. It affects everyone, so it must be taken seriously.

The phrase *would that we had died* is used twice in 14:2 for effect. The theme will appear again in 20:3-5.

The notion of appointing a new *leader* (*head*) in 14:4 makes sense, but Levine argues that the phrase might simply refer to a new direction. So he translates it "Let us head back and return to Egypt."

When Moses and Aaron fall down before the *assembly* (*qhl*, often used in Deuteronomy) of the *congregation*, the gesture could have meant grief or imploring. The final phrase in 14:7 is that *this is a good land, very very*. The double use of *very* indicates the superlative, and has to be translated appropriately. Here the NRSV calls it an *exceedingly good land*. The phrase *if the LORD is pleased with us* functions much as our own idiom, "Lord willing." The plea *do not rebel* (*mrd*) indicates active defiance rather than just giving up. The *people of the land* (Canaanites) will be *bread* (prey). In 14:9 their *protection* (*zl*) could mean whatever gods the Canaanites relied on.

Num 14:11-25 contains a major JE interaction between God and Moses in the spirit of Exod 32:9-14, 30-35; 34:9. God is upset that the people *despise* him (*naz*), and *refuse to believe in* him (*amn*). The first verb means *to have active disdain* or *disrespect*, and the second means *to not trust*. Both verbs have a personal dimension; we are not talking about abstractions of monotheism or doctrine at this point. It is a matter of betraying a covenant partner, a partner for life. The possibility of God using Moses as a replacement for the chosen people is also found in Exod 32:9-10 and Deut 9:14.

Moses' reply is spirited, as it was in Exod 32-33. In Num 14:20 God tells Moses that he agrees to forgive, *according to your words*.

Still, forgiveness, apology, and atonement are always intertwined. The first generation—the veterans of Egypt, the partner in two covenants, the followers of the golden calf, and the ones who complained time after time—will all pass away before their children cross over into the Promised Land. The covenant relationship is still personal, as far as God is concerned. These people *tested me* (*nsh*); they *have not listened to my voice*; they *despised me* (*naz*, as in 14:11). Caleb is the lone exception here, a man with a different spirit, one who was always following the LORD.

God's final instruction in 14:25 is that the people should take the longer but less dangerous route northeast from Kadesh toward Edom, Moab, and the eastern side of the Jordan River. This same route is mentioned in Num 21:4 and Deut 1:40; 2:1.

The final Priestly supplement, Num 14:26–38, reviews this stern topic of the first generation passing away in the wilderness. The sinfulness of the people and the righteous anger of God are painted in intense strokes.

Aaron joins Moses as God begins his speech. Phrases meaning *how long* connect 14:27 with 14:11. The terms *this people* (14:11) and *this wicked congregation* (14:27) indicate that the earlier passage was from JE and the latter from P. The word *complain* or *murmur* is used three times in 14:27, indicating God's rising irritation with their egging each other on in dissatisfaction.

Joshua, in 14:30, joins Caleb as another exception to the fate of this generation. In 14:33 the children of the next generation are described as *shepherds*. The same verb in Hos 12:1 can be translated *Ephraim herds the wind*, meaning that Ephraim is leading an aimless life. Perhaps that is the sense here. Levine translates "your children will *roam about* in the wilderness." The *faithlessness* (*znwt*) comes from a noun meaning *prostitution*, a standard analogy for idolatry.

In 14:34 God's intends to show his *displeasure* (*tnwah*). The verb behind this noun means *to hinder* or *prevent* something. In Num 30:5, 8 it means to prevent a vow from being fulfilled, and in Num 32:7 it means to *discourage* the hearts of the Israelites. Levine uses a circumlocution to connect God's anger with the root of the verb, so he translates "you shall know what the denial of me entails."

God describes the crowd *gathered against* him (*iyd*) in 14:35. The same word will be used in 16:11, where Moses braces some rebellious Levites for *gathering together against the LORD*. The closing phrase of 14:35, *they shall come to a full end, and there they shall die*, uses two verbs with similar consonant patterns. *To come to an end* is from *tmm* and *to die* is from *mwt*. The phrase in Hebrew is *yitammu wesham yamutu*.

Wordplay is not an end in itself; here the play on sounds and vocabulary enhance the solemnity of God's judgment.

At the end (14:36–38) the spies (except for Joshua and Caleb) are called those who *caused others to complain* or *murmur*; the spies brought a *bad report* [*dbh*] *about the land*. It was an *unfavorable report* (literally, *a bad report that was evil*). We can say that it was against the land. This criticism was also raised in 13:32. For this sin they died in a deadly plague.

The response of the crowd in 14:39–45 (JE) makes sense in connection with 14:22–23 (JE). The people *mourned* (*abl*) and admitted that they had *sinned*, but then they wanted to go to battle, the very battle they had feared earlier.

It seems that their conversion to obedience came too late. Moses tells them that now they are *transgressing* God's command. The verb means *to cross over* or *go beyond*; in their haste to patch up their strained relationship with God they are in effect trying to *get around* or *beyond* the decree that all the first generation must die in the wilderness.

Moses spells out his disagreement with them. If they go to battle, it *will not be a success* (*zlh*). The same word in Gen 39:2 is used of Joseph, a *successful man* in Potiphar's house. The chain of dire predictions in Num 14:42–43 is enhanced by the two general statements about the LORD: *he is not among them* and *he will not be with them*.

Despite the clear warning from Moses, and his refusal to go with them or let the ark be put at risk, they *presumed* or *had the audacity* (*ypl*) to go to battle. The verb only appears this one time in the Bible. The final verb in 14:45, *pursuing them* (*ktt*), indicates a very complete, indeed, a smashing victory for the defenders; *Ktt* means *to pulverize*.

The last place name, *Hormah*, means *destruction*. Note 21:1–3, which has an alternate tradition that the name *Hormah* came about as the result of an Israelite victory in another war. There is no way to choose which is the more accurate derivation, if either.

Questions

41. As Moses prepared to send undercover scouts or spies to learn more about the southern regions of Canaan, why did he choose one from each tribe? Even though each one was a chieftain, there were more than twelve of them from whom to choose. How did Moses make his choices?

42. Look at 13:17–24, skipping 13:21. Comment on the style as well as the content of these verses.

43. The scouts' reply continues in 13:27–33. Holding back on 13:32 as an aside from P, comment on the style and content of this passage. Afterward, note the content of 13:32 by itself.

44. How would you characterize the unity of the chosen people as you read 14:1–10?

45. Comment on God's thinking in 14:11–12 and 14:20–25, skipping the intervening verses for the moment.

46. How does Moses line up his pleading in 14:13–19?

47. The Priestly section in 14:26–38 does contain repetitions. What new items do you find in it?

48. How does the final fiasco of 14:39–45 serve to sum up all of chapters 13–14?

Conclusion

The traditions in the JE and P strata behind Num 13–14 just begin to explain the decades-long delay in reaching the Promised Land. For P the delay will be acted out mostly in the wilderness of Paran, while JE indicates more time spent east of Edom and Moab.

Historians have great difficulty reconciling the various conquest traditions, since Joshua, Judges, Numbers, and Deuteronomy have conflicting stories and incomplete information. One example is that Kadesh is not as old as reported; it may have originally been an Israelite border station in Solomon's time, rather than a Canaanite site visited by the scouts reporting to Moses. Num 21:1–3, although brief, indicates that there were some early successful incursions into the Negeb by Israelite tribes (see Num 21:31–35 for more victories, as well as the Danite adventures in Judg 18).

For now we should accept the likelihood of many conquest traditions being pushed back to the time of Moses, and we should realize that most ancient Near Eastern cultures considered the favor and disfavor of their gods as the determining factor in times of war.

As we watch Moses negotiate with God, Levine joins other commentators not only in their respect for Moses' leadership, but also for

God's willingness to allow Moses such active voice. The two are a team, even though they are not always on the same page. Moses keeps trying to hold everything together, whether the people have betrayed God for a golden calf image or betrayed him by being afraid of their assignment to battle.

One final consideration: Levine notes that we cannot allow an individualistic reading of Num 14:18 to lock us into an image of a cruel God. How God balances *not clearing the guilty* with *visiting the iniquity of the parents upon the children to the third and the fourth generation* is always part of his dealing with all Israel. For that matter, the great creed of Exod 34:6–7, reflecting subtle changes from that in Exod 20:5–6, is always part of God's dealings with all peoples and nations worldwide, whether they know it or not. Exod 34:6–7 is a way of claiming that God balances justice and mercy, and a way of admitting that we don't know how to do that ourselves.

To put it simply, nations get themselves into crises, and God needs time to help them out in the best way. Exod 32:33–34 shows God telling Moses to move ahead, even though things are not yet completely solved. In Jer 27:1–7 and 32:1–5 the prophet describes punishments from God that will take years to resolve. So too, Num 13–14 explain delays in the arrival of promised blessings, delays not from a cruel God but from a God who knows what changes of heart his people need to have first.

Section Thirteen

NUMBERS 15:1–41

Introduction

After just a few chapters outlining infighting among those journeying with Moses, we find ourselves with more divine instructions for rituals. The inner logic behind the details is, as usual, assumed but not explained. For priestly editors rituals are as important as stories about the past. Any later reader who prefers to follow the story line of history will just have to try harder to appreciate the importance of laws within a religion of orthopraxis.

The several subdivisions include (following Levine 1:385–86):

Num 15:1–16	Grain offerings, libations to accompany sacrifices
Num 15:17–21	Rules about portions of bread dough in presentation
Num 15:22–31	Atonements for involuntary infractions
Num 15:32–36	Case of a man gathering firewood on Sabbath
Num 15:37–41	Blue fringes and cords on cloaks

In earlier biblical legislation, *grain offerings* (*minhah*) and *drink offerings* or *libations* (*nsk*) could be offered by themselves. In this chapter they are depicted as obligatory supplements to the principal offerings—whole-burnt (*ollah*), shared sacrifice at vow fulfillment (*zbh ndr*), freewill offerings (*ndbh*), offerings at appointed festivals (*meod*), and sin offerings (*hattat*) (see Num 28–29 for regulations on the public sacrifices; Lev 1–3; 6:1–11; 7:11–34 refer to the same topics).

Usually the ceremonial instructions refer to raw grain or flour (see Deut 26:1–11 and Deut 14:22–29). In Num 15:20 *dough* (*arisot*) is specified, apparently for a new ceremony.

The matter of inadvertent infractions comes up in Lev 4–5. The firewood gathering story is like the one in Lev 24, about a blasphemer.

Num 15:1–2 uses the standard covenant style, pushing more legislation all the way back to the time of Moses. Num 15:3 mentions many of the sacrifices involving fire. Calling them *a pleasing odor for the LORD* may sound childish but it is one way to honor the system. In fact incense and other fragrances were added to some sacrifices for the sake of those attending (see Lev 2). The tabernacle was incensed regularly (Exod 30;24–28), and there were daily incense offerings (Exod 30:7–10, 32–33). In Num 19:6 cedar and hyssop are added to the red heifer sacrifice, perhaps for this purpose.

The word for *grain offering* in Num 15:4 (*minhah*) is a generic word that can mean any sort of gift or offering. In Gen 4:3–5 the gifts of Cain and Abel, both plant and animal, were called *minhah*. Aside from Num 15, usually grain or bread offerings were shown at the altar or other sanctuary site, but they were not burnt. The showbreads of Lev 24:5–9 and the firstfruits of Deut 26:1–11 were not burnt. Also, Lev 7:12–15 mentions two loaves for *thanksgiving offerings* (*todah*), which were not burnt. It seems that the custom developed of making grain offerings in the late afternoon or early evening (see 2 Kgs 16:15; Ps 141:2; Ezra 9:4; Dan 9:21).

As far as we can estimate, one tenth of an *ephah* was about 2.2 liters (dry or liquid), and a *hin* was 3.6 liters (liquid). Perhaps the oil was simply poured upon the flour; we do not know how completely they were mixed together.

Sacrifices of *well-being* (*shlmin*) are mentioned in 15:8. Like some of the sacrifices for the fulfillment of a vow, sacrifices of well-being (also called *peace offerings*) were shared with the worshippers (see Lev 7:11–18).

Num 15:13 mentions that the rules apply to every *native Israelite*. The Hebrew word means *one born in the land*. So the author is looking ahead several centuries. Any *alien* (*ger*, a resident non-citizen) could attend ceremonies and make the same sort of offerings. In Jewish custom an alien should not be persecuted or disdained, but was expected to respect local laws and to be mindful of local religious events. This was complicated in that Israelites were monotheistic and allowed no public displays or ceremonies involving other deities. Aliens often included slaves, former

Section Thirteen

slaves, and Canaanite serfs. In the same verse, 15:14, another term, *anyone who takes up permanent residence* (the Hebrew is literally *whoever may be in your midst in coming generations*) seems to have been added for the sake of completeness.

The final four verses, 15:13–16, grow in redundancy for the sake of solemnity.

The next ceremony seems to be a new one. Num 15:19 speaks of *whenever you eat of the bread*. Perhaps this refers to harvest time, as in Josh 5:11–12. At that time a *donation* is made. The Hebrew is *you shall make a presentation offering* [*terumah*]. A round cake or loaf from the first batch or stage of dough will be used, in the same way as grain from the threshing floor is presented in other offerings. The *first* batch might mean *first in quality*, just as for all other sacrificial foods.

Levine suggests that the word for *dough* (*arisot*) in 15:20–21 may refer to a *baking bowl*, the better to parallel with *threshing floor*.

The next section, Num 15:22–31, is not well organized. To some extent these new regulations are like those in Lev 4–5 on community annual atonement ceremonies. In Lev 4:2, 22 both ritual and legal offenses are mentioned, but in any case the action was *unintentional* (two verbs are used, *shgg* and *shgh*). A community could err unintentionally by not understanding details of ritual or law; or it could err by not comprehending the act itself, such as eating a forbidden food when thinking it was a different food. We would call these sins of omission, failure to perform commands. By contrast, in Lev 4–5 the topic is sins of commission.

In these verses the language becomes more serious. The many regulations are called *commandments*, a strong term. The whole community offers a bull as a whole-burnt offering, and a goat for a *sin offering* (*hattat*). They will be forgiven for their *error* (*shgg*).

In Num 15:27–31 the focus switches to individuals (as in Lev 4:27–5:14). But in 15:30–31 we switch to active defiance of God. Here a person *acts with a high hand, affronting* [*gdp*] *the LORD*. By some action, the individual *despises* (*bzh*) the word of God and *breaks* (*prr*) his commandment. All this indicates premeditation. To *bear the guilt* is to bear the punishment.

Describing the process of *cutting someone off* from the people is a reference to shunning, which is a severe procedure of disapproval and isolation. It is not a death threat as such, but in a way it is almost worse.

The public trial of the firewood gatherer reminds one of Lev 24:10–23, wherein a man who cursed using God's name was apprehended and executed. Exod 35:3 clearly outlaws the lighting of any fire on the Sabbath for any reason. In both the Leviticus and Numbers stories the people are not sure about the application of the death penalty, even though the prohibitions against taking the LORD's name in vain and working on the Sabbath are clear. God resolves the situation in each case by simply ordering stoning by the community—end of case.

The instruction about using *fringes* (*zizit*) at certain places on their garments and attaching or interweaving blue *threads* or *cord* (*ptil*) to those fringes is clear enough. Levine assumes that the law may have referred only to the clothing of adult males. A somewhat similar law appears in Deut 22:12, but is not explained.

What is less obvious is the efficacy of these weavings to remind people that they are not to *follow* (*twr*) the *lust* (*znim*) of their hearts and eyes, but instead recall and obey all God's commands. The word for *following* is the same word that has been used for *wandering* in the desert. The word for *lust* can be taken literally to mean sexual excess, but clearly is being used here to represent faithlessness and idolatry. Obeying every command is the only way to uphold the covenant.

The blue dye may have come from murex shells, a very expensive but permanent coloration. Perhaps the few threads or cords interwoven among the fringes would be visually striking. Jewish men still use blue fringes on their prayer shawls at synagogue services in our own day.

Questions

49. In 15:1–16 the use of grain, oil, and wine in various sacrifices is spelled out. What effect does the phrase *a pleasing odor to the Lord* (vv. 3, 7, 10, 13, 14) provide for the reader? What do you know about the resident aliens?

50. When we examine the three cases in 15:22–26, 27–29, and 30–31 how are the priestly editors profiling these failings of the nation and of individuals?

51. Biblical teachers often try to have students broaden their view of the context of a verse, paragraph, or chapter. The brief story of the man gathering firewood on the Sabbath troubles many modern readers, and looking for its context hardly allays their unease. We know nothing about this man. Was he young or old, gathering

firewood for his own meal or for his family, acting carelessly or with impunity? How does his action measure up to the larger acts of defiance in the murmuring stories? Why could he not have been shunned instead, as was just outlined in 15:30–31?

52. How does this pious tradition of using blue piping or cord fit into the overall context of Num 15?

Section Fourteen

NUMBERS 16:1—17:13

Please note: In the Hebrew text Num 16 has just thirty-five verses, and chapter 17 has twenty-eight verses, for a total of sixty-three. Modern English bibles have fifty verses for chapter 16 and thirteen verses for chapter 17, coming to the same total of sixty-three. So the numbering systems come back to agreement at the start of chapter 18.

For the sake of clarity, I will use English chapter and verse numbers exclusively.

Introduction

The next two chapters, 16–17, show more unrest and rebellion, this time led by some Levites. The story of Aaron's rod serves as an appendix. Levine divides the sources as follows:

Num 16:1–2	JE, with Korah's name added by P
Num 16:3–11	P
Num 16:12–15	JE
Num 16:16–24	P, names of Dathan and Abiram in v.24 borrowed from JE
Num 16:25–34	JE, with Korah's name in vv.27, 32 added by P
Num 16:35–50	P
Num 17:1–13	P

In 3:27 we find that Kohath, the ancestor of the main clan of Levites, was grandfather to Korah, Moses, and Aaron. Kohath's son Amram was the father of Moses and Aaron (Exod 6:20), and now we learn that

Kohath's son Izhar was the father of Korah. Thus Korah is a first cousin to Moses and Aaron.

The other three men, Dathan, Abiram, and Or, were Reubenites.

Levine suggests that Priestly editors added Korah's name to a story originally concerning Reubenites. The two groups and their stories were woven together easily. Dathan and Abiram are mentioned briefly in Deut 11:6.

The verb *took* in 16:1 actually has no object expressed. Many emendations have been suggested, but none are completely convincing. The NRSV takes the 250 men of 16:2 to be the object, just to make for a smoother reading in English.

The 250 men are called *chiefs of the congregation, chosen men of the assembly* [*qrai moed*], *men of renown*. The verb form in the second title, *chosen* (*qrai*), is found also in Num 26:9, also which refers to this event. The noun in the second title, *assembly* (*moed*), is the word we have seen used often in the phrase *tent of meeting*, the prayer tent used by Moses. Levine proposes that this title, *chosen men of the assembly*, used only here in the Bible, might refer to a national advisory council of some sort for which we have no other record.

The verb for *assemble* (*qhl*) in 16:3 can also mean *rally* or *demonstrate*. Context indicates that there is tension in the meeting. The Hebrew for *you have gone too far* is actually the verbless phrase *Too much for you!* This emotional interjection is used often (see Deut 1:6; 2:3; 3:19). Moses' gesture of falling is one of submission to God's will rather than to the will of the crowd. Readers are kept in the dark at this point; we do not know what decisions God has already made, or how much Moses knows.

All the pronouns in 16:5 are in the singular. The two phrases for being *allowed to approach* can apply to priests, but they are basically court language, as we find in Gen 45:10; Lev 10:3; Esth 1:14.

At the end of Num 16:7 the translation *You Levites have gone too far* is the same verbless phrase from 16:3, *Too much for you!* The opening question in 16:9, *Is it too little for you?*, is a sarcastic or argumentative twist on the *Too much for you!* phrase. The rest of the verse describes the duties of the Levites to assist the priests, and how much of a privilege and responsibility that is. But even so, these demonstrators seek the rank of *priesthood* (*chnh*).

In Num 16:11 Moses makes it clear that *murmuring* or *railing against* Aaron is the same as *gathering together* [*iyd*] *against* the LORD.

The JE tradition in Num 16:12-15 focuses on the Reubenites. Moses *sends a summons* to Dathan and Abiram, but they refuse to meet with him. Their protest is reported in 16:13-14. Levine notes that the statement *We will not come* in 16:12, 14 might be vague enough to mean that they do not want to continue on the journey at all. The argumentative tone is picked up in 16:13 with *Is it too little that you*, using the phrase from the beginning of 16:9. The argument is the equivalent of saying, "Haven't you done enough harm already?" Num 16:13 ends with the emphatic phrase *you lord it over us and continue to lord*; the verb is built on a noun meaning *ruler* or *leader*. The mention of *putting out the eyes of these men* apparently includes the speakers, Dathan and Abiram, along with their followers. Moses had said nothing about this, but it was a common punishment for runaway slaves or prisoners, or rebellious vassals. The dissatisfaction of these Reubenites has to do with the stress of the wandering in the desert; they do not seen to concern themselves with the problems of who is or is not eligible for the priesthood.

But in 16:15 Moses wants to defend himself before God. The phrase *pay no attention to their offering* might have been an idiom or a curse. It could remind one of Gen 4, where God regards Abel's gift but not Cain's. Moses affirms that he has not gained any wealth from his leadership, and that he has done no harm (see 1 Sam 12:3, where Samuel defends himself with equally dramatic questions).

The P traditions pick up again in 16:16-24. The stage is set for Korah, his 250 fellow Levites, and Aaron to be judged by God himself. In 16:19 we see that, as in 16:3, Korah had *assembled* or *rallied* the whole community *against* Moses and Aaron; they all will get to watch who is holy enough to approach God.

In Num 16:20, as God's determination rises he warns Moses and Aaron to *separate themselves* (*bdl*) from the entire community, lest the two of them be harmed. This verb *bdl* is the main post-exilic term for Jewish people staying apart from social or religious interaction with pagans (see Ezra 9:1; Lev 20:24 for clear examples about separation as an ideal).

In their prayer for mercy, Moses and Aaron speak of *one person* sinning and the whole congregation suffering. Levine suggests that the context covers many persons—Kohar, Dathan, Abiram, their households, and the 250 Levites. The prayer of Moses and Aaron still has its merit even if we were to have them speak of *some individuals* sinning. In the

Section Fourteen

prayer of 16:22 Moses and Aaron address *God, the God of the spirits of all flesh* (*El, Elohe haruhot lekol basar*), combining elements from Gen 33:20 (*God, the God of Israel; El, Elohe Israel*) and Num 27:16 (*the LORD, the God of the spirits of all flesh; YHWH, Elohe haruhot lekol basar*). This method of blending titles and names for God is part of the inclusive approach of Priestly editors.

In response God has Moses warn everyone to *get away* (*ylh*) from the *tent* (*mishkan*) of the three rebel leaders. This is like 16:20, where Moses and Aaron were given their initial warning. The tent may belong to Korah, if we assume that in this verse the names of Dathan and Abiram were inserted by Priestly editors as part of their interweaving of traditions. *Mishkan* is the word has been used for *tabernacle*. Rabbis used to debate whether or not Korah had set up a rival tabernacle, but the word basically means any sort of tent, so there is no need to debate.

The JE tradition resumes in 16:25–34, with Moses and the elders going to meet Dathan and Abiram. This is the first mention of the elders in this chapter. In v. 26 we have another command to the congregation to *turn away* (*swr*) from the *tents* (*ohele*) lest they be *swept away* (*sph*). This last verb appears in Gen 18:23f.; 19:15,17, in the warnings about escaping the destruction of Sodom. In Num 16:27 the *tent* [*mishkan*] *of Korah* is added. Dathan and Abiram then stand at their own *tents* (*ohele*). At the end of 16:28 Moses says that the coming test and punishment has *not been of my own accord*. The Hebrew is has *not been of my own heart*. The test is to prove that all these men have *despised* [*naz*] *the LORD* (16:30). The test will be a *new thing* (*beriah*), a *splitting apart* of the ground itself. The word *beriah*, found only here in the Bible, may mean a *new creation*. Korah's name may have been added again by P in 16:32.

In 16:35, an appendix by P, the 250 men with censers are destroyed by a divinely sent fire, not by the earth swallowing them and their families. The charred but intact censers were strewn amid the ashes and debris. This is quite different from the scene in 16:25–34, and simply reflects how the separate stories were woven together.

The Priestly traditions continue with their relentless logic. God has Eleazar collect the charred censers. These vessels had been used in a rite or trial in God's presence; they were now holy objects (belonging to God) and could no longer be used except by priests or as otherwise directed by God. God wanted the bronze reworked into a new covering for the top of the portable altar. This will serve as a sign and reminder to everyone of the rule that priests be direct descendants of Aaron. No *outsider*, not even a Levite, can perform priestly functions under any circumstances. The Hebrew term for *outsider*, *ish zr*, has a great range of meanings, but they all come down to describing *someone who does not have a right to be there*.

It is hard to imagine that the ordinary Israelites would have enough stubbornness in them for one more tirade, but that is what the next scene brings us. In 16:41 they *murmured against* Moses and *against* Aaron, accusing them of *killing the people of the LORD*. The next verse is somewhat repetitious; the people *assemble* (*qhl*) or *demonstrate*, the same verb used in 16:3, 19. The cloud of God's presence comes to the tent of meeting immediately, and Moses and Aaron are told to *get away* (*rwm*) from everyone else, for their own safety. Moses and Aaron fall down to intercede, but this last action in 16:45 receives no response from God.

At this point Moses apparently knows more than we readers. He seems to be aware that a contagious plague has already begun, and he decides (whether on his own or following divine instructions) that incense can be used *quickly* by Aaron as a way to expiate the sins of the people. Aaron, the one who passed the test that destroyed the 250 opponents, is holy enough to approach the LORD. Here the rite of atoning or cleansing is very place specific: Aaron *runs* (*rwz*) to the boundary line between those already afflicted or dead and those not yet stricken. God's *wrath* (*qzp*) has gone forward; the *plague* (*negep*) has begun. In 16:22 we had the verb *qzp* in Moses and Aaron's plea for God not to *become angry*. In 8:19 the Levites were the ones whose ministry would prevent people from coming too close to holy things and being struck by a *plague*. Now the defenders of the 250 rebels are experiencing a plague for their own stubbornness. Finally the plague was *stopped* (*yzr*). The verb can mean to *hold back*, as in 1 Kgs 8:35; Ps 106:30; 2 Sam 24:25.

As we start the story in Num 17 of the special blessing for Aaron's staff, the writer uses the term *house of the fathers* (or *ancestral house*) to stand for *tribe*. In other biblical accounts there are several such ancestral houses and leaders (*nasi*) for each tribe. Here there seems to be just one house and one leader for each. Given the changes within the tribe of Joseph, these authors may be thinking of twelve staffs in addition to Aaron's. They are to be placed overnight in the tent of meeting, before the ark of the covenant.

In 17:5 God talks about *putting a stop* (*shkk*) to complaints. The verb can mean *to cause to subside* or *calm down*, as in Gen 8:1; Esth 2:1; 7:10. Here God notes that the complaints are against Aaron, but in Num 16:11 Moses equated complaints against Aaron to complaints against the LORD.

In 16:8 the phrase *house of Levi* is used. This is a fairly rare term, used in Exod 2:11 to refer to Moses' lineage. Levine (1:80) suggests that the last part of 17:8, the description of the rod budding, blooming and bearing almonds, is actually in the semi-poetic form of a proverb.

The *rebels* in 17:10 are *sons of rebellion* (*bni mri*). The phrase is used of Israelites often in Ezekiel, Isaiah, and Deuteronomy. The verb form translated by the NRSV as *so that you may make an end* (*clh*) can also be translated in the passive, *so that their complaints against me may cease*.

The final two verses, 17:12–13, are very melodramatic. *Perishing* is mentioned in both verses, from the root *gwy*. The same verb is used in God's stern decree about the flood in the final words of Gen 6:17 and in the plea of the people in Num 20:3. In 17:12 another verb for *dying* or for *being abandoned* or *lost* (*abd*) is used in a forceful double form. A third verb for *dying* (*mwt*, the verb used most often) is associated with the exaggeration in 17:13 that *everyone who approaches the tabernacle of the LORD will die*. The final phrase in 17:13 is *haim tmnw gwy*, which means *are we all going to wind up [tmm] perishing [gwy]?*

Questions

53. If we confine ourselves to 16:1–4 as the introduction to a complex story, who are the people who confront Moses and Aaron, and what is their complaint?

54. In 16:5–7a Moses sets up a holiness test. Who is supposed to participate in it? In 16:7b–11, starting with *You Levites have gone too far*, Moses reviews their complaint and narrows it down. What more do readers learn from 16:7b–11?

55. In 16:12–15 Dathan and Abiram have other complaints. What are they? Consider Moses' reply in 16:15.

56. In 16:16–23 the same Hebrew word is used for *your company* (16), the *whole congregation* (19 twice, 22), *this congregation* (22), and

the congregation (23). In which verses does it mean all of Israel, and in which verses does it mean just the fraction in rebellion?

57. What is Moses doing in 16:26, 28–30, and why is he doing it?
58. How do the people react in 16:26–27, 34?
59. In a separate tradition in 16:35 the 250 Levites with their censers were destroyed by fire, not by the earth swallowing them. How do you react to this story in 16:36–40 of the reuse of the metal from the censers for a new, decorative covering for the tabernacle altar?
60. Public dissatisfaction with Moses and Aaron remained after the miraculous earthquake and fire. How is the scene in 16:41–50 different from those earlier in chapter 16?
61. Is the story of Aaron's staff in 17:1–11 as idealistic as the stories in chapter 16?
62. Is 17:12–13 a reaction to 17:1–11?

Conclusion

One could ask why Priestly editors interwove the stories about the rebellious Levites with those about Dathan and Abiram, who were from the tribe of Reuben. Levine suggests that the Reubenites represent the two and a half tribes that wanted to settle in the Transjordan, the area east of the River Jordan, also called Gilead. The explanation for their decision to settle there, and Moses' conditions and permissions regarding this, will be found in Num 32.

If we look at the Dathan/Abiram core in 16:12–15 and 25–34, their dissatisfaction with the stress of the journey and the lack of a place to settle is deep-seated. In 16:13 they call Egypt the *land of milk and honey*. Twice they refuse to come to meet Moses (16:12, 14), and so (16:25) he goes to meet them instead. As mentioned in the Introduction, their refusal to come could possibly be general enough to indicate a refusal to continue on the journey at all. Perhaps it even hints at a refusal to help the other tribes with the conquest west of the Jordan. So this clash with Moses may have been a harbinger of the complexities of Num 32, where we will find the Priestly editors playing down the Transjordanian settlements as much as possible.

Levine also suggests that the Priestly editors, who wanted to preserve their tradition about Korah and the rebellious Levites, saw a logical connection in Moses' defensive remark to God in 16:15, *pay no attention to their offering*.

Originally this might have been a cursing style rejection of the Reubenites' charges against Moses, but it could serve double duty, and provide a connection or a hook to add the story of another offering, the use of the incense in the censers.

As we take a last overview of the rebellion with Korah and his 250 fellow Levites, we see that their wish to function as priests is simply against the law, and against the chosen priestly line of Aaron. The writers do not debate the principle that *all the congregation are holy* because *the LORD is among them*. No one quotes Exod 19:4–6 about them being *a kingdom of priests, a holy nation*.

Instead the focus goes from *all* (16:3) to the *one* spoken of in all the phrases in 16:5. That *man* will be the *holy one* (16:7), Aaron, against whom *you rail* (16:11). So in 16:16 Korah and his men stand before the LORD along with Aaron by himself.

Our firm knowledge of the gradual ascendancy of Aaron's line and of the development of the system of having most Levites serve as assistants to the priests is very limited. Levine suggests that we are looking at post-exilic rivalries of some sort, pushed back to the lifetime of Moses. He notes some patterns found in Josh 21, but they are too technical to review here. In any case, God defends his own choices. The LORD's glory (16:19) burst forth as flame (16:35), and again (16:42) the glory shot through the congregation as a plague (16:46). Similar language can be found in 14:10–12, when the people feared to invade Canaan. Levine calls the cloud of glory and the wrath, i.e., God's presence and his punishments, a "primitive force." That may well be an impression brought on by the Priestly style, but the other primitive quasi-force in all these stories is the faithlessness, mistrust, and selfishness of the various characters. As in Exod 19, the authors are trying to explain the protective barriers God needs to put between himself and the people so that they are not be overwhelmed by the divine presence. Perhaps the faithlessness harms the barriers as well as it does the covenant itself.

Section Fifteen

NUMBERS 18: 1–32

Introduction

Numbers 18 briefly reviews most of the basic duties of priests and Levites, with an eye to explaining how they were to be supported by the rest of Israel. In these ideal profiles in the Pentateuch some of the meat, grain, oil, etc. used in offerings was set aside to provide for the priests and their families. The tithes of some harvests went to the Levites. There is little mention of practicalities, of how tithes or other special donations were to be converted into money for support or maintenance of these people and the sacred precinct itself. As usual, Levine outlines the details well (1:435–53).

For readers who would like to have a good overview of how the temple system grew and changed down to its last century, I strongly recommend E. P. Sanders' *Judaism: Practice and Belief, 63 BCE–66 CE*.

Num 18 falls into four obvious subdivisions (following Levine, 1:435–37):

Num 18:1–7	Duties of priests and Levites
Num 18:8–20	Income for priests
Num 18:21–24	Income for Levites
Num 18:25–32	Levites must pay a small extra fee to the priests

Section Fifteen

Num 18:1–7 review once again the subordinate role for the Levites, who are not direct descendents of Aaron, and the duties of those who are direct descendents, the Aaronide priests.

All of them, priests and Levites, must beware of *offenses* (*awon*), any ritual neglect or failure to correct the neglect immediately. Aaron is told to *bring* or *cause to come near* (*hqrb*) the Levites, who will be *joined* (*lwh*) to the priests and *serve* (*shrt*) them. The same word for *joined* (*lwh*) is used again in 18:4, where the NRSV translates it as *attached*. This verb appears in Isa 14:1 and 56:6, where it refers to non-Israelites joining Israel. It is in fact a verb that plays on the name Levi, as in Gen 29:34, where Leah says *my husband will be joined to me*. In Num 18:3 Levites must not *approach* or *come near* (*qrb*) the vessels or the altar.

Everyone else is an *outsider*, and must not *approach* (*qrb*) the sacred spaces or those performing duties there. In 18:6 the Levites are *taken* by God and *given* as a *gift* to the priests, but they are still *dedicated to the LORD*. In 18:7 the priesthood is described as a *gift* (for others). The Hebrew has *you shall serve as a service of gift* (*wybdtm ybdt mtnh*). Levine translates, "I will make of your priesthood a service of dedication."

All this vocabulary is standard (see Exod 29:1–37; Lev 8–10; Num 3–4; 8:5–26 for background).

The next section mentions those parts of sacrifices reserved for the priests and their families. The authors speak of (*presentation*) offerings (*terumah*), *holy gifts* (*qdshi*), and *portions* (*mshhh*) in 18:8; the *most holy things* (*qdsh hqdshim*), every *offering* (*qrbn*), *grain offering* (*mnh*), *sin offering* (*htat*), and *guilt offering* (*ashm*) in 18:9; the *gifts* (*terumah*) and the (*presentation*) *offerings* (*tenupot*) in 18:11; the *firstfruits* (*rashit* and *bcri*) in 18:13; and the *devoted things* (*herem*) in 18:14. All these sacrifices, donations, and ceremonial offerings are well known, as well as which parts were reserved for the priests, or for their families with them. Some of the terms such as *qrbn* and *herem* are more generic, some more specific; translating the nuances into English is a difficult process. *Devoted things* (*herem*) involved donations of objects or land, which could not possibly be used in ceremonies. The term itself goes back to grim practices in holy war. *Offerings* (*qrbn*) are mentioned all through Num 7 (e.g., 7:3, 12, 19), where they refer to a mix of supplies and animals for sacrifice. In the New Testament, Jesus criticized a misuse of *qorban* (the word for *offering* in 18:9), a method for donating property in his time. In 18:18 the priests apparently get all of the meat from the sacrifices of firstborn animals.

This seems to indicate a change from the original laws in Lev 7:11–34, wherein the priest was given the right breast and thigh of these offerings of well-being. At times small changes in regulations such as this are not resolved within the Old Testament, nor can we tell how temple practice and custom developed in the long run.

The rules for redeeming firstborn sons and unclean animals involve donations of money, but the firstborn of clean animals are sacrificed or redeemed in the normal fashion.

The passage ends with a reminder that the priests did not have large allotted tribal territories within Israel; the Hebrew words are *nhlh* (*inheritance*) and *hlq* (*share*). So this system of providing meat, produce, and the occasional monetary donation was the way that Israel paid for the services of the priests. In 18:19 the system is called a *covenant of salt*, an apparently favorable reference to Lev 2:13, where salt is presumed to be used in every sacrifice. Salt was a preservative, an essential to life; it's opposite, yeast, was misunderstood and feared, even though it was used in baking and fermenting. It was never used in sacrifices.

It would be distracting here to give all the cross-references to the original sources for these laws elsewhere in the Pentateuch and the Old Testament. Leviticus 6–7 could be a place to start for those who want more detail.

The next few verses, Num 18:21–24, indicate divine approval of supporting the Levites through a system of annual tithes of produce (see Deut 12:17–19; 14:22–29; 26:12–15; Lev 27:30–32 for the basic laws). There are small discrepancies among these references, which we will not try to iron out here. Some of the tithed produce was eaten, and some shared with Levites living nearby. Some of it would normally be sold, and the profit could be spent on pilgrimages to Jerusalem, but somehow the appropriate share of that money was distributed to Levites as pay for their services. Most commentators assume that generally Levites were less financially secure than the priests, but we do not have as much information about either group as we would like. As far as we know, Levites may have lived in towns with small common grazing areas. Levine notes the typical royal taxation system described harshly by Samuel in 1 Sam 8:15–17. He assumes that the kings of Israel eventually came to actually collect and administer the tax payments to Levites.

Finally, in Num 18:25–32 we come to the one entirely new regulation in this chapter. The Levites are to set apart a tithe of their own income, and present that tithe to Aaron. This may seem odd to us, but it is called an *offering for the LORD* five times in 18:25–29. In 18:26 it is called *a tithe of the tithe*, meaning the tithe of the Levites' income. In 18:27 it is called a *gift* (*terumah*), the equivalent of the grains and wine tithed by the people of the other tribes. Having made this tithe, the rest of their income, in edibles or in monetary form, can be freely used (18:31). Paying this tithe has made the rest of their income available to them, in the same way that tithes work for everyone else. Scholars use the term *desacralization*, meaning that by some initial sacrifice we have acknowledged God's ownership of these things as creator.

18:32 ends in a very solemn fashion, referring to their tithing of the *best* of the *holy things of the sons of Israel*, a tithing that has kept everyone's tithes from being *profaned*, a tithing that must be done *on pain of death*. The Priestly editors of Numbers use inflated language at times, but, for a florid description of generous benefactions to priests, Levites and temple, none of them can match what we read in 2 Chr 31.

Questions

63. Comment on the style of 18:1–7. Do you find this depiction of God encouraging?
64. How does God treat his priests in 18:8–20, and why?
65. If priests and Levites are supported by a complex system of sacrifices and tithes, why is it necessary for the Levites to contribute a small percentage of their income to the priests?

Conclusion

As I mentioned above, E. P. Sanders can help correct misimpressions many readers might have about the temple in its last century of service. He doubts that the priests and Levites were paid salaries directly by the government, and notes that most of the large number of priests and Levites were only able to serve part-time. While they did not become farmers or shepherds, many did work as scribes, minor magistrates (paralegals?), teachers and craftsmen.

He also points out that many donations due them could have been made in their hometowns; only a part of the gifts would need to be brought to Jerusalem. Over the centuries various tithing routines were worked out to support priests, Levites, and the disabled and destitute.

Sanders is especially vigilant in defending the temple system as one that served its nation well. Expenses were kept at a reasonable level, since everyone had to be accommodated, including many poor people. Most priests and Levites were sincere in their calling, and served with integrity. In 70 CE, when the Roman soldiers finally invaded the temple itself, they found the regular shift of priests serving at the altar. The priests made no attempt to defend themselves or stop what they were doing. They were slaughtered where they stood.

Section Sixteen

NUMBERS 19:1–22

Introduction

In Num 19 we are told of the various ways of becoming unclean by contact with a corpse or with human remains such as bones from a grave. We are also given the ceremonial procedure to make a combination of ashes and fresh water used to make the people in these cases clean again, i.e., to make them eligible to attend community worship. In 19:1–10 we find the procedure to make the ashes, and in 19:11–13 there is a warning about how necessary it is to use the special water. The remaining verses, 19:14–22, review the larger topic of who and what becomes unclean in these cases, with the associated quarantines and the proper method of using the special holy water. The writers do not explain why corpses and human remains are so defiling, nor why the special holy water with ashes can counteract the defilement.

The second section, 19:14–22, has some significant differences in vocabulary from the first section, but the entire chapter is clearly from Priestly editors.

The animal to be burnt is to be a heifer or young cow, never bred or used as a work animal. The Hebrew word for *red* (*adm*) may be related to the word for *blood* (*dm*). The animal is to be slaughtered outside the camp, and burnt to ashes in its entirety. This case is very different from most worship sacrifices, in which the skin and hooves are removed, the blood drained, and the animal properly gutted beforehand. 19:4 indicates that the priest, in this case Eleazar, must *sprinkle* (*nzh*) some of the blood seven times toward the front of the tent of meeting. It does not matter how many yards or miles lay between the slaughtered animal and the tent. As the fire consumes the animal, cedar chips and red cloth are also thrown in, along with some hyssop fronds. Hyssop is mentioned in Ps 57:6, in David's confession and prayer for forgiveness.

Each person involved in this rite—the priest, the one tending the fire, and the clean person who collects and moves the ashes—becomes unclean for the rest of the day, and has to wash his clothing as well. No other ceremony takes place like this outside the camp or has this immediate consequence.

There are other sin offerings mentioned in Leviticus where blood or oil is sprinkled seven times, or where some animals are burnt in a similar fashion. The rules of those rites are endless and far beyond our scope, but they do provide some context for us; see Lev 4:1–6 (sin offering for a priest); Lev 8–10 (ordination rites); Lev 14 (cleansing for lepers); Lev 16, especially vv. 27–28 (rites at *Yom Kippur*).

In Num 19:9 the holy water is called *water for cleansing* (*mi ndh*). In fact the word *ndh* usually is taken to mean *impurity* or *menstrual flow*, so the idiom must mean *water for cleansing from impurity*. Levine argues for relating the noun to another Hebrew word *nzh*, which means to *sprinkle* (as in 19:4, *sprinkling the blood*). So Levine calls it *water of lustration*.

Also in 19:9 the rite is called a *purification offering* (*hattat*), which actually means *sin offering*, so the idiom must mean *offering for purification from sin*. Most scholars do not link the phrase in 8:7, *water of purification* (*mi hattat*, used at Aaron's ordination), with this water in chapter 19.

Note that this holy water must be used on Israelites and aliens alike (19:0). The warnings in 19:11–13 are for everyone living in the land; see the opening word *all* in 19:13. Also in 19:13 a major concern is mentioned: that an unclean person *defiles the tabernacle of the LORD* merely by entering that sacred space. A different word for *sprinkle* (*zrq*) is used in 19:13, 20. The NRSV uses *dash* to preserve this variation. An unclean person who declines to be sprinkled with this water is to be *cut off* (*shunned*). This punishment is used elsewhere for those who violate Sabbath rules, who partake of blood or fat from sacrifices, who fail to circumcise their sons, or who commit certain sexual wrongdoings.

The customs mentioned in the second part of the chapter, 19:14–22, are clear. Anyone present indoors near a corpse, and any open vessels in the same room, becomes unclean. Outdoors, one becomes unclean by touching any dead person or any human remains, bone or grave. In addition to a seven-day quarantine, these unclean people need to by sprinkled with holy water on the third and seventh day of that period. A clean person, not necessarily a priest, sprinkles the tent, furnishings, and people as needed. After these sprinklings the person bathes and washes his clothes and becomes clean again.

In the closing passage, 19:21 refers to the one who did the sprinkling, and 19:22 refers to anyone else involved.

Obviously, ordinary people could fall under these rules from time to time. Anyone caring for a family member who was seriously ill could wind up at a deathbed. Workers in fields or with their flocks might have to retrieve a co-worker who has died of a sudden heart attack or stroke. Soldiers in battle and pallbearers at a burial would have no choice. None of these people would have thereby sinned, even though the purification rite partially resembles rites for atonement from sin. The underlying concern was that unclean people must not attend community worship in that state. Even during Jesus' lifetime this sprinkling ceremony with the water for cleansing was in use. A few weeks before Passover Levites would fan out through all the villages to do these third- and seventh-day sprinklings, so that when the pilgrims came down to Jerusalem they would not have to have the ceremony there and stay another seven days away from home.

Questions

66. Although the editors of 19:1–10 do not give the rationale for any of these steps in preparing this special holy water, can you explain why these steps were taken? You might think about ancient folk medicine as well as ancient religions.

67. As you read of the regulations in 19:11–22, how does the uncleanness of any human corpse or bone reach out to the community?

Conclusion

Numbers 19, along with 31:19–24, erects a high wall against the dead, whether recently deceased, or found as unearthed skeletons or in their gravesites. Their remains never cease to be defiling.

Those impure by contact with the dead endanger the tabernacle or temple, even if they do no go there. In other purification rites, the one cleansed comes to offer something at the tabernacle or temple, but, after being sprinkled with this mix of water and ashes, the cleansed person simply returns to everyday life.

In Lev 21:1–15 we read of priests being restricted in attendance at burials. They may only attend those of immediate family, and the high priest can never attend any burial at all. Even the Nazirites we read about in Num 6 were under a restriction similar to that of the high priest. Given these restrictions, priests would not have been officiants at any funeral services; burials were family affairs for the laity.

As worshippers of the same God, modern readers might wonder why such a high wall came to be. We can guess about the danger of disease for those who need to bury someone, or those who have gone through the carnage of a battle, but a dry bone or an undisturbed ancient gravesite could hardly have contagious consequences. Today we might think of loved ones in their afterlife, and we respect gravesites, but we do not go through such purifications.

Levine suggests that we have overlooked one custom common in the world of the ancient Near East, namely, cults of the dead. He makes a clear distinction between the normal honor paid to the deceased in most cultures and a cult. He defines a cult as a system of propitiation of the dead through sacrifice and other forms of ritual activity, as well as by magic. This cult system has two goals. First, one tries to provide the dead with some comfort in the afterlife. Second, one ensures that the powerful dead will not forget the living, and will act benevolently toward them. Their approval is sought for major decisions by the living, and their presence is desired at major events.

The Old Testament writers oppose this in many places. The dead have no power and no active presence. We can honor their deeds and their memory, but we cannot contact them in their passive state in Sheol. Much of the Old Testament was written before the ideas of an active afterlife in God's presence began to develop. This might be surprising to many Christians, who read of Jesus and the Pharisees speaking about life after death on many occasions in the Gospels.

One group throughout the ancient Near East that seems to have had more interest in departed ancestors was the ruling class. Leaders sought to contact deceased monarchs and heroes. Royal burials took place close to palaces, often within the walls of palace complexes. Even Jewish kings were buried this way, as we see in 2 Chr 21:20; 24:25; 35:24.

Ezekiel strongly criticized this in Ezek 43:6–9, saying that the royal burials were too near the temple. His remarks indicate a change in attitude about the custom. In Lev 19:26–28 several pagan customs are banned, including *making any gashes in your flesh for the dead*. In Deut 18:10–11 we find similar warnings against *consulting ghosts or spirits* or *seeking oracles from the dead*. See also Isa 8:16–22; 65:3–4.

In 2 Kgs 22–23 King Josiah reformed a very corrupt system of worship. These two chapters are worth reading as a reality check from all the idealism of the Priestly editors of Numbers. In 2 Kgs 23: 6, 14, 15–20 Josiah used ancient human bones to desecrate shrines for idols, and destroyed an offending graveyard at the shrine of Bethel. In Deut 26:5–15 there are well-known prayers to be used at the presentation of firstfruits and at the time of the tithe of produce in the third year. During the second prayer, the speaker attests that he has not used any of this food as offerings to the dead (Deut 26:14).

Clearly, cults of the dead are incompatible with monotheism. The belief that the dead have power as individuals to assist the living undercuts belief in an all-powerful God. Further, the dead to whom one offers gifts and seeks favors can, in the long run, appear more and more divine in themselves. So the high wall we find in Num 19 and in these other biblical citations had sound reasons behind it. The distinction between proper burials and improper contact with the deceased was legitimately enhanced by the quarantines and the special holy water.

Section Seventeen

NUMBERS 20:1–22

Introduction

In the next two chapters several brief incidents are mentioned that describe events closer to the time of the wanderers' entrance into Canaan. Levine (1:483–95) keeps track of the variations in the geographical terms and the competing traditions of how much time was spent and where during the forty years.

We will study each chapter separately for the sake of simplicity.

In Num 20 the four incidents are easily divided. Except for the JE passage in 20:14–21, the rest are Priestly traditions (Levine, 1:483–85).

Num 20:1–2	Miriam dies
Num 20:3–13	Water provided from a rocky site
Num 20:14–21	Edomites refuse passage
Num 20:22–29	Aaron dies

Many commentators assume that in Num 20 the Priestly editors start to wrap up the wilderness period. In Num 27:12–14 and Deut 32:48–52 God reminds Moses near the end of his life about this gift of water in Num 20, and about the wrong done by Moses and Aaron at that time. It would be logical to think of Miriam, Aaron, and Moses serving the people until very near the end of the journey. According to P, the command to go by a Red Sea route comes in 21:4.

According to JE (13:26; 32:8) the people came to Kadesh about a year after the exodus, where the spies returned after scouting the land.

Section Seventeen

On the other hand, the Priestly editors thought that the people spent most of their years in the wilderness of Paran, as near Sinai as possible. So in Num 20 they are just coming near Edom for the first time.

In JE they left Kadesh soon after the spying and wandered for many years before winding up at Wadi Zered (21:12). They were told to go by a Red Sea route in Num 14:25, but the clearest JE statement about where they spent most of the forty years of wandering is found in Deut 2:14, which specifies that the trip from Kadesh to Wadi Zered took thirty-eight years, *until the entire generation of warriors had perished*.

The biblical sources have many discrepancies like this. In Num 20:21 the Edomites resist the wanderers, so they go around Edom instead. In Deut 2:1-8 the people pass peacefully right through Edom, with no battles at all. Biblical editors tried to retain all ancient traditions, although they had to use the occasional exaggeration or fuzzy remark to put conflicting information in close proximity.

As mentioned earlier, the Priestly traditions are set in either the wilderness of Sinai or the wilderness of Paran, broad names for southern and central regions of the Sinai Peninsula. The wilderness of Zin is more to the northeast. In 20:1 the people arrive in the wilderness of Zin in *the first month*, but no year is mentioned and we are not told when or how long they stayed in Kadesh.

The notice that they stayed in Kadesh could have been borrowed from the start of the JE story in 20:14. The term *wilderness of Zin* is often used by Priestly editors (see Num 27:14; 33:36; Deut 32:51). It can mean the southernmost part of Canaan, as in Num 13:21; 34:3-4; Josh 15:1-3. In Num 13:26 Priestly editors squeeze Kadesh back into Paran, rather than Zin. This could be an example of a deliberately fuzzy remark; we will look at this again with regard to the death of Aaron.

While Miriam's death is mentioned at this point, we are given no details.

The next story, obviously related in significant ways to the JE account in Exod 17:1-7, starts quickly; a shortage of water leads to another hostile gathering against Moses and Aaron. In Num 20:3 the people *quarrel* or *contend* (*rib*), starting with a despairing remark about wishing to be dead. The noun form of *rib* is commonly used to refer to a *formal complaint* or *lawsuit*, especially in matters of covenant. Their wishing to be dead may pick up the sayings in 17:12-13. In 20:4 the wilderness can be Zin, but in Priestly thinking all the events of Sinai and Paran still contribute to the stressful experiences of these people.

In 20:8, in answer to the prayer of Moses and Aaron, God comes in his glory. The conjunction of Moses and Aaron praying and God's glory coming in response is quite common. We have seen this in Exod 16 and Num 14, 16, 17. Now God tells them to *speak* to or *command the rock* (NRSV) in the presence of all the people to yield water. *Speaking* to a rock could be more dramatic than hitting it with a staff. It could emphasize God's powerful word working through Moses' word. Levine suggests that *speaking to the rock* has been added in 20:8 to explain what Moses (and Aaron) did not do in 20:11-12. There Moses used the staff and spoke no words, which may have made less of a religious impression on the people than if appropriate words had been used.

Geologists are familiar with wells of water deep within mountain crevices, as well as underground rivers and even channels or tubes carved by running water just inches under a vertical rock surface. Travelers not familiar with such things might pass a few feet from a water source without any idea that water was nearby. It is possible that Moses was directed by God to such an apparently dry place.

In 20:10 Moses calls the people *rebels* (*mrh*), but even so the question he puts to them seems counterproductive, i.e., ironic or argumentative. Levine calls it a taunt. We might have expected a simple statement by Moses of what will happen next, with credit given to God for the miracle. As it stands, the question in 20:10 is not self-explanatory.

Moving right along with the story, modern readers might pay little attention to the fact that Moses used the staff to strike the rock, or that he struck it twice. Ample amounts of water gushed out, and all the people and animals were given what they needed.

Jumping ahead to 20:13 for a moment, the place was named *Meribah*, derived from the word *rib* for *quarrel*. This place name is mentioned in Deut 33:8; Pss 81:8; 106:32. A longer place name, *Meribah-kadesh*, is found in Num 27:14; Deut 32:51; Ezek 47:19; 48:28. In Exod 17:7 there is the compound place name *Massah and Meribah*, with *Massah* meaning a *place of testing* (from the verb *nsh*). Massah is mentioned without detail in Deut 6:16; 9:22; 33:8. The frequent allusions, no matter how brief, to these places of testing (based on Exod 17 and Num 20) recapitulate the harmful effects of murmuring.

The other statement in Num 20:13, that there God *showed his holiness* (*qdsh*), makes sense; a merciful God provided the needed water even while his people were challenging him as much as they were challenging Moses and Aaron.

The verse that is hard to understand is 20:12. God accuses Moses and Aaron of *not trusting* in him, and of *not showing God's holiness* to the people. The accusation, unexplained to us, is followed by the sentence of punishment that neither Moses nor Aaron will enter the Holy Land. After the trauma of leading the exodus and the many years of wandering in the wilderness, these two shall not make it to the last step, the ultimate goal (see Deut 3:23–29 for a variant tradition).

Given the guessing about Num 20:12 and the quite different context of Deut 3:23–29, many scholars assume that 20:12 is an interpolation of some sort. Taking the story humorously, we might say that the rebels won one this time; they got their water, and Moses and Aaron got in hot water at the same time. In fact, at many of the citations of the place names *Meribah*, *Meribah-kadesh*, and *Massah* listed above, writers did not take any humor; they recalled this as a significant rebellion in which all their ancestors failed to trust God once again. In those citations Moses and Aaron are not the ones blamed.

In the next story, from JE, Moses sends messengers to the king of Edom, the territory to the southeast of the Dead Sea. Levine notes that this account could only have come from a time around the mid-eight century BCE, when Edom was a much larger and more secure realm than it was during Moses' era. The messengers' request begins with the title *your brother Israel*, which seems to be a normal diplomatic greeting. In Deut 23:8 Edomites are called the *kin* (*brothers*) of the chosen people. This goes back to Esau, ancestor of the Edomites (according to Genesis) and brother to Jacob in Gen 25:23, 30; 27:39–40; 32:3; 33:16.

As he recounts their history for the king, Moses speaks of an angel God had sent with them on their journey (see Exod 14:19; 23:20; 33:2). In Hebrew the word for *messenger* and *angel* is the same (*malach*).

The king of Edom refused to let them enter, and the show of force by his army convinced the people to move further east on their journey. In Amos 1:11 Edom's resistance is mentioned, leading Levine to speculate that this depiction of Edom is an eighth-century-BCE tradition.

In the request for safe passage, Moses mentions the King's *Highway* or *Road* (*derek*), one of the well-known main roads from Damascus to Egypt, running east of the Jordan. In Num 20:19 JE has a different word for *highway* (*mslh*), a term used for rock-free roads with some grading or maintenance. JE also has another word for *livestock* (*mqnh*). *It is only a small matter* translates the unique phrase *surely there will not be harm* (*rq ain dbr*). Levine suggests that the phrase *passing through by foot* could mean *with foot soldiers*.

At their next stop, Mt. Hor, God exacts his punishment for Aaron decreed at Meribah.

In the Priestly tradition, Mt. Hor, presumably not far from Kadesh, is outside Edomite territory. The statement *you rebelled* in 20:24 is in the plural to include both Moses and Aaron.

Questions

68. Compare this story of water made to come from a rocky site with that of Exod 17:1–7. Why would the two traditions both be used, instead of just one?
69. Comment on the elements of dialog in 20:2–13.
70. Why is God upset with Moses and Aaron in 20:12?
71. What is the tone of Moses' negotiations with the king of Edom?
72. What impressions do you get from the scene in 20:22–29?

Conclusion

In the Priestly tradition of 20:23 Aaron dies at *Mt. Hor* (*hor hahar*). Levine does not translate the Hebrew, guessing that the term is somewhat contrived, and might simply mean something like *the top of the mountain* (see Num 33:38–39; Deut 32:50). Num 20:28 uses a slightly different phrase.

This death scene keeps the people near Kadesh a little longer. Kadesh is in the Paran wilderness (13:26), or in the wilderness of Zin, as here. Priestly editors overlap Zin and Paran just enough to include Kadesh in each but to keep Kadesh outside the territories of Canaan or Edom. Thus God's promise is fulfilled that Aaron would not make it to the Promised Land. In 14:30–32 Caleb and Joshua are exempt from the command that the older generation will die in the wilderness, and in Deut 3:23–29 Moses will be allowed to view the land from Mt. Pisgah, just outside the border.

Section Eighteen

NUMBERS 21:1–35

Introduction

Numbers 21 mentions one more murmuring incident, several battles, and several individual stages on the journey. Most of the accounts are from JE traditions (possibly E in 20:12–35); the first three verses might be Priestly, along with the mention of the Red Sea route in 20:4. Three ancient poetic fragments are included at appropriate points. The subdivisions are (following Levine, 2:79–80):

Num 21:1–3	Battle at Hormah with Negeb Canaanites
Num 21:4–9	Bronze serpent incident
Num 21:10–13	Stages and remarks about Moab
Num 21:14–18	Ancient poetic fragments inserted
Num 21:19–26	Stages and battle with Amorites
Num 21:27–30	Third ancient poem inserted
Num 21:31–35	Victories and settlements in Amorite and Bashanite lands

Consulting biblical atlases, we can see the regions under discussion, mostly to the east of the Dead Sea and the Lake of Galilee and the Jordan, which connects them. Ignore for now atlas map legends regarding the tribes of Reuben, Gad, and Manasseh. Levine's interest in geographical sites is invaluable here (2:79–133).

Edom lies to the southeast of the bottom of the Dead Sea, with the Wadi Zered as a northern boundary. Moab is next, running from the

Zered to the river Arnon, just about halfway along the Dead Sea. Amorite territory goes from there to the River Jabbok, a little less than halfway between the Dead Sea and the Sea of Galilee. We are told in 21:26 that the Amorites had taken large territories from what would have been formerly the northern half of a larger realm of Moab.

Mt. Pisgah is within this territory, just northeast of the top of the Dead Sea. That is where Moses died, after viewing the Holy Land from afar. Heshbon is mentioned, wich is a significant city just east of Mt. Pisgah. Areas controlled by Amorites, Ammonites (further east of the Jordan), or Bashan cover the rest of the region from the Jabbok to the top of the Sea of Galilee. Levine assumes that Bashan was an Amorite province.

The only exception to this eastward and northward pattern is the first battle with the king of Arad at Hormah. This is twenty miles or so to the northwest of the southern end of the Dead Sea.

Several of the other sites mentioned in this chapter, such as Ar, Mattanah, Dibon, Nahaliel, Medeba, Jazer, and Edrei (roughly going from south to north), are usually marked on atlas maps.

Levine raises many questions about the geography and the historicity of these stories; we will treat some of his research at the end of this chapter.

21:1-3 might be a Priestly tradition; some think it to be from the Elohist. This conflict is mentioned briefly in 33:40. This victory seems to be in conflict with 14:44-45, where the Amalekites defeated the Israelites, *pursuing them as far as Hormah*. Perhaps the story in chapter 21 is from a later period, projected back to this era.

The vow to *utterly destroy* in 21:2 and the actual *destruction* in 21:3 are verb forms of *hrm*. The verb, and its noun form, *herem*, are the common words used in depictions of holy war, where the conquered are put under the *ban* (the sentence of destruction) or, at times, deportation. The place name *Hormah* (*Destruction*) is built on this same verb.

Styles are a bit mixed in 21:2-3. The Israelites first make a vow, but in 21:3 *the LORD listened to their voice*, as though they had offered a prayer.

The story of the bronze serpent, which starts in 21:4, could easily have come right after 20:21 or 20:29. This is another indicator that 21:1-3 may well have been inserted by editors. The instruction to go by the Red Sea or easterly route comes from 14:25. The Hebrew phrase for the people *becoming impatient* is *the soul of the people became short*.

Their frustration with the journey, and with limited food and water, comes to a head in 21:5, where they say *our soul hates [qwz] this miserable food [lhm qlql]*. The last word may come from the verb *qll*, which can mean *to ignore* or *to treat with contempt* or *to curse*. Many think rather that it comes from cognate languages and refers to a species of very bitter bean. To capture the spirit of the sayin NRSV translators use *wretched* or *miserable food*; Levine uses the term *putrid food*.

Two different words are used to describe the poisonous or fiery serpents. They are called *serpents which are fiery (nhshim seraphim)* in 21:6 and *fiery one (seraph)* in 21:8. The singular *nhsh* appears in the other verses. The word *poisonous* may be used instead of *fiery* if we consider the toxic venom to have caused a burning sensation. Our word *seraphim*, meaning *good angels of fiery appearance*, comes from this same adjective. The words for *bronze (nehushet)* and the *bronze figure (nehustan)* that king Hezekiah destroys in 2 Kgs 18:4 are very close in sound to this word for *serpent*. 2 Kgs 18:4 identifies that bronze figure with this serpent that Moses made in Num 21, but it is hard to imagine that the artifact, if not legendary, was preserved for so long. By the time of Hezekiah the figure, however old, was being used in a superstitious fashion and had to be eliminated.

In 21:12 the people arrive at Zered. This point in time traditionally marks the end of the forty years of wandering (see Deut 2:13–14). The ancient poetry of Num 21:14–15 acts as a prooftext for 21:12–13. 21:16 refers to *Beer* (a *well* where Moses received some orders from God). Here it functions as a place name. 21:17–18 is the prooftext for 21:16. The *leaders (sarim)* and *nobles (ndibi)* could have been tribal officials rather than royalty.

In the rest of the chapter we see more conquests. Moses' request to King Sihon resembles the request to the king of Edom in 20:14–21. Sihon also refused to cooperate, and the Israelites fought his army at Jahaz. The Amorites had held Heshbon, the city from which one would have to proceed west to invade Canaan. The Israelites had to conquer Heshbon to advance.

The picture we get in Num 21 does not agree in all details with that of Num 32, wherein we read that the tribes of Reuben, Gad, and half of Manasseh were specifically involved in many of the conquests in these regions east of the Jordan.

In 21:26 we are told that Sihon and the Amorites had conquered northern Moab years before, from Heshbon south to the Arnon. There is no historical proof for this.

Levine pays close attention to every word in the poem in 21:27–30. In some places his translations are refinements of the existing Hebrew. In the opening line he offers, *Come to Heshbon; how it is fortified! How firmly founded is Sihon's town.* Levine argues that, in context, this is a taunt. In 21:28 he modifies *the lords of the high places of Arnon* to a place name, *Bamoth Baal of Arnon*. This matches the names *Bamoth* in 21:19–20 and *Bamoth Baal* in 22:41. In 21:29 he drops *to an Amorite king Sihon*, taking it out because it violates the meter of the poetry.

In the remaining verses a good deal of ground is covered. More Amorites are displaced from the region of Jazer, a well-known site near Rabbah, slightly northeast of Heshbon. The battle with Bashanites at Edrei was slightly south but quite far to the east of the southern end of the Sea of Galilee. The Israelites then made the long trek back from Edrei to the Plains of Moab, a point just east of the Jordan, across from Jericho on the west side (22:1).

Levine argues that the poetic sections of Num 21 refer to what we would call greater Moab, the area from Heshbon down to the Wadi Zered. The prose of much of the rest of the chapter focuses on the Amorites, who had taken the northern half of greater Moab for themselves, from Heshbon down to the Arnon.

The result of mentioning all of these battles is that the first generation after the exodus is seen as conqueror of much of the Transjordanian regions near the Holy Land. These are the very areas that biblical atlas maps mark out in sweeps of capital letters for the tribes of Reuben, Gad, and the Manasseh half-tribe, coming up in order from the Arnon to Galilee.

Questions

73. Compare the story of the bronze serpent in 21:4–9 with earlier murmuring stories.
74. In 21:21–35 what do the people do after many of the victories?

Section Eighteen

Conclusion

The picture we get in Num 21 of the various battles is clear enough, but we are not professional historians or archaeologists, nor do we have instant recall of the fine details in other biblical books such as Deuteronomy, Joshua, Judges, Samuel, and Kings. Learning from professionals in these areas makes Num 21 quite complex. I want to share some of Levine's overviews at this point, because of his own interest in archaeology and his mastery of biblical cross-references. There are two parts to the overview: what we know about the regions at the time of Moses (1200 BCE, for the sake of argument), and what we know of the centuries much closer to the time of the final post-exilic editing of the book of Numbers.

Part One (2:110–26)

Place names for Moab can be a bit confusing. The main area always included that part from Wadi Zered up to the Arnon. The area above that, as far as Heshbon, is sometimes called the *Plains of Moab*. Scholars use terms such as "northern Moab" for the Plains, or "greater Moab" for both sections. The principal ancient city of greater Moab was Medeba (or Madaba). Heshbon also became an important town as time went by. One small problem has to do with the location of the city of *Ar* (21:15). Levine thinks that the place name Ar is so close to the Hebrew word for *city* (*ayr*) that we cannot be certain of the site. Setting the problem of Ar aside, Num 21 is concerned with northern Moab.

Archaeologists find no ruins at Heshbon dated to before 1000 BCE. They suspect that what they have found there indicates that Heshbon may originally have been built as an Israelite military outpost during the reigns of David or Solomon (that era is often called the united monarchy). By 700 BCE it was held by the Ammonites. Some partially fortified cities near Heshbon do date back earlier than 1000 BCE; perhaps Heshbon was simply used as a representative name by later biblical writers.

Other cities mentioned in Numbers are not as old as thought. Hebron was abandoned for centuries before being reoccupied. The information about Hebron in 13:22 is completely incorrect. Kadesh may have been first built by Israelites during the united monarchy.

Levine notes that for centuries Canaan and regions east of the Jordan were host countries, refugee zones for outcasts from northern Syrian regimes. In Num 21 all Israel is described as winning battles as a united force. In fact, it may be that individual tribes fought separately. So in 32:34–42 the tribes of Reuben, Gad, and the half-tribe of the clans of Machir and Jair, belonging to Manasseh, occupied various towns near the Jordan, on the east side. The same facts are mentioned at length in Deut 3 and Josh 13. Some towns, such as Ataroth and Nebo, had very early Israelite roots. Nebo even had a shrine of *Yahweh*.

Levine agrees that Edom, Moab, and Ammon were cohesive cultures over the centuries, but he argues that the Amorites were simply sporadic refugees from regions in Syria, such as the kingdom of Amurru on the Orontes. Levine denies any credibility to the idea of an Amorite kingdom conquering all of North Moab, as we have in 21:26.

In 21:18 mention is made of *leaders* (*sarim*) and *nobles* (*ndibi*). The same subject of leadership is found in the blessing for Gad in Deut 33:20–21, and in Judg 5:14, referring to magistrates from the Machir clan of Manasseh. So it is possible that early Israelites around the time of the united monarchy could have dominated Amorite refugees east of the Jordan.

One final side issue has to do with the initial account in Num 21:1–3 of a victory over Canaanites from Arad at Hormah, a site near Beer-Sheba. There is little archaeological evidence so far about occupations this far west in the Negeb. Levine notes the citation in Judg 1:16–17 about a town called Zephath, which was renamed Hormah. If Zephath was close to Arad, this could represent a somewhat more reliable tradition, but a battle there might have been a tribal affair, and not one that involved all of Israel. In Num 21:4 we return to the main tradition of the eastern Red Sea route.

Clearly, archaeologists cannot and should not try to verify every biblical claim about the years wandering in the desert after leaving Egypt, nor about the earliest conquests east or west of the Jordan. So we could proceed to the next question: What do we know from the time from David's reign down to the post-exilic era?

Part Two (2:126–33)

Levine notes that 21:4–11 could be connected easily with 22:1. That would continue the tradition that the people went around Edom and the lower part of Moab, and then came directly west to the Plains of Moab in order to cross the Jordan.

Section Eighteen

This could indicate that 21:12–35 came from a different source, perhaps from the E level of the JE traditions. It is likely that Deut 2–3 derives from Num 21:12–35, except for Deut 3:1–3, which may be the source for Num 21:33–35, the battle with Bashanites. In Deut 2:17–29 Moses firmly claims that the people went directly across Edom and Moab rather than around them. Moses also reports God's word that they should not clash with the Ammonites, who were descendents of Lot according to Genesis.

In looking for information closer to the times of the authors and editors of Numbers, the Edomites rebelled against Israel after the death of King Jotham in the eighth century BCE. This may form the allusion in Amos 1:11–12.

The Ammonites probably broke free of Israelite influence soon after the united monarchy. They were far enough to the east to be left alone. Their strongest presence in the area was in the seventh and sixth centuries BCE. In Judg 11 there is an interesting dispute attributed to Jephthah and the king of the Ammonites. In Judg 11:13 the king accuses Moses and the Israelite ancestors of having taken *my land from the Arnon and up to the Jabbok, and to the Jordan*. This king wants this land returned by Jephthah. In reply (Judg 11:14–27), Jephthah notes (11:20–23) that the Amorites—not the Ammonites—occupied all the territory when Moses came. The claim of Jephthah is based on the Num 21 tradition of winning a war with Sihon.

With regard to the Moabites, historians have a famous stele, a stone monument from about 850 BCE with writing carved on it. It is called the Mesha Stele, named after the king of Moab who commissioned it. On the column Mesha speaks of the people of Gad, living near Ataroth longer than anyone can remember. He mentions King Omri of Israel (r. 882–71 BCE), who occupied large parts of Moab during his reign. According to the stele, Moab remained tributary to Israel until the death of King Ahab in 852 BCE. Around 845 BCE Mesha rebelled and retook parts of Moab.

Given that Omri and Ahab after him dominated much of the area east of the Jordan, it is possible that Israelites built or rebuilt Heshbon during that era and conquered southward. It is possible that Omri was the original subject of the poetic ballad fragment in Num 21:27–30. If we drop the reference to Sihon in Num 21:29 as an addition that upsets the meter, then Omri could have been the *fire from Heshbon* that *devoured* Moab, and made its *sons fugitives* and its *daughters captives*.

Now in Numbers this ballad is pushed back to the time of Moses. Moses was the first Omri, so to speak, and later Israelite influence east of the Jordan is a legitimate extension of the way Moses exerted force in the same area. Such recycling of history was common in most ancient Near Eastern societies. It was almost an unconscious process, given that facts and legends were of equal weight, and given that there were no good ways to date ruins in themselves.

We can also observe, however, that Num 21 is a very condensed version of many details in Deuteronomy, Joshua, and Judges. Num 21 puts no emphasis on the efforts of individual tribes. There may be more reason for this brevity than the simple economics of scale in the narrative.

Numbers 22:1—24:25

Section Nineteen

NUMBERS 22:1–41

Introduction

The next three chapters, Num 22–24, contain a special narrative of curses turned into blessings. We will look at each chapter individually because of their length and complexity, and then end with some overviews of all three chapters together. While we can find some JE or P vocabulary in certain verses, it is wiser to simply take the three chapters as a separate source in their entirety.

Levine (2:137–275) will point to some elements of polytheism within the oracles and to the counterbalancing orthodoxy of the framework in order to remind us of significant traces of syncretism (sincerely held) in various Jewish regions in those centuries.

With the exception of Num 22:2, which mentions victories over the Amorites, there are no other editorial links to what has gone on in Num 1–21. One could easily move from the JE traditions ending in 21:35 right to the JE story in 25:1. The mention of Mt. Peor in 23:28 is only a minor allusion to the events of Num 25, and is not weighty enough to help us find sources for the texts.

We can also note that the story of the talking donkey in 22:22–35, while amusing, is a fable that has been inserted within another story. One could easily move from 22:21 to 22:36 without the intervening verses.

The plot of all three chapters might be called a spiritual battle with the Moabites, told from their point of view. The four oracles of Balaam, lyric poetry in 23:7–10; 18–24 and 24:3–9; 15–24, are the heart of the tradition. They differ in several important ways from the surrounding prose framework.

Numbers 22:1—24:25

Num 22 can be subdivided as follows:

Num 22:1	The people come from Bashan to the site near Jericho
Num 22:2–21	Balaam tries to avoid Balak's invitation, until God sends him
Num 22:22–35	Inserted fable; 22:22 does not fit well with 22:20
Num 22:36–41	Balaam is under pressure to begin curses

We start with a note of the panic among Moabites, especially their king, Balak. The people were *in dread (gwr)* and *overcome with great fear (qwz)*. The second verb appeared in 21:5, where the people *detested* the miserable food. The mention of Midianite elders in 22:4 could be an addition by P. The two uses of the verb *lick (lhk)* in 22:4 mean that the Israelites will use up all the vegetation, one way or the other. Balak is mentioned in three cross-references to this story in Josh 24:9; Judg 11:25; Mic 6:5.

Num 22:5 is quite difficult to translate. The Hebrew has *Pethor, which is beside the river in the land of the sons of his people*. NRSV takes *of his people* to be a location instead, *Amaw*. Levine emends *of his people* to *Ammonites*. Often in ancient texts *the river* is the *Euphrates*, the second biggest river in the entire Near East (aside from the Nile). There are conflicting theories about Balaam's origins. He is certainly not Jewish. In Num 23:7 Balaam himself says that he is from *Aram* (Syria).

In 31:8 Balaam is executed along with many Midianites (some manuscripts have *Ammonites* instead). Gen 36:31–32 mentions an Edomite king's name, *Bela*, which may be related. Levine speculates that the king (Bela/Balaam) might have been in alliance with Balak, the king of Moab. Levine also raises the question that the river might be the nearby Jabbok, rather than the far off Euphrates. These broad guesses stem in part from Levine's interest in Balaam as a local figure, as we will see later.

In Num 22:5 the people from Egypt *have spread [csh] over the face [ayn] of the earth*. This specific phrase in found in Exod 10:5, 15 about the plague of locusts; it may indicate that Balak knows of the exodus story in some detail.

Balaam is asked to *curse (arr)* the Israelites; maybe the curse will weaken them enough to be defeated in battle. We should not consider curses like these simply a useless hex or voodoo, looking at them from our standpoint. In ancient cultures curses invoked the gods and were taken seriously. In the Near East archaeologists often find execration bowls. These were curse formulas painted onto shallow clay bowls, which were then glazed and fired. The one wishing to impose the curse would then secretly bury the bowl on his enemy's land, after shattering it. The bowls are easily reassembled now, but serve only as quaint reminders of long-gone hard feelings.

The mention of Midianites in 22:7 may be another addition from the P level. The same verse speaks of *(fees for) divination (qsm)*. In Josh 13:22 Balaam is called a *diviner (qosm)*; this is the only biblical reference to Balaam that mentions his profession specifically.

In 22:8–12 Balaam speaks with God. In 22:11 Balaam uses a new word for *curse (qbb)*, but in 22:12 God goes back to using the common verb *arr*. *Qbb* will used several times in the next few chapters, probably for variety. In 22:13 Balaam reports that God has *refused* to let Balaam go to see Balak; in 22:14 the messengers report back that Balaam *refused* to come.

In 22:16 Balak says, *do not let anything hinder you [mny] from coming*. The same verb will appear in 24:11 where Balak says that God has *denied* Balaam any reward. There the verb means *kept back*.

Note that Balaam refers to *the LORD my God* in 22:18. 22:21 concludes the first section of the story, which can be easily picked up again by context at 22:36.

The story of the talking female donkey is now inserted. This odd reversal story raises questions about Balaam, as we can see in Deut 23:3–5; Josh 13:22; 24:9–10; Num 31:8, 16. Deut 23:3–5 may be behind the other negative references. Geza Vermes has an excellent chapter on the divergent attitudes about Balaam in later Jewish traditions in pp.127–77 of his book *Scripture and Tradition in Judaism*.

In Num 22:22 God was *enraged*, and gave his angel orders to set himself as an *opponent (stn)* to stop Balaam. While we get the name *Satan* from the same verb, the opposing angel is clearly not Satan in this account. Seeing the angel, the donkey *turned aside (nth)*—the same word will be used in 24:6 to refer to groves (or valleys) *stretching away*.

When the angel eventually explained things to Balaam, he says that he was an *adversary (stn)* to Balaam because *your way was perverse [irt] before me*. These last words are quite difficult to translate. The Hebrew has *the way was steep for me*. A very small change can make *the way* into *your way*, and *steep* could be thought of as *perverse* in context. Levine comes at it from another perspective, thinking of the angel describing his own *way*, his own *assignment*. He translates the phrase as *the mission was pressing upon me*. The angel's mission was to stop Balaam at all costs, even if it involved killing Balaam with his sword. Num 22:35 folds the fable back into the main story line.

22:36 speaks of a *city* [*yir*] *of Moab*. This might have been the capitol, or an unnamed city, or the city called Ar in 21:15, 28. The NRSV leaves it as a place name, *Ir-Moab*. Some biblical atlas maps display a site east of the Arnon called "City of Moab."

In Num 22:38 the NRSV has *I have come to you now, but do I have power to say just anything?* Levine takes the word *now* (*yth*) not simply as a mark of the present, but rather as the introduction of a wholly new statement. So he translates it as *I have come to you. Now then: Can I really make any pronouncement?* It is difficult to read Balaam's mind as he makes statements like this. Is he comfortable or frustrated with God controlling his words? The text simply has him following orders, and letting everyone know what his orders were.

Kiriath-huzoth may be a place name for a certain hilltop. In 22:40 Balak's sacrifice of oxen and sheep may simply have been a dinner for Balaam and the emissaries, rather than a formal worship service. *Bamoth Baal* can be left as a place name, or it can be translated as *the high places of Baal*. Levine relates it to the location in Num 21:28, which the NRSV calls *the heights of the Arnon*. The Hebrew in 21:28 has *the lords* [*baals*] *of the high places of the Arnon*. The word for *high place(s)* (*bmh, bmot*) can mean either a natural hilltop or a manmade earth or stone platform for a shrine or altar.

Questions

75. What do you find most unusual as you read the first two sections of the Balaam story (22:1–6, 7–14)?

76. Does the story line in 22:15–21 make sense?

77. The talking donkey story in 22:22–35 may have been added later on. It is based on the premise that Balaam was wrong to undertake this trip, but we don't know why that is the case. What do we learn about Balaam in the first section, 22:22–30?

78. Evaluate Balaam's reactions in 22:31–35.

79. What is your impression of King Balak, based on 22:36–41?

Section Twenty

NUMBERS 23:1–30

Introduction

In Num 23 we find the first two oracles of Balaam, introduced by preliminary sacrifices and followed by the king's frustration in each case. In the final four verses the king makes preparations for a third attempt to get a curse past the lips of Balaam. The subdivisions are quite easy to outline (Levine, 2:139–40):

Num 23:1–6	Sacrifices offered at Bamoth Baal
Num 23:7–10	First oracle
Num 23:11–12	Balak upset
Num 23:13–17	Sacrifices offered at Mt. Pisgah
Num 23:18–24	Second oracle
Num 23:25–26	Balak upset
Num 23:27–30	Sacrifices offered at Mt. Peor

The whole-burnt offerings of the seven bulls and seven rams at each site involved Balaam as well as Balak. In 23:2 they were co-officiants. Balaam stood by the king for part of the second ceremony and proclaimed his second oracle next to the altar. In 23:29 Balaam says the altars and animals are for his use.

So here at each sacrifice Balaam searches for God nearby, first at a *bare height* (23:3) and later *over there* (23:15). In 24:1, by contrast, Balaam will be confident that he does not have to continue to search for

God nearby, so he just stays next to the altars. In 24:1 the narrator says that Balaam *did not go, as at other times, to look for omens.*

Another detail that is not immediately explained is any reason for the different venues and vistas that Balak chooses. At the start Balaam can see only a fraction of the Israelites (22:41). In 23:13 the king moves Balaam to Mt. Pisgah, though he knows that from this second vantage point Balaam will still see only a fraction, but not all, of the Israelites. In 23:27 the king moves his party to Mt. Peor, and here Balaam can see the encampment of all the tribes of Israel (24:2). Does the king expect God to act differently at one of these places? Does he expect Balaam to have more influence with God in a different location?

23:3 ends with a note that Balaam walked by himself *to a bare height* (*shpi*) or *bare pathway*. In that solitude God spoke to Balaam. This is the sole usage of *shpi* in the Old Testament. Levine suggests that a rare verb may be behind the phrase, meaning that Balaam walked *in silence*. After receiving another directive from God, Balaam returned to the king and *uttered his oracle*. The Hebrew is that he raised up his *saying* or *proverb* (*mashal*). A *mashal* can be any sort of well-prepared or well-crafted speech or saying, no matter the length. As we look at the oracles I am indebted to Levine once again, for his skills with the very complex technicalities of Hebrew poetic style.

In this first oracle, 23:7, 9, 10, each have two full lines, with each line made up of two halves. Most Hebrew poetry is in blank verse, with sophisticated meters of long and short syllables. Readers may recognize some stylistic points in common with the Psalms, mainly the pattern of two halves to each line, with the second repeating and adding small points to the first half. Num 23:8, which looks equally long in English, is actually only one full line. So the total is seven lines and fourteen half-lines.

23:7–8 can be taken as introductory, identifying Balak, Balaam's roots, the commission to curse, and the fact that the God of Israel does not want to curse his own people at all. Then 23:9–10 moves on to describe the destiny and the great number of Israelites, and Balaam's admiration for them.

In 23:7 *curse* (*arr*) and *denounce* (*zym*) are forceful verbs. The other word for *curse* (*qbb*) appears in 23:8. The word for *God* in 23:8 is *El*, not the standard plural, *Elohim*.

The interjection *for* (*ki*) at the start of 23:9 always indicates a shift in content. There are many words in English covered by the one word

Section Twenty

ki. In this case Levine prefers *when* or *as* rather than *because* or *for*. The people living or encamping *alone*, and *not reckoning themselves among the nations* are not *lonely*. They are physically secluded to an extent in their wilderness journey, but self-sufficient, not needing alliances with other nations or peoples. Levine prefers to think of Balaam's focus on Israel's military and political independence, rather than traditional interpretations of this oracle, which emphasize Israel's being alone in having a unique call to monotheism and a high moral code.

As Balaam uses *dust* and *dust cloud* to describe Israel, we might think of the great numbers of people with Moses. But *dust* (*aphr*) can mean *land*, and *dust cloud* (used just this one time in the Bible) is close in form to a word that means *fourth part* (*rby*). In keeping with the military and political independence just mentioned, Levine offers *who can chart the terrain of Jacob, and who can measure Israel's quarterland?* Balaam admires these people, and wants to die the death of the *upright* (*yshrim*), like them. The Hebrew word *yshr* can mean *upright* or *righteous*, but it can also mean *valiant*. Levine prefers this less religious meaning. He cites Ps 112:2, where *the mighty* and *the upright* are in parallel.

When Balaam concludes this first oracle, the king is furious and uncomprehending, in spite of the several caveats that Balaam had given him. He decides to try again after moving to a new location. His decision to have Balaam see only a *part* (*aps*) of the Israelites may well be in reaction to Balaam's admiring remarks in 23:9–10, even though in 22:41 we had already been told that only a partial view could be had from Bamoth Baal. Levine reworks the place name *field of Zophim* in 23:14 to come up with a suggestion to call it *Lookout Plateau*.

In 23:15 Balaam again goes off by himself to meet with God, going *over there* (*ch*). Levine has *hereabouts* for this. When Balaam returns to the altars, the king asks him, *What has the LORD said?* This could indicate that Balak is beginning to realize that *the LORD* is in charge.

In the second oracle the first few verses (23:18–21a) show God's desire to bless Israel. 23:21b, describing God as a king among his people, serves as a transitional phrase to the last few verses (23:22–24), where Israel is a God-empowered force that can win any battle. The name *El* is used for *God* in 23:19, 22, 23, and the name *Yahweh* is used in 23:21.

The form of the oracle is again poetry in blank verse. 23:19, 21, 23, 24 are double lines with two halves each, and 23:18, 20, 22 are single lines with two halves each for a total of eleven lines and twenty-two half lines.

23:19 says that God will not *lie* (*czb*), i.e., he will not promise to bless and then *prove false* or *fail* to do so. The same verb (*czb*) is found in Isa 58:11, about a spring whose waters *never fail*. God will not *change his mind* (*nhm*). The verb has to do with *regret*, and here it means God will never *let himself come to sorrow* by neglect; he will never *renege*.

Balaam's claim in 23:20, *I received a command to bless; he has blessed*, is a bit confusing. The first word can be translated as a passive: *I was brought* or *summoned to bless*. The next phrase, *he has blessed*, can instead be translated as an infinitive, reduplicating the form right before it, *to bless*. So we could have *I was brought to bless, indeed, to bless*. One advantage of this reconstruction is that *God* (*El*, 23:19) has not yet completed his blessings. So far he has simply prevented Balaam from invoking any curses.

At times in Hebrew nouns do double duty; they specify something and include its consequence in the same word. So in 23:21 the Israelites have done no *wrong* (*awon*) so God will not send *misfortune*; they have done no *evil* (*yml*) so God will not send *trouble*. *God is acclaimed as a king* is a loose translation for *the battle cry [trwyt] of a king is among them*.

23:22 acts as a refrain; in a way it interrupts the flow. It may have been borrowed from 24:8. Why would anyone compare God to the horns of a wild ox? The horns stand for the whole animal, and a common ancient Near Eastern practice was to use young bull figurines and images to serve as pedestals or icons of powerful male gods. Levine drops the phrase *for them* at the end of the verse, keeping the focus on God himself.

In 23:23 we can speak of enchantment and divination *against* Israel, but the same preposition can simply mean *in* or *among*. The people with Moses need no auguries because they know God's plans for them already.

Questions

80. In 22:41–23:6 what is the purpose of the various procedures?
81. For these questions from Num 23–24 about the four oracles, we will use the NRSV translation exactly. (In Levine's concluding overview of all three chapters a new wrinkle will be added regarding Balaam's consideration of other gods). As you study the four verses of the first oracle, 23:7–10, what do you learn about those

wandering in the wilderness with Moses? What do you learn about Balaam himself?

82. In 23:11–17 how does Balak react?

83. Contrast the style and content of the second oracle, 23:18–24, with that of the first, 23:7–10.

84. In 23:25–30 how does Balak react?

Section Twenty-One

NUMBERS 24:1–25

Introduction

In this chapter we find two more oracles from Balaam, followed by three very brief citations of words of Balaam against other nations. The second oracle in this chapter, the fourth oracle of the series, is cast more as a prediction or prophecy, although the topic is as military as it is religious. At the end Balak and Balaam go their separate ways. The verses can be outlined as follows (Levine, 2:140–41):

Num 24:1–2	Brief introduction to the third oracle
Num 24:3–9	Third oracle
Num 24:10–13	Protestations by Balak and Balaam
Num 24:14	Introduction to fourth oracle
Num 24:15–19	Fourth oracle (or prophecy)
Num 24:20–24	Three additional examples of Balaam's predictions
Num 24:25	Balaam and king depart separately

In 24:1 we are told that Balaam had even less trouble than before getting the words from God for this third oracle. He did not have to use *omens* (*nshim*), an apparent reference to what he might have done at the *bare heights* (23:3) or *over there* (23:15). 24:2 speaks of the *spirit of God* [*ruah Elohim*] *being on him.*

The third oracle consists of twelve lines of poetry, including the larger portion of 24:3. 24:4 and 6–9 have two lines each, while 24:3 and 5 have one line each. Strictly speaking, in our text 24:4 has three half lines, instead of the expected four. Levine suggests that we should repeat the phrase *and knows the knowledge of the Most High [Elyon]* as we have it in 24:16; then 24:4 and 24:16 would be identical in vocabulary, length, and form.

In 24:16 we find three divine names. They are *El* (*God*), *Elyon* (*the Most High*), and *Shaddai* (*the Almighty*). The first and last are also found in 24:4. The name *Yahweh* (*LORD*) is used in 24:6.

Most readers might note a more solemn or perhaps self-centered style in 24:3-4. Balaam speaks of his *clear* (*shtm*) eye, his hearing of the words of God, his *seeing* (*hzh*) the *vision* [*mhzh*] *of the Almighty*, and his having *uncovered* or *open* (*glh*) eyes. There are some small translation problems. Slight variations in the Hebrew allow for *clear* to mean *closed* or *open*. The Septuagint and Vulgate translators had trouble with the same phrase. We will stay with the word *clear*. The verb used for his *uncovered* (*glh*) eyes was used in 22:31, when the LORD *opened* Balaam's eyes so that he finally saw the angel with the sword. Levine suggests that Balaam *falls down* in a trance or dream vision, and that all of 24:3-4 emphasizes Balaam's privileged access to divine plans.

24:5-7a describes the beauty and fertility of the camps of Israel. The opening exclamation *How fair* (*mh tbw*) in 24:5 only appears elsewhere in the Bible at Song 4:10, *how much better is your love than wine*. Levine proposes the word *boughs* instead of *buckets* in 24:7a.

The mention of Agag in 24:7b refers to 1 Sam 15, where this king of the Amalekites and his people were slain by king Saul centuries later.

In Balak's anger at this third blessing, he *struck* (*spq*) his hands together in disapproval. A similar phrase is found in Lam 2:15: *all . . . clap their hands at you; they hiss and wag their heads*. Balak said that Balaam had not cursed as he should have, but *instead* (*hinneh*) blessed them three times. *Hinneh* is more dramatic than the word *instead*; it usually is translated *behold*. In the next verse, 24:11, Balak gets in a second dig, to the effect that Balaam has lost promised rewards by all this, and that that is the LORD's fault. The Hebrew has *Behold, the LORD has denied you any reward*. Balaam gives his standard reply to the king.

But in 24:14 Balaam goes further, and foretells doom for the Moabites. He begins with *And now, behold me* [*hinneni*], *I am going to my people*. Balaam offers *advice* (*iyz*). The verb can mean *to give counsel* or *plan together*, but here Balaam seems to simply be *giving bad news*.

In other biblical traditions Balaam will be considered a co-conspirator regarding the events in Num 25, and that judgment could go back to the broad range of meanings for this verb *iyz*.

The fourth oracle is nine lines long. 24:15 and 19 are one line each, while 24:16 has two lines and 24:18 one and a half lines. 24:17 has three full lines. The divine names *El*, *Elyon*, and *Shaddai* appear in 24:16, as we have already noted.

In 24:17 there are no special vocabulary words, but the male figure being discussed, the *star* or the *scepter*, is clouded in mystery. Levine takes the scepter or rod as a *comet* or *meteor*, with the tail being like a rod attached to the heavenly body. This could be justified by the parallelism with the star within this verse. In the Hebrew this figure strikes the *brow* or *forehead* of Moab, and the *pate* (*qdqd*) of all the people of Seth. Seth was the third son of Adam and Eve; it is not clear why the Moabites would be called the people of Seth (or Shethites). Most commentators assume that the star or scepter stands for king David, who kept Moab under control during his reign.

24:18 is choppy in the Hebrew, but the meaning is clear enough: Edom will be conquered by the same star or scepter. It is not clear whether or not 24:19 continues to speak of Edom, but the victor in battle will destroy or deport the survivors of *Ir*. The city of *Ir* (*yir*) might be the city of *Ar* mentioned in 21:15, 28.

The brief references to other cities and peoples in 24:20–24 might be intended to enhance Balaam's reputation as an international diviner. Amalek, to the west, had once been first in status, but now it will be last in its fate—destroyed or losing its identity.

The Kenites are well located in their mountains, but their capital, *Kain* will fall to *Asshur* (Assyria). The verb for *burning* can also mean *falling into ruin and becoming a place for wild animals to graze.*

24:23–24 is quite confusing. Levine changes links among consonants to read *who shall live from the Northland?* instead of *who shall live when God [El] does this?* The *Kittim* are Cypriots, who will conquer *Asshur* (Assyria) and *Eber* (Syria), but then the Cypriots will be defeated by someone else. All these references are too brief to indicate specific battles or events.

Section Twenty-One

Questions

85. Note any new or different details in 24:1–2.

86. How is the third oracle, 24:3–9, different from the first two? Note 24:3–4 and 24:7–8 in your reply.

87. Characterize both Balak and Balaam, based on their remarks in 24:10–14.

88. What does Balaam describe in the fourth oracle, 24:15–19?

89. Let us consider the four oracles by themselves, setting aside all the prose verses in Num 22–24. Point out the one or two verses in each oracle that you consider to most directly point to the timeless destiny of the chosen people. We surely will not agree on each and every verse, but the exercise is worthwhile.

Review of the Balaam Traditions

Levine (2:206–40) does a thorough job of evaluating the three chapters about Balaam. He starts by saying that we cannot find consistent criteria in these chapters for sources such as JE or P, but that instead we should consider the four oracles by themselves, and then review all the surrounding prose as possibly the work of later editors. Levine speculates that the four oracles may be from the same era as the Heshbon Ballad of 21:27–30. That was around the time of King Omri's victories in the first half of the ninth century BCE.

Levine is enthusiastic about some archaeological finds at Deir 'Alla in the valley of Sukkoth, slightly east of the Jordan and about halfway between the Dead Sea and the Sea of Galilee. These writings on plaster fragments mention a *Balaam, son of Beor*. We will come back to these fragments later.

The four oracles themselves have internal links and commonalities. The pairing of the names Jacob and Israel occurs twice in each of the first two oracles, once in each of the other two, and once in reverse order, in 24:18–19. Balak is mentioned by name at the start of the first two oracles.

The pair of verbs *I see* (*rah*) and *I behold* (*shwr*) in 23:9 is paralleled in 24:17, where they are used again to describe Balaam seeing the star and scepter. In 23:24 there is an image of a rising lion, while in 24:9 a lion lies down to gnaw on its prey. The image of a powerful ox is used in 23:22 and also in 24:8. Israel is called a *people* (*am*) once in 23:9 and again in 23:24, but no other specific terms are used to describe all the Israelites, beyond the pair of names Jacob and Israel.

The result of these links and commonalities is that the short-term goal of the first two oracles (blessing) fits in well with the long-term predictions in the third and fourth oracles of future Jewish victories on each side of the Jordan. The pairing of Jacob and Israel now stands for all Israelites, even those who settled on the eastern or Transjordanian side.

An unusual feature of the oracles is the various divine names involved. The word *El* is used for *God* in 23:8, 19, 22, 23 and 24:4, 8, 16. Another name, *Elyon*, appears in 24:16 and seems to be mistakenly dropped from 24:8. In 24:16 we use the title *the Most High* for this name. A third name, *Shaddai*, is found in those same two verses, 24:8, 16, where we use the title *the Almighty*. The name *Yahweh*, which by custom we always replace with the title LORD, occurs in 23:8 and in a lesser role in 24:6, but the most prominent citation of *Yahweh* in the oracles is in 23:21, *The LORD their God [Yahweh Elohim] is with them.*

The usual practice in the Old Testament is that we have two words used for the Jewish (and Christian) God. One is the proper name, *Yahweh* (replaced by LORD in translations), and the other is *Elohim*, which is actually the plural form of *El*. Propp, in his commentary on Exodus, considers the biblical use of the plural form to be a cultural claim that there is only one God, even if we use plural terms. The words *el* and *elohim* can mean another *god* or other *gods* in a few passages.

But Levine reminds us that *El*, *Elyon*, and *Shaddai* were also proper names for specific gods in the ancient Near East, and that we are caught at times by whether to translate these as proper names or simply as titles for *Yahweh*.

The process of making a proper name, or a phrase developed from that name's meaning, into a title for someone else is called assimilation. Priestly editors combined divine names and titles in the Pentateuch. For example, they felt the need to explain why we have the older name *El Shaddai* and the newer name *Yahweh*. So in Exod 6:3 Moses was told by God, *I appeared to Abraham, Isaac, and Jacob as God Almighty [El Shaddai], but by my name The LORD [Yawheh] I did not make myself known to them.*

The story in Gen 14:18–21 is surprising. There Abraham greets Melchizedek, the pagan king of Salem, who is also a priest of *God Most High (El Elyon)*. The king uses this name, *God Most High*, twice in his blessing of Abraham, identifying this god as *maker of heaven and earth* and as the one who delivered Abraham from his enemies. Abraham gives the king a tithe of his gains in the recent battle, and refers to his own oath to *the LORD, God Most High (Yahweh, El Elyon), maker of heaven and earth*. In this account the implication is that Melchizedek is heading along the right track toward monotheism. The authors would not have used this to show Abraham getting too cozy with polytheism.

Numbers 22:1—24:25

For the sake of argument, Levine suggests that the Balaam oracles are not examples of assimilation. He thinks we should read the four oracles with the various divine names included, instead of replacing them with the word *God* or the other usual titles. Thus in 23:8 we would have a parallel: *How can I curse whom El has not cursed?* and *How can I denounce those whom Yahweh has not denounced?* In 23:19 we would have *El is not a human being, that he should lie.* In 23:22 (and in 24:8) we would read that *El brought them out of Egypt*, and in 23:23 we would have the exclamation *See what El has done!* In 24:4 and 16 we would have references to the *words of El*, the *knowledge of Elyon*, and the *vision of El Shaddai*.

Returning to Num 23:8 for a moment, Levine states that this is the only case in the Old Testament, where *El* and *Yahweh* are in clear synonymous parallel in sequential half-lines (setting aside a complex text in Ps 10:11–12). But even if such parallelism is rare, Levine wants to retain the parallel in 23:8 as referring to two separate deities.

Levine notes the case of Deut 33:26–28, where the name *El* is used at the start, *There is none like God (El)*. The first two verses invoke storm god imagery, and may be very old. But in Deut 33:29 we find an expanded ending, which calls Israel *a people saved by the LORD*. The mention of the LORD tones down any misgivings about the use of an old word like *El* in 33:26. Much of Deut 32 deals with the same topic—competition between one and many gods (note 32:8–9).

Levine argues that our Balaam oracle references to other gods are not toned down by any verses like Deut 33:29. In the Balaam poems *El* is an individual, not a common noun, and not a synonym for *Yahweh*. In all these oracles *Yahweh* is just one part of the picture, while *El* gets more mention.

Levine claims Balaam is invoking the entire regional pantheon, in addition to the national god of the Israelites. So in Num 23:8 neither *El* nor *Yahweh* will allow curses to come upon these people. In 23:19–21 *El* has commissioned Balaam to bless Israel, a people protected by *Yahweh* (23:21). People will say of them, *See what El has done!* (23:23). In later times Saul will defeat the Amalekites west of the Jordan, and David will subdue the Moabites and Edomites east of the Jordan. All these outcomes were predicted by Balaam before any Israelites had crossed the Jordan.

Levine notes that diviners would often call on more than one god, using formulae. He notes the formula for moving the ark in battle, in Num 10:35–36. We would call this a prayer; nonetheless it is cast as a formula, in balanced lines. Balak wanted Balaam to get divine cooperation and empowerment, something like the formula in 10:35–36, in order to defeat or weaken the Israelites.

Diviners had to seek permission of the gods for curses to work; they could not pressure the gods, but had to placate and entreat them. This subservience is not the same thing as simply promising to be obedient. Without divine authorization, no curse could be effective.

So Balaam invoked the regional pantheon, a coalition of divine powers common to Transjordan, Phoenicia, and Syria, and including *Yahweh*, the god particular to the Israelites. In context, *El* would have been Balaam's own chief god.

Who would have written such oracles? Levine concludes that Balaam's oracles represent Transjordanian Jewish authors who also had not yet assimilated the local pantheon into a strict Yahwistic monotheism. Even if they held *Yahweh* to be their particular patron, they projected their own heterodox ideas onto Balaam.

This loose polytheism is harder for us to grasp, perhaps, than the image of Abraham in Gen 14, eating with the pagan priest-king Melchizedek and getting blessed by *El Elyon*.

Levine argues that a consistently serious monotheism was not firm in Israel until right before the Babylonian captivity at the earliest. Some components of local polytheism were rooted out early, namely *Baal* worship and cults to the goddess *Asherah*. But we have less information on the gradual decline of *El* worship and its assimilation into Yahwism. There are references to shrines to *Baal-berith* in Judg 9:4, the story of Abimelech's reign as an unworthy judge in Israel, and to a shrine of *El-berith* in Judg 9:46, where Abimelech slaughtered many enemies. *Berith* is the Hebrew word for *covenant*; one may wonder at how these two shrines got their names. In Isa 14:4–21 the king of Babylon is depicted as wanting to raise his throne above the stars of *God* (*El*), and making himself like the *Most High* (*Elyon*) (Isa 14:13–14). But the LORD breaks the staff of the wicked (14:5).

Levine argues that we can call many ancient Transjordanian Jews heterodox; a few of them might even have been unfamiliar with *Yahweh* worship. Many probably practiced cultic coexistence, worshipping different gods in addition to *Yahweh* at different shrines and ceremonies.

By contrast with the four oracles, the surrounding prose narratives of Num 22–24 are strictly monotheistic, using *Yahweh* and *Elohim* all the time. They are apparently the work of a single author who had the poems and other sources at hand. There is no use of *El/el* in the narrative sections. In 22:8, 13, 18 *Yahweh* gives all the orders. In 22:18 Balaam refers to *the LORD, my God*. This shows him as a devotee. Balaam offers many sacrifices of attraction to *Yahweh*, who shows up and speaks to him often. The searching about on *bare hill* and *over there* might be a sign of Balaam's uncertainty that he will get audiences. In 24:1-2 Balaam gets *the spirit of God*, as do prophets and judges or military heroes.

The name *Yahweh* dominates at important points, such as 23:5, 16-17; 24:2, 13. References to divination fees, omens, auguries etc. might be local color, fees a non-Israelite divine might expect. Balak's whining about how much he would pay highlights a panicky king and greedy divines in general. Balaam's refusal to accept the rewards for something he cannot deliver makes him look professional and ethical.

In a way Balaam and Barak interact like Moses and Pharaoh; their dialogs go back and forth until finally the king begins to see that *Yahweh* is really in charge and wants to protect his people. All the emphasis on where Balaam is to stand and what he is to see may be a bit of a spoof on the poems, where Balaam also speaks about what he sees, as in 23:9.

The first two oracles speak of blessings, and then the third and fourth speak more of future battles. On the other hand, the prose author highlights the theme of blessing and cursing until after the third oracle, at 24:13.

From the narrator's point of view, the issue never changes; Balaam was always forbidden to curse, but he was not forbidden to tell Balak of future defeats for the Moabites, as in the fourth oracle.

The Balaam stories are supposed to take place during the time of Moses, but Moses himself gets no mention anywhere in Num 22-24. In the prose of Num 22-23 the Israelites are consistently called the *people* (*am*), except for the term *horde* or *assembly* (*qahal*) in 22:4. In 24:1-2 the narrator finally uses *Israel* twice. This change may be an indicator that the oracles in Num 24 will be about future victories.

The other odd thing about the prose framework is the denigration of Balaam in the talking donkey story. Other denigrations will come in 31:8, deriving from Num 25, where Peor is mentioned in 25:3, 6, 18 (see also Josh 13:22). Further criticism of Balaam can be found in Deut 23:5-6; Josh 24:9-10; Neh 13:2. Perhaps the denigrations grew from later history, when attitudes hardened against the Midianites or other Transjordanians, or even against Transjordanian Israelites.

Levine concludes,

> When all is said and done, The Balaam Pericope celebrates the glory days of the Transjordanian Israelite communities. Like so much of Torah literature, it retrojects later events and situations into the Wilderness period, and lays a foundation for the actual historical relations of the Israelite kingdoms with neighboring peoples. There was a time when the Transjordanian Israelites were blessed by JHWH, their national God, and also by El, the dominant deity of Transjordan. (2:240)

Levine (2:241–75) comments at great length on the Deir 'Alla plaster fragments. They came from the walls of a building in what may have been a crafts center in the valley of Sukkoth in the late ninth to eighth century BCE. This would be just prior to the Assyrian campaigns around 730 BCE, when the Assyrians deported many Transjordanian Israelites, and Ammonites moved into the region. The fragments were located not far from Moabite and Ammonite territories. The language of the inscriptions is a local dialect, which Levine calls Gileadite.

One of the fragments very clearly has the name *Balaam, son of Beor, a diviner*. In the inscriptions Balaam foretells cosmic and earthly doom for his region, and uses spells and the help of some gods to save one goddess from being forced to carry out the sentence of doom, as she had been ordered to do by other gods.

The story is completely polytheistic; *El* and *Shaddai* gods (*Shaddayim*) are mentioned. Levine argues that despite the polytheistic content there are several strong factors in favor of the texts actually being of popular Transjordanian Israelite authorship. After presenting these technical arguments he concludes,

> It must be remembered, however, that the official or strictly monotheistic views expressed primarily in biblical law and prophecy speak for only certain circles within the Israelite society. Based merely on what prophets and other spokesmen for Israelite monotheism had to say, and what they condemned, we have the impression that the sort of divination and mythological conflict that the Deir 'Alla inscriptions relate were not foreign to the Israelite ethos, on both sides of the Jordan. (2:271–72)

I find Levine's arguments for Balaam's use in the oracles of the local pantheon of *El, Elyon,* and *Shaddai* along with *Yahweh* to be helpful. It highlights the irony of the pagan Balaam being used by the LORD in the first place. Balaam's polytheism may have added to his own peace of mind and to his admiration of the people whom he was hired to curse. The questions we have asked about these oracles and their prose settings are not hampered by the thought that some Transjordanian Jewish authors not only depicted the regional polytheism of someone like Balaam but also thought that way themselves. A clear reminder of the persistence of polytheism within Israel can be found by scanning Ezek 8.

Numbers 25:1—36:13

Section Twenty-Two

NUMBERS 25:1–18

Introduction

After reading of the providence of God in Balaam's oracles, it is jarring to return to another grim outbreak of Israelite idolatry and divine wrath. In Num 22:1 the Israelites were camped in the plains of Moab, just east of the Jordan. The site mentioned in 25:1, *Shittim* (*acacia trees*), may be the same as that in 33:49, *Abel-shittim* [*the brook at the acacia trees*] *in the plains of Moab*. By this link to 22:1 we are reminded again that the entire Balaam cycle was inserted just in front of Num 25.

The chapter has two parts:

Num 25:1–5   JE story about intermarriage and idolatry with Moabites
Num 25:6–18   P retelling of same event, shifting focus to Midianites

In 25:1 *camping* (*ishb*) could mean *staying somewhere temporarily*, but it could also mean *settling down*, as in 21:31. Levine prefers the latter, since he takes 25:1–5 to be a JE account about the Transjordanian Israelites who never did cross over the Jordan. The verb for *having sexual relations* (*znh*) does not normally take an object. When it does, as here, it is used metaphorically to refer to participation in idolatry (see Ezek 16:26, 28 for good examples). In this context, the reference to sexual relations could refer to intermarriage with Moabites and subsequent participation in their polytheistic ceremonies. The two problems, intermarriage with those of other ethnic and religious roots and eventual involvement in their religions, are basically one and the same problem.

The problem of intermarriage is raised often in the Old Testament. In Num 31:13-20 Moses condemns Balaam and many Midianite women because of the events at Baal Peor (31:16), and a law about the same topic can be seen in Deut 23:4, where marriages with Moabites or Ammonites are prohibited. In Deut 7:1-6 the link between intermarriage and idolatry is starkly drawn. In 1 Kgs 11:1-8 Solomon himself is criticized for his disgraceful example in getting involved with the religions of some of his wives.

The Moabites had a high god, Kemosh (or Chemosh), who might be the one worshipped here, even though the reference to *gods* is in the plural. Another possibility is that *Baal of Peor* is an unnamed local deity, or the name of the site or shrine. The site, Mt. Peor, was mentioned in Num 23:8. When the women *invited* the men *to the sacrifices*, the reference might be to formal rites on holy days. In saying that *Israel yoked itself* (*zmd*) to the *Baal of Peor*, the author is using a strong verb, indicating *commitment*. Levine, studying the verb in ancient Near Eastern magical texts, adds the notion that Israel allowed itself to become *spellbound*, or *entranced*, or *addicted*. There is no emphasis here on ceremonial or ritual prostitution, which is spoken of elsewhere in the Bible.

God's command to Moses to impale the chiefs reminds one of 2 Sam 21:1-9, where descendents of Saul were impaled in satisfaction for his betrayal of a pact with Gibeonites. In Num 25:5 Moses may even have broadened the command to include all the men who had worshipped the *Baal of Peor*. This reminds us of his stern command in Exod 32:26-29.

Cross-references to this story vary somewhat in ascribing blame to the Moabite women, but most admit that this yoking to Baal was a great failing on the part of Israel (see Num 31:15-16; Deut 4:3; Josh 22:16-18; Ps 106:28-31; Hos 9:10).

In Num 25:6-18 Priestly authors add the complex details about the impudence of the Israelite man and the Midianite woman, and about Aaron's grandson Phineas, son of Eleazar, who executed them on the spot. Their deaths ended a plague from God, which had not been mentioned before 25:8. This entire section of the chapter focuses on Midianites, not Moabites.

The scene takes place in front of the *whole congregation* (*kol adat*), as they were weeping at the entrance of the tent of meeting. The weeping could have been an act of repentance, or of grief for those executed, or for those dying in the plague.

In 25:8 the two very rare words *tent* (*qubbah*) and *belly* (*qebah*) are used in a word play. Levine argues that the traditional image of Phineas using one thrust of the lance inside a large tent may be overly graphic or sensational because of the use of such rare words. He suggests that the *cubbah* could have been a small, doghouse-sized shrine tent (*cubbe*) holding sacred relics or talismans, as in many pre-Arabic cultures. Phineas could have come to the area *in front of* the tent, and instead of piercing the woman *through her belly* (*al qebatah*), the text could easily be reconstructed to read *in front of her tent* (*al qobbatah*). The area in front of this small, perhaps portable shrine would have been the prayer site where the man and woman chose to confront the congregation with their polytheism; so Phineas slew them there. The man and woman, Zimri and Cozbi, were from high-ranking families; this adds to the importance of the event. The mention that their deaths ended the plague, which had already caused 24,000 deaths, adds another somber note.

In 25:11 the Hebrew says that Phineas' *zeal* [*qna*] *was with my zeal so that I did not consume the Israelites in my zeal*. The meaning is clear: Phineas expressed in action God's own zeal; he acted on God's behalf. For this he receives a *covenant of peace* or *fellowship*, a *covenant of perpetual priesthood* (*berit kehunnat olam*). This last phrase is similar in form to *the covenant of salt forever* (*berit melah olam*) in 18:19. 25:13 speaks of Phineas *being zealous* (*qna*) for his God, and *making atonement* (*kpr*) for the Israelites. We might also think of Aaron frantically atoning with his censer in 16:47–48.

In 25:1–5 Israel was to blame for the Baal Peor incident, but in 25:16–18 blame is shifted to the Midianites to a large extent. God commands, *Harass* [*zrr*] *the Midianites and defeat them, because they have harassed you*. The verb means *to take military action*. It is used in Exod 23:22; Num 10:9; 33:35. The Midianites used *trickery* and *deceived*; both noun and verb come from *ncl*, meaning *to be clever* or *cunning*. A good example is Gen 37:18, where Joseph's brothers *cunningly plotted* to kill him when he arrived at their campsite.

Later, in Num 31, a war will be won against the Midianites. That account is also from Priestly sources.

Numbers 25:1—36:13

Questions

90. How many important details are left unexplained in 25:1-5? Why are the authors so stingy with information in this paragraph?

91. In 25:6-9 how driven were the man and woman who opposed the whole congregation of Israel? Why would they act this way?

92. In 25:8-13 how can God go through this large mood swing, from sending down a plague with 24,000 deaths to showering Phineas with exuberant praises for turning back God's wrath from consuming even more people?

93. Explain how 25:17-18 does or does not fit in with earlier components of the same chapter.

Conclusion

Levine reminds us that in the JE traditions the older generation of those who left Egypt died out by Num 21:12, the arrival of the people at Wadi Zered. See also Deut 2:14. In order to reach Abel-shittim in the plains of Moab the Israelites had to get through Moabite (or Amorite) territories. Thus the new generation was already victorious in some battles, and all the more to blame for their sins at Baal Peor.

If we take Num 25:1-5 as an insight drawn by JE authors, rather than something entirely fictitious, we can look at Hos 9:10, where Baal Peor represents Israel's main sin in the wilderness, after much blessing and protection (see Hos 13:1-6 and Deut 32: 10-18 for more of the same theme). In this tradition something went wrong during the wilderness years after a good start from Egypt.

On the other hand, in Exodus and Numbers lots of things went wrong very early.

Think of all the murmurings and rebellions, such as Num 13-14. These resulted in the divine sentence of forty years to wander in the first place.

Perhaps the JE editors of Num 25:1-5 took into account Hos 9:10 and themes in Deut 32, traditions about northern Israel of the ninth to eighth centuries BCE, and retrojected them back into the time before the conquest of the Holy Land.

Section Twenty-Two

The lesson would be that northern Israelites and Transjordanian Israelites were doing many things wrong even before Moses died; living in Transjordan would always lead to idolatry.

Hos 11:12—12:14 has many more judgments against the northern and Transjordanian Israelites. After the northern King Jeroboam died in 746 BCE, the next few kings were Transjordanian pretenders: Shallum, Menaham, and Pekahiah. The country was falling apart by the time the Assyrians arrived.

The topic of the wisdom of staying in Transjordan will come up again in Num 32, where those tribes will seek Moses' permission to stay east of the Jordan.

Levine notes that the rise of Aaron's line to the priesthood may be post-exilic. There are now links between the later line of Zadokite priests and Aaron in Ezra 7:1–5 and 1 Chr 24:1–5. A special passage is Mal 2:4–6. There the prophet describes ideal priests from the tribe of Levi. They have *a covenant of life and well being* with God; they *reverence* him, teach his truths, and walk in *integrity (shalom)*, and they *turn many from iniquity*. Levine suggests that the description of Phineas is based on the themes of Mal 2:4–6, especially where Phineas made atonement and *turned away God's wrath* from consuming all of Israel (Num 25:11).

Section Twenty-Three

Numbers 26:1–65

Introduction

There are several censuses and genealogies found in the Old Testament, most from Priestly traditions. While modern readers may find them dull, they served several social purposes within nomadic and tribal cultures, and formed the basis for military conscription and land distribution. For one example among many of military mustering, see Judg 20–21, a sorry story of civil war with the Benjaminites. The counting for soldiers was done by tribes. Scholars may question the high numbers in such accounts at times, but we should be patient enough to give these lists their moment in the spotlight. Working with such lists is another of Levine's strengths (2:307–37)

The contents of Num 26 can be outlined as follows (2:308):

Num 26:1–4a	Introduction; this census is to count able-bodied soldiers
Num 26:4b–51	Main body of information gathered
Num 26:52–56	Additional instruction to use the census for land distribution
Num 26:57–62	Levite clansmen counted from age of one month
Num 26:63–65	Caleb and Joshua were sole survivors from the exodus

Most readers would assume that this census logically follows on that in Num 1; the forces were counted as soon as they got out of Egypt, and then again forty years later, as they prepared to cross the Jordan. But

Levine argues that the census in Num 1 was actually derived from this one. We will come back to this matter later, in the Conclusion.

The main population categories in Num 26 will be *ancestral houses* and *clans*, but the totals are listed by the names of Jacob's sons. The various censuses use different classifications. The one in Gen 46 does not mention *clans*; the one in Num 1 considers *clans* and *ancestral houses*; this one in Num 26 mentions *ancestral houses* only in 26:2, and does not actually use the word *tribe* itself, although it uses the individual names of Jacob's sons.

The Hebrew of Num 26:4 is garbled. It says . . . *as the LORD commanded Moses and the sons of Israel who came out of the land of Egypt*. This seems to combine the people with Moses in an odd way, and leaves the next verse about Reuben with no introduction. The NRSV drops the word *and*, and in a new sentence calls the sons of Israel *Israelites*. Levine drops the word *and*, and in a new sentence calls the sons of Israel *the descendants of the Israelites*. In English we can try to distinguish *descendents* from *sons*, where Hebrew only has the one word (*sons*) for both.

In the list of Reuben's clans, we find Dathan and Abiram, who rebelled along with the Levite Korah and were swallowed up by earthquakes, at the same time as the 250 men with censers were burned by fire from the LORD. These rebels are called a *warning* (*nes*) in 26:10. The word *nes* can mean *standard* or *symbol* or a *pole holding a standard or symbol*. In 21:9 the bronze serpent was attached to such a *pole*. 26:11 notes that some descendents of Korah survived. The name occurs again in 26:58, and in several psalm titles as part of music directives.

The number of Simeonites, 22,200 as mentioned in 26:14, is noticeably lower than it was in 1:23, where they totaled 59,300. All the counts in Num 26 are slightly different from the counts in Num 1. The tribe of Joseph is subdivided into the half-tribes of Manasseh and Ephraim. One clan of Manasseh, Machir, later joined with the Reubenites and Gadites in seeking permission to settle in Transjordan (Num 32). The Gileadites, direct descendents of Machir through his son Gilead, settled in Transjordan (Josh 17:1–6). Levine notes that some of these proper names, such as Gilead, were originally names of regions or towns, not of individual people. But, in the process of tracing genealogies and charting censuses, some site names were personified. Thus the tribe of Joseph was the only tribe eventually to have clans legally reside on both sides of the Jordan (see Num 32:33–42, esp. 32:39–40, for Gilead as a site, and Josh 17:1–6, where some of these traditions are repeated). Another descendent of

Manasseh, Zelophehad, had no sons but five daughters (26:33). Matters relating to the daughters' inheritance on the western side of the Jordan will be recounted in Num 27. Some of the daughters' names are also site names, in context supporting the claims for land west of the Jordan.

The total count for able-bodied men in these twelve tribes (counting Manasseh and Ephraim as two, and not counting Levi) was 601,730. This is relatively close to the total in Num 1:46, where the count was 603,550. The estimate in Exod 12:37 was *about six hundred thousand men on foot, besides women and children.*

In Num 26:52–56 God gives instructions about dividing the land proportionately and by lot among the tribes. The lots may have been cast, or drawn one by one from a bowl. Strictly speaking, these few verses do not take into account the fact that the Reubenites, the Gadites, and many of the clans of Mannaseh will eventually remain outside the Promised Land, east of the Jordan. Beside the question of some groups staying east of the Jordan spoken of in Num 27, 32, 34, the extensive details of land distribution are also found in Josh 14–17, including the observation in Josh 14:2–3 that the nine and one-half tribes who moved west of the Jordan used the system of lots, and the two and one-half tribes that stayed east of the Jordan were given properties by Moses.

The census of Levites by clans in Num 26:57–62 is a condensation of information in Num 3–4. The clansmen were numbered from the age of one month, since they inherited their ceremonial duties, and had no military obligations or large land allotments as did the other tribes. In 26:59–61 we are reminded of the genealogy for Moses, Aaron, and Miriam, and of the fate of two of Aaron's sons who committed sacrilege.

In accord with the tradition of the forty years of wandering as a punishment, the Priestly editors assure us in 26:64–65 that the older generation had all died out, to the last man, with the special exception of Caleb and Joshua. Moses was still alive, of course, but he had been told that he too would not see the Promised Land.

Questions

94. Looking at 26:1–56 in its entirety, point out any unusual information or points of style that you find.

95. What is the main contribution that the entire census in 26:5–51 makes to the story of Numbers?

Conclusion

Levine (2:330–37) studied other biblical lists, starting with those in our book of Numbers. We could now look back at the census in Num 1, the order of march in Num 2, and the divisions of Levitical clans in Num 3–4. Tribal patterns also occur in chapters 7 (donations of vessels), 10 (order of march), 13 (spy trip to Canaan), and 34 (land distribution by lot).

Levine suggests that the census in Num 1 was distilled from Num 26; Num 1 is skeletal by comparison, focusing on tribal totals for able-bodied soldiers. A much longer tally of clans and warriors can be found in 1 Chr 5–7. The information in Num 26:57–62 was distilled from chapters 3–4.

Num 26 is much like Gen 46, the list of Jacob's immediate family. Later, during the conquest, many details about towns and territories will be worked out (Josh 13–22). In these genealogical lists clans are often mentioned, but not ancestral houses. The traditional biblical model is to think of the list of the sons of Jacob in Gen 46 as the start of small tribes that grew larger and subdivided over the centuries. Most scholars realize that the entire tradition of tribes, clans, and houses is much more complex than that.

Levine takes Num 26:4b–51 to be the underlying basis (along with elements of 13:1–16) for much of Num 1 and for Exod 6:14–25. Num 26 may well rest on Gen 46:8–37. He concludes that Num 26 was originally a record of those who left Egypt, not of their descendents forty years later. The bulk of Num 26 was shifted to this point in the story, very close to the time of the new generation crossing the Jordan, because editors felt free to move it here rather than let it stand at the start of the book. Levine calls the shift a "time warp," but there needs to be some more explanation.

Levine notes the that Transjordanian traditions in Num 21 and 32 are from JE; the majority of the Priestly traditions in Numbers favors the narrower definition of the Promised Land as only that land which is west of the Jordan. As he studied the vocabulary of many of these genealogies and censuses, Levine noted that mention of *clans* and *tribes* are quite common in the older lists, and that talk of *ancestral houses* seems to come in later, mainly in Priestly texts. The key is the word *house*. Tribal and clan relationships are part of one's broader identity, but one's *house* always includes its buildings and its land, no matter how large or small. An *ancestral house* is a household, a place of residence of a patriarchal family or larger unit founded or headed by a father, or by fathers related to each other. Royal families and dynasties used the same vocabulary.

The Hebrew for *ancestral house* or *patriarchal house* is *bet ab* (*house of the father*) or *bet abot* (*house of the fathers*). The increasing use of the plural *abot* was a slow, stylistic process in later Hebrew, especially found in P sections of Joshua, Ezra-Nehemia, and Chronicles. Perhaps such terms as *ancestral houses* and *chiefs* were used in later writings to lend an aura of antiquity to contemporary socioeconomic structures. Levine remarks,

> It is reasonable to suggest that the term *bet'abot* was introduced by postexilic writers to designate the ancestral clans of the returning Judeans, now repossessing the lands they had owned before the Exile. (2:335)

When the Persians under Cyrus let Jewish detainees return from Babylon to Jerusalem, not many were willing to go. They had managed to put down roots in the area around Babylon, and knew there would be financial insecurity in the return, and even land disputes to regain title to their old properties. As an example, Levine points to Ezra 2:59–60, which mentions some returnees *who could not prove their families [bet abot] or their descent*, and to Ezra 2:61–63, where some priests *looked for their entries in the genealogical records, but they were not found there, and so they were excluded from the priesthood as unclean*. The same events are mentioned in Neh 7:61–65.

The later the post-exilic writing, the more we find mention of ancestral houses and the less we find of clans. So Numbers and Josh 13–22 may antedate Chronicles. Joshua uses lists of towns and territories; Numbers uses genealogies; but both books are concerned with property rights.

The mention of clans in the Pentateuch is more consistent; those traditions might be post-exilic or older. Levine concludes,

> It is now proper to inquire as to what it is that we are reading about in Numbers 26, realistically speaking. We are reading priestly expressions of a postexilic mentality, one that developed in several stages, and that retrojected contemporary ideologies of the postexilic restoration to Jerusalem and Judea, subsequent to the Edict of Cyrus, into the early history of Israel. The legitimation of the restoration was expressed in many modes, including traditions of the Exodus, the wilderness migrations, and the conquest and settlement of Canaan. We are being told that like the several waves of returnees from Babylonia, those early ancestors who entered Canaan after the death of Moses had also been mustered and identified according to tribes and clans, and

patriarchal 'houses.' In fact, they were the direct descendents of the Patriarchs, the original *'abot* . . . (2:337)

Levine's analysis of census and genealogy vocabulary is masterful, although beyond the scope of our book. He does make us think about how writers, editors, and archivists centuries later were awash with the names of ancestors, warrior heroes and kings, priests, prophets, tribes, clans, and ancestral and familial houses. As heirs to massive legal and liturgical lore, they could reimage or reimagine some of the complexities of their religious lives back to that more ideal time of Moses. They could think of a time when Moses and those who had fled Egypt had the same problems of trusting God, building up the community, passing on the faith, and figuring out what might happen next.

Section Twenty-Four

NUMBERS 27:1–23

Introduction

There are two fairly straightforward accounts in this chapter:

Num 27:1–11   Change in inheritance rules for women with no brothers
Num 27:12–23 Instructions for Moses to commission Joshua as next leader

The tribe of Joseph was subdivided into the half-tribes of Manasseh and Ephraim. One clan of Manasseh, Machir, later joined with the Reubenites and Gadites in seeking permission to settle in Transjordan (Num 32). The Gileadites, traditionally taken as direct descendents of Machir through his son Gilead, also settled in Transjordan (Josh 17:1).

As mentioned earlier, Levine notes that some of these proper names, such as Gilead, were originally names of regions or towns, not of individual people, but in the process of tracing genealogies and charting censuses some site names were personified. Thus the tribe of Joseph was the only tribe eventually to have clans legally reside on both sides of the Jordan.

In Josh 17:2–13, esp. 17:5, we learn of the larger portion of land given to the tribe of Manasseh west of the Jordan, a broad swath ranging northwest of Shechem.

Another descendent of Manasseh, Zelophehad, had no sons but five daughters (26:33). Matters relating to the daughters' inheritance on the western side of the Jordan are recounted here in Num 27. Some of the daughters' names are also site names, in context supporting the claims for land west of the Jordan.

The permission for the daughters to inherit in their own names, which they receive in this chapter, will be seriously modified later on in Num 36. The story as we have it in Num 27 may simply underscore the legitimacy of Manassite settlements on the western side of the Jordan, in addition to the settlements in Transjordan. In the Samaritan Ostraca (notes on clay) of the eighth century BCE we find *Hoglah* and *Noah* as town or district names in Samaria. Thus two of Zelophehad's daughters' names may represent Samaritan settlements.

Their request for changes in inheritance law was a very public event; all the important figures heard their case at the entrance to the tent of meeting (27:2). The daughters point out that their father had not been a rebel, but simply *died for his own sin*. In context this simply means that, like all the others of his generation, he was not allowed to survive to see the Promised Land.

The verb *taken away* or *subtracted* will appear again in 36:3, where other members of this clan are concerned that when the daughters marry, they might in fact transfer property from this clan or tribe to others, namely the clans and tribes of their new husbands. The clan's concern is clearly for Zelophehad's property, not his memory.

In 27:4 the women request a *possession* (*ahzh*). This is the main word for real estate or other real property, inherited or acquired. In 27:7 God allows them to have a possession of the *inheritance* (*nhlh*), otherwise belonging to the brothers of their father. This latter word means an *inalienable heritage*. In 36:2–4 the word *inheritance* (*nhlh*) is used ten times; what the daughters wish to acquire is what the clansmen do not wish to be alienated from their control. Levine polishes 27:7 to read *grant them an ancestral holding among their father's brothers, and transfer their father's ancestral territory to them.*

At the start of 27:7 God says the women have spoken *rightly* (*ken*); the same phrase will be used in 36:5 as Moses says the same (perhaps relaying God's words) about the clansmen who protested what had happened in Num 27. *The descendants of Joseph are right [ken] in what they are saying.* Levine suggests that this second use of *ken* in 36:5 indicates that Num 36 is the derivative passage, and that Num 27 is its foundation.

27:11 calls this a *statute and ordinance* (*huqat mishpat*). The only other biblical use of this compound term will be in 35:29, in reference to cities of refuge. There are many cultures today where tribal real estate laws still prevail. Among American Natives and Samoan Islanders certain sales of long-held clan property require the signatures of each and every first cousin of the seller. Any one first cousin can hold up the proceedings.

God then instructs Moses to *go up this mountain of the Abarim range.* The exact location is a bit less specific than we might have expected. In 21:11 and 33:44 there is a camping place called *Iye-abarim*, which seems to be nearby. In Num 33:47–48 the mountains of Abarim are described as facing Mt. Nebo. In Deut 32:49 this *mountain of the Abarim* is Mt. Nebo itself. For some reason the traditions seem unsure of exactly where Moses went to view the Promised Land.

God recalls the scene in Num 20:11–13 where Moses did not trust God and did not show God's holiness to the people. For that reason Moses could not cross the Jordan. The elaborate phrase *the LORD, the God of the spirits of all flesh* (*Yahweh, Elohe haruoth lekol basar*) is similar to that in 16:22, when Moses made a desperate plea for the people. Gen 18:25 has a similar dramatic title, *the judge of all the earth*; this was part of Abraham's plea to save any just people in Sodom.

Moses thinks of his successor as someone who shall *go out* and *come in*, who shall *lead them out* and *bring them in*. These idioms are often used in military contexts.

God selected Joshua, a man in whom is the *spirit* (*ruah*). This could be some of God's spirit, so to speak, which gives Joshua skill and wisdom. In Deut 34:9 Joshua has the *spirit of wisdom*.

In Num 27:20 Moses is to give Joshua some of his own *authority* (*hod*); the word can mean *height*, *weight*, *power*, *majesty*, or *dignity*, and can refer to God or to a human in various contexts. Eleazar's role will be to guide some of Joshua's decisions by using lots. Saul used such assistance in 1 Sam 14:41–42. There is no tradition of Moses using them.

Questions

96. As you read 26:33 and 27:1–4, what do you learn about property rights and inheritance law in ancient Israel?

97. As you read 27:5–11, how does the story end? Would you call 27:1–11 a story that promotes women's rights?
98. In 27:12–17 how does Moses conduct himself?
99. Comment on the style of 27:18–23.

Conclusion

Levine contrasts the scene where Aaron dies and Eleazar is made high priest (20:22–29) with this scene where Joshua becomes Moses' successor-to-be. Eleazar assumed full priestly powers, sanctioned by Moses' involvement at that transfer; Joshua receives the duties of leadership at a public ceremony sanctioned by Eleazar's presence. Eleazar will provide future assistance to Joshua (20:21). The understanding is that Joshua will not have the direct access to God that Moses had, and so will need more help from the high priest. Moses will remain a unique figure in Jewish thought.

Levine notes that this profile of Joshua's leadership and cooperation with priests is a fair reflection of what we see in all the historical books. Priests became an important part of the nation's monarchic system of governance, along with royal officials, generals, and other advisors. One example is found in Deut 20:1–9, esp. 1–4, where a priest (or the high priest) is to encourage soldiers right before battle.

Section Twenty-Five

NUMBERS 28:1—29:40

Introduction

The next two chapters review details concerning the annual liturgical calendar, repeating matters found elsewhere (e.g., Exod 23:12–17 and Lev 23) yet also adding in new information. Levine's overviews are well organized, and his attention to the vocabulary is impressive (2:365–422). The various daily, weekly, seasonal, and annual rituals can be outlined as follows (2:366–67):

Num 28:1–2	Introduction
Num 28:3–8	Daily offering of two lambs, flour, oil, and wine
Num 28:9–10	Sabbath offerings of four lambs, flour, etc.
Num 28:11–15	Sacrifices at new moons, the first day of each month
Num 28:16–25	Sacrifices for Passover and Unleavened Bread (*Mazzot*)
Num 28:26–31	Sacrifices for Festival of Weeks (Pentecost)
Num 29:1–6	Sacrifices for New Year (*Rosh Hashanna*)
Num 29:7–11	Sacrifices and fast for *Yom Kippur* (Day of Atonement)
Num 29:12–38	Sacrifices for *Succoth* (Booths, the final holy week)
Num 29:39–40	Conclusion

Note that Num 28–29 does not specify where the ceremonies are to be held. Given that in the storyline they are wandering in the desert, the editors imply that the sacrifices take place at the tabernacle, the portable shrine. Even the references to *pilgrimages* could refer to this tabernacle by default, although the pilgrimages were in fact made to local shrines for centuries after the time of Moses. There is a brief reference to the *sanctuary* (*qadesh*) in 28:7, and to a *holy convocation* (*miqra qodesh*) in 28:18. Levine calls this a *sanctuary convocation*. Either translation can be taken as an indicator of the importance of the ceremonies, and as a call to attend if possible. In Lev 23, unlike Num 28–29, there are references to some ceremonies taking place in everyone's home village.

Levine assumes that most sacrifices took place in the cooler morning hours (e.g., 28:4) unless otherwise indicated. In the section on Passover the text fails to mention that that ceremony took place in the late afternoon. What is most different in our Num 28 passage is the mention of the daily sacrifice of two lambs, even when a Sabbath or holy day brings additional obligations. The doubling of the number of animals on the Sabbath and the additional sacrifices at the new moons also go beyond Leviticus and other Torah passages (see Exod 29:38–46 and Lev 6:12–16, which are likely borrowed from Num 28).

Most of the other Torah cultic passages refer to annual holy days, and do not focus on daily, Sabbath, and new moon details. So Num 28:3–15 is new; none of these ceremonies are called *holy convocations*, and the topic of abstaining from labor is not discussed. The rest, 28:16–31 (spring holy days) and 29:1–38 (autumnal holy days), are all *holy convocations*, with notice about abstaining from labor.

28:2b ends with reference to *moed*, a *set* or *appointed* time. The schedule for ceremonies was always a vital point in Priestly regulations. 28:2 literally says *you must take care to present to me my offering, my food, for my aromatic offerings by fire, at its set time*. The style is solemn and legalistic in tone. The words for *offering* (*qorban*), *offerings by fire* (*ashh*—may or may not be whole-burnt), and *soothing odors* are all stock phrases. In Lev 2:1, 15 incense granules were actually added to some sacrifices of grain.

Num 28:3–8 refers to whole-burnt offerings (see also Exod 29:38–46). The *burnt offering* (*ylh*) is always the main item at ceremonies in which it is used. The NRSV calls it either the *regular offering* or the *regular burnt offering*. Levine does the same. With each of the two daily lambs, there is an added mixture of grain or flour and oil (*minhah*), and a wine offering (*nesek*). On new moons and annual holy days a *sin offering* (*hattat*) is added; this is usually a he-goat offered for the sins of the people in general.

The two daily whole-burnt lambs are unblemished yearling males, echoing the many sacrifices by fire in Lev 23:8, 25, 27, 36-37. The burnt animals (minus hides, hooves and entrails) ascend as a smoke or essence, perhaps more easily sensed by spiritual beings. The word *daily* (*tamid*) can mean *continual* or *regular*. The amounts of flour and oil are specific (see Lev 2 and Num 15:1-16).

In Num 28:6 the reference to Mt. Sinai is puzzling since the only offering made there was in Exod 24:5. Or perhaps we should consider the laws in Exod 29:38-42. So we could understand the mention of Sinai to refer to sacrifices ordained or prescribed, or to sacrifices actually performed back then.

The grain offerings were burnt, and the drink offering was wine (not beer).

28:10 makes it clear that the total sacrifice for Sabbaths was twice the daily amount; thus four lambs and the accompanying grain, oil, and wine offerings.

In the regulations for the first day of each month, the Hebrew refers to the *new moon* (*hdsh*), derived from a word meaning *new*; by extension the new moon represents the entire lunar month that follows. In a sentence where the word is used twice, such as 28:14, we could use both terms, as *every new moon throughout the months of the year*.

In 28:15 a *sin offering* is mentioned. There were several types of these sacrifices. Some, such as in Lev 4-5, used whole-burnt bulls to atone for inadvertent priestly or community failures. Others represented the failures of tribal leaders or individuals; these used a male goat for the sacrifice, and some of that meat was given to the priests. This one in Num 28 may be similar to that in Lev 9:15, a minor offering for the people to assure their purity in the sanctuary area. Usually the sin offering was the very first in the series of offerings for a particular day.

Moving to the annual sequence of feasts, Passover and the week of Unleavened Bread are now described. The term *pesach* (*passover*) basically refers to the lamb itself. The current consensus is that the sacrifice represents God's *protection* for the flocks and the people. Isa 31:5 uses the same verb in the phrase *he will spare and rescue it*.

In Num 28:17-18, the first day of the seven for *Unleavened Bread* (*Mazzot*) is called a *festival* (*hag*), originally meaning a one-day pilgrimage to a local shrine. This day is also called a *holy convocation* or *sanctuary convocation*. The one-day restriction from *any work at your occupations* may be slightly less comprehensive than the shorter phrase *any work*, found elsewhere (see Lev 23:6, 34 and Deut 16:1–7). Levine argues that after this first day of the festival the people who traveled far would return home; the priests would continue with the required sacrifices and final convocation, and most of the people would simply observe the final day of abstention from work in their home towns.

Num 28:26–31 describes *Weeks* (Pentecost), the early harvest rite celebrating the *firstfruits*. Strictly speaking, in 28:26 this is not called a *hag* or *pilgrimage*; the Hebrew simply refers to a period of weeks. In Deut 16:9–10 and Exod 34:22 the same holy day is called a *hag*. These firstfruits were presented and then given to the priests (see Num 18:12–13).

In Num 29:1–6 the new moon of the seventh month involves additional sacrifices, and a *blaring* (*trwyh*) of trumpets (see Ps 81:3). No rationale for the horns is given; perhaps we should take this as a preparation for the feast of Booths at the middle of the month. While the title is not used here, this is the gist of the New Year rite, also known as *Rosh Hashanna*. Num 29:6 notes that the sacrifices just mentioned are above and beyond those for a regular new moon and for the daily sacrifices due each and every day of the year.

In 29:7–11 we find regulations for what we now call *Yom Kippur*, the *Day of Atonement* (see Lev 16; 23:26–32). It is another *holy (sanctuary) convocation* on which no work should be done. The reference to *denying* [*ynh*] *yourselves* in 29:7 can also be taken to mean *fasting* or *humbling your souls* or even *mortifying your bodies*. Similar phrases can be found in Lev 16:21; 23:27; Isa 58:3–5; Ps 35:13. Fasting is the traditional custom representing communal atonement. Num 29:11 mentions a male goat as a sin offering in addition to the sin offering of *atonement* (*kippurim*) (see Exod 30:10). In Lev 16:27–34 we find the he-goat and one bull used in these sacrifices on *Yom Kippur*. The blood of the goat and the bull were taken into the outer tent to sprinkle on the shrine incense altar; then the high priest took more blood, as well as incense and fire, into the holy of holies, where he put blood on the mercy seat and used the incense. On the way out of the tent of meeting he put more blood on the horns of the outdoor altar (see Lev 16:12–19).

Num 29:12–38 describes the most elaborate annual rite, *Ingathering* or *Booths* (*Succoth*), at the end of the full harvest of all the crops, excluding the grains that had matured a few months earlier.

This *pilgrimage festival* (*hag*) was to last for seven days. The abstention from assigned work mentioned in 29:12 was just for the first day. Over the seven days the number of bulls sacrificed went down by one a day, from thirteen to seven, but that still came to a total of seventy bulls in all, not to count the rams, lambs, goats, grain, etc.

In 29:35–38 further sacrifices were held on the eighth day, another day of abstention from assigned work. In 29:35 this day is also called an *azeret*, a *solemn assembly*. The term derives from a verb *azr*, which might mean *to continue to assemble* or *to abstain from labor*, in this context. Levine suggests that this one-day ceremony may have had older roots, but was later merged with the seven-day *Succoth* ceremonies.

29:39 notes that the preceding list of public liturgies is paramount. All other individual vows and individual offerings for sacrifice were always voluntary, and could take place at any convenient time, often near holy days. Some of the meat of many of these individual sacrifices was shared with family members.

Questions

100. Comment on the style of 28:1–8.
101. Why would anyone want to have special religious rituals for the first day of each lunar month (new moon), as we have in 28:9–15?
102. In 28:16–25 why is there so much emphasis on the seven days of Unleavened Bread, and so little detail about the Passover meal?
103. Assuming that the day of Firstfruits (28:26–31) was originally a harvest ceremony celebrating the first portion of early-ripening types of grain, how is this ceremony outlined now in chapter 28?
104. Ancient societies have chosen dates for New Year's Day in various ways, generally favoring a day in the spring or fall. In our own Roman system of the names of months, the new year originally began in March; thus September to December were the seventh to tenth months. We have kept the original names even though the New Year date was later moved back to January. What is the religious focus of the Jewish New Year as found in 29:1–6?

105. What is the religious focus of the day of atonement and fasting described in 29:7–11?

106. As a present day reader of 29:12–38, what impressions or feelings do you have as you read these regulations?

Conclusion

Readers might be forgiven for skimming over the many details in this Conclusion section, but I think there is some value to considering Levine's comparison of these two chapters of Numbers with their counterparts elsewhere in the Pentateuch. Levine searches for the post-exilic setting for most of these regulations, and estimates how calendars and procedures underwent modifications over time. He does admit that the focus of the authors is on the rituals themselves, leaving us with little explanation of how helpful these experiences were supposed to be for ordinary Jewish people. But there is a theological maxim that rituals reach people on many levels, and in that sense rituals justify themselves, so to speak. The more we read of these ancient fine points, even though we have no expectations of ever watching a lamb being offered in whole-burnt sacrifice or the like, we (Jewish and Christian believers) are in contact with our "ancestors in the faith." Through circumstance and history we have developed other rituals to adore the same God, and we take them just as seriously.

Levine proposes that the precise regulations of Num 28–29 in fact represent worship at the temple during the Persian period (538–323 BCE). Much of the passage is Priestly in style (post-exilic). In comparing liturgical calendars we can look at Lev 23 and Num 15 (and also Ezek 45:18–46:15), but Num 28–29 is the most detailed. We can say Num 28–29 complements Lev 23, without precisely endorsing every detail in Leviticus.

Biblical scholars can find dozens of minor discrepancies in these texts. One example is the way to measure the days before the festival of Weeks. Deut 16:9–10 speaks of counting seven *weeks* (*shabot*) from the time the sickle is first put to the standing grain. Harvest times could vary by region and by conditions each year. In Lev 23:9–16 the seven weeks start on the day after a Sabbath, so they are full *Sabbath weeks* (*shabatoth*, i.e., weeks that end on a Sabbath), plus one extra day. In Num 28:26 the text simply refers to *your festival of weeks*, a general phrase like that in Deuteronomy. Another discrepancy is that only Deuteronomy calls Weeks a *hag* (Deut 16:10). Levine considers minutiae such as these to reflect actual changes in liturgical theology.

The unexpected details in Num 28–29 involve the regulations for daily, Sabbath, and new moon sacrifices. Many ancient Near Eastern religions required regular food offerings in their temples (not necessarily daily, but scheduled in precise ways). Such rites were covered by temple budgets, not dependent on free will offerings.

Levine searched for evidence as to when the daily morning and evening sacrifices became standard temple customs. In Lev 6:12–16 daily grain offerings are divided between what is burnt and what is given to the priests. In 2 Kgs 16:15 daily morning burnt offerings and evening grain offerings are mentioned, but not in detail. In 1 Kgs 18:29, 36 *offerings of oblation* are spoken of, apparently offered sometime later in the day. Ezek 46:13–15 refers to morning burnt and grain offerings. Ezekiel uses the word *tamid* in 46:15. This was probably written well after 586 BCE. One could conclude that components of the two-part *tamid* system in Num 28:3–8; Exod 29:38–42; Lev 6:12–16 are most likely post-exilic. Later, passages such as 1 Chr 16:40 (a late comment on 2 Sam 6) also mentions daily burnt offerings, morning and evening. So Lev 23 in general is used in Lev 6:12–16 and Num 28–29, and all are post-exilic. Levine postulates that Exod 29 generally relies on Lev 8, and is cast back to the time of Moses. Exod 29:38–42 is most likely a reuse of Num 28:3–8. Thus the two-part daily *tamid* in Num 28 now echoes the Mosaic passage of Exod 29:38–42, even though daily sacrifices do not appear in Leviticus.

In Num 28:9–10 Sabbaths (not called *holy convocations*) require two additional lamb sacrifices, with grain, wine, etc. These offerings may be assumed to take place along with the morning *tamid*; so the evening *tamid* would just be the second regular daily lamb, etc.

The other Torah sources for the Sabbath differ in details. In Lev 23:2–3 the term *holy convocation* is used twice. In Lev 23:2–3; Exod 20:8–11; 23:12; 31:12–17; 35:1–3; and Deut 5:12–16 there are no references to Sabbath animal offerings at all, just to the ban on work. In 2 Kgs 4:23 there is a hint that one could visit holy people or sites on the Sabbath, and in Hos 2:11 and Isa 1:12–13 there are hints of public worship on Sabbaths and new moons. Levine admits that in Num 28:9–10 the focus is on the offerings themselves, rather than on the community of worshippers.

In 28:11–15 the rites for new moons are detailed, again without much focus on the community of worship. These rites were offered by the priests, but they were not *holy* or *sanctuary convocations*.

In 28:15 the mention of a sin offering at the new moon is unexpected; most likely it was a sin offering by and for the people, not like the one for the priests in Lev 16. Other references to these sin offerings can be found in Ezek 45:21–25; Neh 10:34. These were gifts from people to priests, insuring the people's status before God. They expiated for inadvertent offenses that might detract from the efficacy of the rituals. Levine suggests that using the he-goat might represent the wilderness in some way, the land of desert and demons (see Isa 13:21; Lev 16:22; Lev 17:7). So an animal signifying sin could be sacrificed for purification from sin; this is another example of *like correcting like*, an ancient concept.

Levine suggests that we should look at Deuteronomic liturgical reforms, considering them as older than the passages in Leviticus and Numbers. Starting with Exod 12:21–27; 13:1–10; 23:15–19, we find simple descriptions of three one-day *hags*, namely Unleavened Bread, Firstfruits (Weeks), and Ingathering (*Succoth*). Even for *Mazzot*, the week of Unleavened Bread, only the first day was a *hag*; the rest of the days were spent back home. Such pilgrimages were all to local shrines, not necessarily major shrines such as Bethel or Jerusalem.

While King David began to consolidate worship in Jerusalem, it took a long time for that to be established, partly because of the secession of the Northern tribes. As we read in 2 Kgs 22–23, King Josia firmly closed many illegitimate shrines and exalted the temple in Jerusalem. See Deut 12–16 for a grand overview of how worship was to affect all of daily life.

Given that the Passover meal began with the sacrifices at home on the afternoon of the fourteenth day of Nisan (March/April), the week of Unleavened Bread (*Mazzot*) started at the full moon on the fifteenth. Exod 13:6 indicated that on the seventh day of that week there would be a *hag*. Many scholars consider both these rites as commemorative of the ancient nomadic shepherd lifestyle. The young male lambs represented all the flocks, and their sacrifice was for the safety of the newborn lambs, soon to be moved to summer grazing grounds, and for the safety of all the people. It was also a way of celebrating their lives as shepherds.

With the changes involving Jerusalem and the closing of local shrines, both ceremonies had to be centered in Jerusalem itself. In order to spare people the great inconvenience of being away from home until the last day of the week of Unleavened Bread, Deut 16:7 allows the Israelites to go home the morning after Passover. Deut 16:4, 6 also speaks of sacrificing the Passover lamb in the *evening* (*byrb*), thereby splicing the two rites, Passover and the first day of Unleavened Bread, into one overnight event. After they had gone back home, the people would celebrate the final day of *Mazzot* as a *solemn assembly* (*ezeret*), not a *hag*. Exod 23:16a refers to a firstfruits (barley) festival or pilgrimage (*hag*). This blessing of firstfruits is understood to honor God as the true cause of the harvest, and so to release the rest of the harvest for use. In a sense, the offering renders the harvest no longer holy to God alone, but now holy to all, i.e., available for people to eat. Another theological term is that the blessing of the firstfruits *desacralizes* what belongs to God by right. At times this early harvest offering could have occurred about three weeks after the week of *Mazzot*.

Since the Deuteronomists wanted to move this local celebration to the temple in Jerusalem, it was impractical to hold it so soon after *Mazzot*. Deut 16:9–12 simply legislated a seven-week period prior to the ritual. This *festival* (*hag*) of *weeks* (*shabuot*) was also inserted in Exod 34:22, along with a reference to the *hag* for Ingathering. In Deut 16:10 the faithful are encouraged to *contribute a freewill offering in proportion to the blessing that you have received*. So now the rite of presenting actual firstfruits at the start of that harvest has been transformed to one that takes place several weeks later, and a monetary offering in some proportion to the total value of the crop has become the practical substitute. The rite of desacralization has been changed to the equivalent of a tithe of thanksgiving.

Exod 34:22 mentions the festival of *Ingathering*; in context it could have been another single day of pilgrimage to celebrate the final harvests, another rite of desacralizing that which belongs to God by right. In Deut 16:13–15 this became the major festival, the one that could be attended by many who lived far from Jerusalem. Phrases are repeated in Deut 16:13–15; the celebration is called a *hag* three times, and twice we are reminded that it is to last *seven days*. Deut 16:13 speaks of the produce from the *threshing floor* (*minrana*) and *wine press* (*miqboha*). This is much more specific than the reference in Exod 23:16b, which simply speaks of *produce from the field*. So Deut 16 considers all the harvest, including fully winnowed grain stocks and pressed olive oil or wine.

Lev 23:39-43 describes Ingathering or Booths (*Succoth*) in even greater detail. Visitors to Jerusalem and residents alike are to live in booths (temporary huts made of branches), in honor of the primitive shelters imagined to have been used in the wilderness by Moses and the people with him. This custom of using booths is enthusiastically described in Neh 8, especially vv. 13-18. Modern versions of the booths and harvest symbols are still used today at Jewish *Succoth* ceremonies.

Having studied passages from Deuteronomy and Exodus that were close to the time of Josiah, just before the exile, Levine then looks at Lev 23 and Num 28-29. This is the next step in liturgical modifications, representing the post-exilic Second Temple system.

Lev 23 precisely counts months and days for rituals, starting with Passover in the first month (Lev 23:5, 6, 11, 15-16, 24, 27, 34, 36, 39). Another Lev 23 innovation is calling some of these festivals, and even the Sabbath, *holy* or *sanctuary convocations* (*miqra qodesh*). So now we have two terms, *hag* and *miqra qodesh*, as alternatives to encourage compulsory attendance. Levine suggests that *miqra qodesh* might be a specification of *solemn assembly* (*ezeret*). So for those living near Jerusalem the call to attend could be reasonable, while in towns further away it might have been understood as a call to abstain from assigned labor. Lev 23:3, 13-14, 21 refer to *your settlements*, the towns at a distance. For many ordinary Israelites, tied to shepherding and farming, one trip per year to Jerusalem was very probably all they could manage. The description of the sacrifices for Weeks (23:15-21) could be understood as comprising formal offerings of loaves of bread and animal sacrifices in Jerusalem, while many in the far towns would simply observe the abstention from labor, as mentioned in 23:21.

In Lev 23:10-14 we find what seems to be a revival of the desacralizing of firstfruits. Representative sheaves of new grain will be offered, along with one lamb and its flour, oil, and wine. Lev 23:14 makes it clear that no new grain is to be eaten before this ceremony takes place, but the same verse may also allow that many in the distant towns will not be able to attend this service in Jerusalem.

Lev 23:39 (like Exod 23:16) speaks of the gathering of produce at the final harvests, but does not use the terms in Deut 16:13 for *threshing floor* and *wine press*. This might be another echo of the original desacralizing notion for this harvest ceremony. Levine favors the theory that the eighth day of the *Succoth* festival (Lev 23:36) may actually be a remnant of a much older New Year ritual.

So Lev 23 may agree with regulations in Deuteronomy in calling the first day of *Mazzot* a *hag*, in deferring Weeks for fifty days (while not calling it a *hag*), and in extending *Succoth* to seven days.

On the other hand, Lev 23:5 moves Passover back to its own afternoon time slot, no longer overlapping that with the first evening of *Mazzot*. Lev 23:15–21 adds the sheaf-raising ceremony for firstfruits, and counts the seven weeks as weeks that start on the morning after a Sabbath (Lev 23:15–16). In 23:36 details are added regarding the eighth day of *Succoth*, but in 23:42–43 the details are not repeated.

Lev 23:24–25 makes much of the new moon solemnity for the seventh month (*Rosh Hashanna*), calling it a *shabaton*, a day of *complete rest*. The word can mean *a day equal to the Sabbath in importance*. 23:26–32 introduces *Yom Kippur* on the tenth of the same month, calling the day a *shabat shabaton*, a *sabbath of sabbath rest* or a *sabbath of complete rest*.

Using Lev 23 as a base, Num 28–29 adds some details and omits others. It serves as the final Priestly fine-tuning of the liturgical calendar within the Pentateuch. But, as we have noted before, the Numbers focus is mainly on the sacrifices themselves, and chapters 28–29 do not explain the theological meanings behind the rites.

Finally, Levine notes that Lev 23 and Num 28–29 indicate "that there was a degree of diversity in religious observance during the Persian post-exilic period, as well as considerable innovation in religious experience" (2:422).

Section Twenty-Six

Numbers 30:1–16

Note: Num 29:40 in English is 30:1 in Hebrew, so the Hebrew of 30:2–17 is 30:1–16 in English. Both English and Hebrew numbering will coincide again at the start of Num 31. We will use the English numbering at all times in Num 30.

Introduction

The mention of votive and freewill offerings in 29:39 may have been the hook for Priestly editors to add comments on religious vows and oaths. While no examples are offered of specific vows, the subdivisions of the chapter are clear (Levine, 2:425–26):

Num 30:1–2	Men obligated to fulfill any vow or oath they make
Num 30:3–5	Fathers may override vows made by unmarried daughters
Num 30:6–8	Husbands may override vows made by their wives
Num 30:9	Widows and divorcees must fulfill any vow they make
Num 30:10–15	Further explanations of how the husband must proceed
Num 30:16	Conclusion

Levine suggests that this chapter combines elements of the theology of vows with elements of family law. The combination might be a late innovation by Priestly editors. In the ancient Near East a *vow* (*neder*) to a god was a promise to do something in return for having received a divine favor or mercy. While we might consider such a promise as a questionable attempt to "bargain with God"—a way of dealing that demeans both God and ourselves—the biblical view is that these religious vows are entirely honorable and compatible with human freedom. One is never forced to take a vow, but one should fulfill any vow taken.

Two terms are used to describe oaths. The verb *shby* and its noun *shbwyh* mean *to swear*, and the verb *asr* and its noun *aissar* mean *to bind*. The verb *asr* is well developed in Aramaic contracts, and can refer to positive obligations to pay or perform, as well as to negative obligations to stop or abstain from something.

Family lines of authority are presumed throughout this chapter. Adult males are free agents; they can make any vow they wish. Most women continue to fall under the control of their fathers or their husbands; few owned property in their own name. The daughters spoken of are likely in their early teens, living at home and not yet married. Widows and divorcees had no male relative directly responsible for them; if financially destitute, they could appeal for help from brothers or sons, but that help had to be voluntary.

A man must not *break his word* regarding any vow or oath; the Hebrew means he must not *profane* or *invalidate* (*hll*) his word. The second commandment (Exod 20:7) may cover improper oaths, and Deut 23:21–23 highlights the importance of fulfilling any vow or oath to God.

The responsible father or husband could challenge any vow made by a daughter or wife, but he had to do so early on. The man could not *keep silent* (*hrsh*); if he did, he would become responsible for the vow himself. The verb *to express disapproval to her* (*nwa*) in Num 30:5 (twice), 8, 11 is forceful; it can mean *to prevent* or *to thwart*, and in a sense refers to control of the person as well as of the content of the vow or oath. Levine uses the terms *disavow her* or *deny her*, meaning to *deny her* (*permission*), all in order to remind us of the forceful nuance of controlling the person. The same verb, *nwa*, is used in 32:7, 9 to describe the Gadites and the Reubenites (and their ancestors) *discouraging* the hearts of the Israelites. In 14:34 the related noun *tnwah* describes God's *displeasure* or *denial* of the people, as he condemned them to wandering forty years in the wilderness.

In 30:8, 12, 13, 15 the phrase about *nullifying* or *breaking* (*prr*) the vow also supports the distinction between overriding the person and canceling the vow itself.

There is one more phrase, used twice, to characterize a wife's vow that a husband might choose to annul. In 30:6, 8 the wife is described as being capable of making a *thoughtless utterance* (*mbta*). The verbal root *bta* may refer to something said *rashly* (Lev 5:4; Ps 106:33; Prov 12:16), but can clearly be used of men and women alike. The reference in Ps 106 is to Moses himself. The general phrases in 30:2, 12 about whatever comes from the man's mouth or from the woman's lips could include rash vows also.

Given the topic of controlling wives and daughters and their vows, I think the word *rash* is a more appropriate translation than the word *thoughtless*. Levine goes even further, using the term *any verbal statement* instead of *thoughtless* or *rash utterance*. One could justifiably leave out the NRSV word *thoughtless* altogether, and not replace it with any other adjective.

The reference to self-denial in 30:13 is usually taken as referring to fasting, although it might include other forms of asceticism that would affect only the one making the vow.

Questions

107. 30:5–8, 10–14 refer to vows made by dependent daughters of marriageable age or dependent wives. Did women have the religious right to make vows? Why did the father or husband have the religious authority to confirm or nullify such vows?

108. Why is there mention of God *forgiving* the woman in 30:5, 8, 12 or of having the man *bear guilt* in 30:15?

Conclusion

Levine observes that vows and oaths were always free acts, sometimes offered for the benefit of others. They were never obligatory cultic regulations, although they could be attested or completed at a public ceremony or sacred site at times. Num 30 provides no examples of what such vows might concern. We can guess that people might have made vows for the safe delivery of a child, for the health or safety or rescue of a loved one, for success in farming or shepherding, or for survival or victory in battle.

From Num 30 we can conclude that women had the right to make such vows and oaths without prior permission; they were independent on some level, and had direct access to God in prayer. The question is rather to what extent the unmarried daughter or wife could commit family resources to these vows. Given the few rights accorded to women, the fact is that the father or husband would be responsible in the long run for such expenses.

So Priestly editors came up with this compromise; perhaps it was a late innovation. Levine speculates that they may have been reacting to advances in property rights for women, or to the complexities of the rules for donations found in Lev 27. This line of inquiry goes beyond our scope in studying Numbers at this point.

Section Twenty-Seven

NUMBERS 31:1–54

Introduction

Shifting from the fine points of public worship ceremonies and the various obligations when making individual vows to God, readers are thrust back into a violent war against the Midianites. Not only was the battle sanctioned by God; its cruel aftermath was made all the more severe by Moses. The account ends with ritual cleansings and donations to the priests, Levites, and sanctuary.

The great idolatry of Num 25 looms in the background. Balaam, taken by some traditions (e.g., Josh 13:22; 24:9–10) as the instigator of that event, is slain here in Num 31:8. Many Midianite wives will be condemned by Moses (31:15–17), as was the Midianite woman Cozbi in Num 25. Her father, Zur, identified as a clan leader in Num 25, is likely the same Zur, one of the five slain kings of Midian in 31:8.

The battle in Num 31 can be understood as the direct wish of God, based on 25:16–18, even though different verbs are used in 31:2–3.

The chapter can be divided into three subsections, all from Priestly traditions (Levine, 2:445–46):

Num 31:1–12	Details of the battle itself, the slain, and the spoils
Num 31:13–20	Moses orders executions and rites of purification
Num 31:21–54	Distribution of spoils, donations assessed, and officers' gifts

Levine argues that this intense enmity with Midianites has been projected back to the wilderness period as a way of explaining later hostilities at the time of Judges (Judg 6–8), or perhaps even at the time of Nehemiah. He suggests that the ethnic name *Midianite* may have gradually become more of a general geographic or regional reference, and by the time of Priestly editors the term may have been used to refer to various hostile Arab clans, as hinted at in a few places in Ezra, Nehemia, and Chronicles.

Priestly writers were also interested in purification ceremonies and methods of assessing some of the value of the spoils of war as sanctuary donations.

If this is an example of "history" being retold in a quite exaggerated style in order to confirm later theological or cultural standards, it is our task to sort out what is overdrawn, to critique the cultural standards, and to salvage any lasting theological values. Num 31 has lessons for us, but we must find them ourselves.

God's opening command to Moses is harsh; he is to *avenge the vengeance (nqm nqmt)* on Midian. The phrase *the vengeance of the LORD* is used again in 31:3. The verb for *conscripted* or *numbered (msr)* is a late Aramaicism. Phineas may have gone to the battle because his father, Eleazar, as high priest, should not be near the dead for any reason. The *holy vessels* or the *vessels of the sanctuary* are not identified. In some battles the ark of the covenant was brought along. The verb in 31:7 for *serving in battle (zba)* is also used for *serving in worship* at the tabernacle.

The five names in Num 31:8 are close to those in Josh 13:21. In Num 31:10 the *encampments (mwshbt)* might mean *territories of settlement*; Levine takes this as a way of adding a flavor of the nomadic life of the wilderness period. The *booty (mlqwt)* 31:11, 12, 26, 27, 32 is based on the verb *lqh*, meaning *to take*. The only other use is in Isa 49:24–25.

Moses and Eleazar met the soldiers outside the camp, since the soldiers (and many of the captives) were ritually impure because of contact with the dead. While Moses' anger was directed at the commanders, the context indicates that all the soldiers were responsible for allowing the Midianite wives and young boys to be taken alive. Moses says these wives *became an unfaithfulness [msr myl] against the LORD*. This *msr* is a late Aramaic form, oddly also used to mean *conscripted* in 31:5. The NSRV has *they made the Israelites act treacherously*; Levine puts it that *they instigated sacrilegious rebellion.* The call for the deaths of wives and boys can also be found in Judg 21:11–12, and has its roots in Deuteronomy.

The purification ceremonies for contact with the dead will apply to all the soldiers and their captives. The mention in Num 31:20 of garments, leather, and wood anticipate the additional remarks in 31:23–24. The phrase *statute of the law* is found only here in 31:21 and in 19:2, the beginning of the ritual of burning the red heifer. Non-flammable items can be purified by briefly holding them over flames, and all items and people involved must be sprinkled with the water of purification derived from the ashes of the heifer. Clothing must also be washed.

The *tribute* or *impost (mekes)* is found only in 31:28, 36, 38–41. The *spoil (baz)* spoken of in 31:32 likely refers to small confiscated objects such as jewelry, which were kept by individual soldiers and not taxed or counted. The related verb, *bzz*, is used in 31:9, 53.

The final passage, 31:48–54, is striking. The officers seem proud that no soldiers died in this battle. The exact wording of 31:49 is *Your servants have counted the heads of the men of the battle who were at our hand [under our command], and not is missing from us a man!* They now bring *the LORD's offering (qorban)*, which seems to be a freewill offering, not a tax or assessed tribute or impost. The same donations are called an *offering (terumah)* in 31:52 and a *memorial (zkrin)* in 31:54.

In 31:50 the officers explain that their gifts are given *to make atonement [kpr] for ourselves* (or *our lives* or *souls*; NRSV). As we have seen elsewhere, the verb *kpr* has a wide range of meanings. Levine notes the phrase in Exod 21:30, where a *ransom (kpr)* can be paid by a *redemption fee (pdin)*, in the case of an ox killing a person. In Exod 30:12–16 mention is made of a tax for the sanctuary; it is called a *ransom* in 30:12, and the same verb and noun forms in 30:15–16 are translated as *to make atonement, atonement money,* and *ransom*. The root in all three verses is this verb *kpr*. In 35:31–32 murderers and dwellers in cities of refuge may not provide *ransoms* to evade the punishments due them.

Taking all this into account, Levine proposes that the officers are giving gifts *as ransom for our lives*. They may feel that, since God spared their lives and the lives of their soldiers in battle, they "owe" God a freewill gift in substitution or in gratitude. Levine's translation has the merit of enhancing the freedom behind the officers' very large donation, rather than having readers think simply of atonement for unspecified wrongdoings.

Questions

109. Comment on the style of 31:1-8.

110. How does 31:9-12 strike you as a modern reader?

111. Comment on the style and content of 31:13-18.

112. What is the focus in 31:19-24?

113. What do the authors assume in 31:25-47?

114. What is unexpected in 31:48-54?

115. Can we question the historical accuracy of Num 31? What were the cultural standards of the time? Are there any lasting theological lessons or values for us today?

Conclusion

The main wars with Midianites are found in Judg 6-8, along with a few brief references to them in Gen 25, 36. The Priestly editors of the Pentateuch often look for precursors of ethnic relationships during the patriarchal or wilderness periods that might explain or justify the wars of later centuries. Hostilities with a Midianite profile might even have endured to the Persian period, when the Priestly editors were active.

The rules for executing captured soldiers or civilians are upsetting to us, but they were applied in varying ways in biblical sources. In Judg 21:1-12 the citizens of a Jewish town, Jabesh-gilead, were executed, with the exception of the unmarried daughters. Those four hundred young women were then given in marriage to members of the tribe of Benjamin. Deuteronomy speaks quite often of such mass executions in war, especially with regard to Canaanites. When conquering the Canaanites, there were to be no treaties, no sparing of shrines, no intermarriage with survivors, and no taking of gold or silver by individual soldiers (see Deut 7:1-11, 17-26). In the most stark examples, where all humans and even livestock were condemned, the only thing gained in a battle would be the land itself, to be used by tribe or clan in redistribution. As far as we know, other ancient Near Eastern cultures had similar attitudes. In the famous Moabite Stone inscription the Moabite king Mesha exterminated everyone in the Israelite city of Nebo.

The notion of having each tribe contribute the same number of troops may well be an oversimplified or romantic touch of the tribal era; Jeremia and Ezekiel do the same.

In Deut 13:6–11 individual Israelites who promote idolatry are to be executed immediately; in 13:12–18 entire Israelite towns that promote idolatry are put under the same punishment. These hypothetical cases or examples are drawn in extreme strokes; you should strike an immediate family member, or burn everyone and every animal in the town, and make sure the town is never rebuilt for any reason. In Deut 20–21 (esp 20:10–18) rules allow for the humane treatment of those conquered outside of Canaan, but not inside the borders. Deut 21:10–14 seems to allow for intermarriage with non-Jewish maidens conquered in battles outside of Canaan. In Num 31 these Midianites do not dwell within the borders of Canaan, and are never classified as Canaanites. So the women and young children of both genders should have been spared, but the harsher ideals of the Deuteronomists seem to have prevailed here.

In fact, over the centuries most Canaanites seem to have become serfs within Israel. Some may have moved away as refugees. As time went by Jewish people intermarried with Canaanites and had more compromising contacts with polytheism. The prophets had plenty of work to do in trying to reform vast numbers of their own people.

Section Twenty-Eight

NUMBERS 32:1–42

Introduction

This chapter of Numbers continues the JE narrative or historical strand last seen in depth in 25:1–5. Since that point we have seen many Priestly traditions—Phineas executing some of those doing wrong at Peor, condemnation of Midianites, census information before the crossing of the Jordan, claims of clans of Manasseh to land in Canaan, the liturgical calendar, rules about vows and oaths, and the war of vengeance against the Midianites. Much of the final chapters of Numbers (33–36) will also be the work of Priestly editors. The Priestly material in all these chapters has to do with the coming conquest of Canaan proper (west of the Jordan), and with the antiquity of ceremonies and holy days, etc. There is very little about Transjordanian conquests and settlements, last mentioned in detail in Num 21. Levine, of course, is interested in these Transjordan traditions, since they are related to the Balaam traditions in some ways (2:477–507).

The details and negotiations of Num 32 can be easily outlined (Levine, 2:479–80):

Num 32:1–5	Initial request by tribes of Reuben and Gad
Num 32:6–15	Moses refuses at first
Num 32:16–19	Reuben/Gad promise military service
Num 32:20–24	Moses then agrees to this condition
Num 32:25–27	Reuben/Gad confirm their promise again

Section Twenty-Eight

Num 32:28-32   These arrangements are told to everyone
Num 32:33-42   Many towns mentioned, and news of the clan of Machir

The Machir clan of Manasseh (Num 32:39-40, 41-42) is called *the half tribe of Manasseh* in Deut 3:13. The same term is used in Num 32:33 and at various points in Joshua. Num 32:1 speaks of Reuben and Gad desiring land in Gilead; 32:39-40 associates Gilead with the Machir clan. Perhaps 32:33 was an edited mention of the two tribes, Reuben and Gad, and the clan of Machir, in order to combine all the traditions smoothly.

Throughout Num 32 there are style and vocabulary characteristics of JE, P, and even Deuteronomic levels. The town name *Kadesh-barnea* in Num 32:8 is found in Deut, and the various mentions of *armed men* in Num 32:21, 27, 29, 30, 32 echo Deut 3:18. Levine concludes that a late Priestly editor aware of the traditions in Num 13-14, 21 and Deut 3 wove the traditions into this form in Num 32.

Priestly editors seem to have been reluctant to give much approval to the Transjordanian territories; that reluctance can be seen somewhat in Num 32:22b, 28-32.

In Num 32:1 the mention of Reuben and then Gad is as we find in Deut 3:12, 16 and often in Joshua. Elsewhere, as in the rest of Num 32, Gad is often mentioned first. This is a minor point, but it might indicate a deliberate nod toward Deut 3. The mention of the *land* (*eretz*) of Jazer and the *land* of Gilead might refer to local districts rather than to the entire expanse of a nation or culture. Jazer, north of the Dead Sea, is first mentioned in 31:32. Gilead can refer to a large area east of the Jordan between the Dead Sea and the Sea of Galilee. It is also at times a clan name (26:29-33; 27:1; 36:1), and may refer to one single town in Hos 6:8. In Num 32 it is quite difficult to pin down the exact territories the two tribes desire.

The towns named in 32:3 are to the immediate northeast of the Dead Sea, between the Arnon and Jabbok Rivers, generally near Heshbon. The two tribes ask for this territory as a *possession* (*ahuzzah*), a term also used in 27:4.

The reaction of Moses is signaled by his first question in 32:6, *Shall your brothers go into battle, and you will you sit here?* The same phrase for *going into battle* was used in 31:21. Moses says that their remaining behind would *discourage* (*nwa*) the heart(s) of the other tribes. *Discourage* might be a weak translation, especially in light of 32:6; in context it could mean *to hinder* or *thwart* others. In 30:6 it is the verb for *nullifying* a vow. Levine suggests we translate the question, "Why would you turn the will of the Israelites?"

In 32:8-13 Moses recalls the story of the spies and the fearful people from Num 13-14. He is flatly comparing the request of these two tribes to the lack of dedication shown in the earlier event. This seems to be a stern judgment, perhaps indicating the consistent Priestly preference to focus on the land west of the Jordan.

The mention of Caleb's Kenizzite roots points to Josh 14:6-15. In Josh 14-15 and Judg 1, 3 the Kenizzites and others allied themselves with Judah in the conquest of the land. Josh 14:6-15 shows Caleb's devotion and bravery, the same characteristics Moses is challenging the two tribes to exhibit at this juncture.

Moses claims that not only will the cowardice of these two tribes not crossing the Jordan discourage or harm the goals of all the people, it will also cause God to become more angry with everyone. Moses calls them a *brood* (*trbwt*) of sinners. The word *brood* only appears here, and may be derived from the verb meaning *multiply* (*rbb/rbh*).

The verb (*swp*) is used to mean *increasing* God's anger (32:14) and causing God to *again* abandon the people in the wilderness (32:15). Moses ends by saying that this request will *destroy* (*shht*) or *ruin* everyone. 32:15 certainly puts a lot of blame on the tribes who asked to settle to the east of the Jordan!

There is another wordplay in Hebrew between God making the people *wander* (*nwy*) and *abandoning* them (*nwh*) in the wilderness. It is often impossible to preserve these word plays outside the original language, but they do point to the artistry of the authors and traditions.

The tribal leaders may have been stung by this harsh judgment, or perhaps they had not made their intentions entirely clear. In any case they volunteer to do their fair share of military service during the entire conquest. They propose promptly building the usual sheepfolds or enclosures for flocks, and building, or more likely repairing, the walls of captured towns for their own families. Then they will *take up arms* (*hlz*) and act as a *vanguard* (*hwsh*) in the coming battles. The latter term, which only appears here, might grow from the basic meaning of the verb meaning *to hurry*, and also from the context, where they promise to *bring* the Israelites to *their place*. 32:19 restates the heart of the proposal: the two tribes will serve in order to gain permission to settle east of the Jordan at the end—and only at the end—of the Israelite conquest west of the Jordan.

At this point (32:20-27) Moses agrees to the proposal, although he includes precise warnings, which might indicate his own doubts (or the doubts in the Priestly traditions). Moses uses *if* (*im*) twice in 32:20, *after that* in 32:22, and *if not* (*im lo*) in 32:23. He notes that failure to live up to this promise to do military service will be a *sin* against God. The remark can be seen as gratuitous or insulting in a way. The two tribes speak well of the LORD in 32:4, 27, and their full participation in the battles was never subsequently criticized.

Throughout this chapter there are no doubts that battles will need to be fought. 32:4 mentions towns east of the Jordan already conquered, calling them *the land that the LORD subdued before the congregation of Israel*. The basic image is also found in Deut 1:30, where Moses says, *The LORD your God, who goes before you, is the one who will fight for you . . .* In Num 32:17 the Reubenites and Gadites promise to *take up arms as a vanguard before the Israelites*. The same is said in Deut 3:18: *all your troops shall cross over armed as the vanguard before your brothers, the sons of Israel*. In other places, such as Deut 20:4, the preposition *with* is used instead of *before*, to the same effect: *. . . it is the LORD your God who goes with you, to fight for you against your enemies . . .*

Further, the phrase *before* [*liphne*] *the LORD* is used seven times in Num 32:20, 21, 22, 23, 27, 29, 32 (the NRSV has *for the LORD* instead of *before the LORD* in 32:27). In all these cases the two tribes are the ones *going before the LORD*. We might ignore these as pious phrases, perhaps added for solemnity, but Levine takes them as parallel in meaning to the phrases in 32:4, 17. He takes the preposition *before* in a spatial sense, picturing God and the rest of the tribes marching side by side, with the two tribes (and the Machir clan) out in front. They may have been eager to fulfill their agreement with Moses, but Levine asks us to consider that the tradition might indicate that those who wanted to stay east of the Jordan were being allowed or directed by God and the other tribes to take more of a risk and have less protection during their difficult maneuvers as the vanguard. The effect of the emphasis on being out in front may be then not so much a compliment for the generosity or good faith of the warriors of the two tribes, but rather a carping reminder that the two tribes will pay extra dues for extra privileges. They have made the entire conquest a much more complex task, and it is only fair for them to take the brunt of some of the battles.

In 32:22 Moses says these two tribes will be *free of obligation* [*nqh*] *to the LORD and to Israel* if they participate in the battles of conquest. The verb can also mean *to be guiltless* or *to be free from punishment*. The rest of 32:22 could well be a Priestly gloss; it is not needed for the context. 32:23 adds the note of *sin against the LORD* to any failure to fulfill this promise to provide a fair share of military aid. That sin will *find them out* or *overtake* them. Another prodding is found in 32:24, where Moses tells them, *what has come from your mouths—do that*. Similar phrases can be found in Judg 11:36 and Num 30:3.

Moses and the leaders of the two tribes now relay the details of this arrangement to the rest of the people. What is surprising is Moses' proviso in Num 32:30 that failure to act as a vanguard will result in the two tribes sharing the land to be conquered west of the Jordan, the land of Canaan proper. One way or the other they must do their duty to the rest of Israel, but if they shirk their promises to cross the Jordan and do battle they will not be allowed to remain in Transjordanian territories. Moses seems quite firm in issuing this warning; it is hard to imagine how they could have been forced to come along if they did not comply. In response (32:32), the leaders restate their desire to do their duty and then to remain east of the Jordan afterward.

Num 32:33 mentions the half-tribe of Manasseh (the Machir clan) for the first time. A similar account is in Deut 3:12–20. The kingdoms of Sihon and Og are mentioned in Num 21, Deut 1–4, often in Josh, and in Judg 11. The *building* or *rebuilding* or *fortifying* of various towns is hard to follow in detail.

The final verses of the chapter, 32:39–42, might have come from a separate source. The Machir clan drove out the Amorites, apparently overlords of many small farming villages. Levine notes that these few verses generally agree with what we know from other sources, and indicates an ongoing interest regarding Transjordanian settlements.

Questions

116. What is your first impression about the request of the two tribes to Moses in 32:1–5?

117. How fair is Moses' reaction in 32:6-15?

118. Is the response by the two tribes in 32:16-19 fair or just?

119. What is the tone as Moses relents in 32:20-24 and the tribes respond in 32:25-27?

120. What is the tone in the public announcement in 32:28-30, along with the official reply in 32:31-32? Note especially 32:30.

121. What is the focus of the opening (32:1-5) and the closing of the chapter (32:33-42)? You can almost bracket the intervening verses for a moment.

Conclusion

For some reason I find Levine's respect for and interest in the Transjordanian Jews (and in Balaam) refreshing. Every major religion has experienced breakaway groups, people who wind up on the fringes of the mainstream. However "we," the mainstreamers, should admit that "they," the fringe groups, are "ours" more than not. Perhaps "we" are part of the reason that "they" broke away.

Num 32 stems from some of the Israelite Transjordanian conquests mentioned in Num 21. Some Jewish settlers remained in those regions from times before king David to around 730 BCE, the time of the Assyrian deportation. Thus, for two centuries or so after Solomon they were part of the northern kingdom of Israel.

Early biblical passages such as Num 21 simply record the settlements, without much concern that they were east of the Jordan (see the blessings of Reuben and Gad in Deut 33:6, 20-21; Judg 5:14-16; also the good fortune of Jacob in some of these regions in Gen 31-33). It is in Deuteronomy that the Jordan becomes the inland or eastern boundary of the Promised Land (see Deut 1-4; 12:8-12). Deut 3 does recount the special exception for the tribes of Reuben and Gad and for the Machir clan. Num 32 probably draws many details from Deut 3.

Following Levine (2:498-507), later biblical passages can be sorted into those that accept the Transjordanian settlements without much discussion and those that focus on the problems of these lands east of the Jordan. Num 34:13-15 simply mentions the settlements granted by Moses. Josh 1:12-18; 12:6; 18:7 repeat basic information. Josh 12-13 provides extensive accounts of the villages and towns on both sides of the Jordan that were captured in early battles, but does not repeat the negotiations that Moses had with the leaders of the tribes of Reuben and Gad and the Machir clan. In Josh 20 cities of refuge were designated for both sides of the Jordan, and in Josh 21 towns from both sides were set aside for the Levites. In Josh 22:1–9 Joshua blesses the tribes of Reuben and Gad and the clan of Machir for living up to their promises to Moses and to Israel, and he confirms Moses' permission for them to live in their own territories east of the Jordan.

On the other hand, one incident that comes on suddenly in Josh 22:10–34 has to do with an altar set up by the Transjordanian Jews. The opening text (22:10–11) is not clear as to the exact location of the altar, but Levine argues that it was to the east of the Jordan. He suggests that the phrase *in the land of Canaan* in 22:10 was a scribal error, a mistaken copying of the same words from 22:9. Though we have no variant texts that would prove the mistaken copying, the context of the entire chapter supports Levine's argument that this altar was to the east of the Jordan.

The uproar caused by the construction of this altar was extensive. War almost broke out against the Transjordanians; they were accused of turning away from God, of rebelling against him, and of causing great guilt to come upon all of Israel. In Num 32:15 Moses used some of the same language about *turning away* and bringing God's wrath on the whole nation.

In Josh 22:21–29 the Transjordanians offered a complex excuse: that the altar was no more than a replica to be used as a *testimony* or *witness* (*yd*) for the benefit of future generations. They said it was to provide proof of good intentions, of faith shared by all, and not to be used as an actual altar of worship in competition with Jerusalem. The excuse worked; war was avoided. But we can surely see that making such a replica on their own caused the confusion in the first place. Replicas can be misunderstood; if something looks like an altar, perhaps future generations will start using it for that purpose. The religious peace attained at the end of Josh 22 may have been no more than a truce. Anyone can turn away from a great relationship with God, as Joshua notes in 23:12–13, 16.

The story in Num 32 was set right before the conquest, and harked back to the earlier incident of the cowardly reactions to the spying mission in Canaan. The upset Israelites in Josh 22:17 hark back to the sin of Peor. The verse is dramatic: *Have we not had enough of the sin at Peor from which even yet we have not cleansed ourselves, and for which a plague came upon the congregation of the LORD?*

The references to *the altar of the LORD our God* in Josh 22:19,28, 29 echoe the term used throughout Deuteronomy (12:27; 16:21; 26:4; 27:5, etc.). Levine argues that Josh 22:10–34 is a late Priestly extension of the Deuteronomic centralization of the cult in Jerusalem, specifically designed to include the Transjordanians. The added force of the phrase *if your land is unclean (tmah)* in Josh 22:19 is also a dramatic, perhaps insulting editorial addition. The same adjective occurs in Amos 7:17, where Amos condemns the priest Amaziah to die in exile, in *an unclean land*.

Levine notes that the Josh 22 passage may be from the post-exilic Persian period, and may reflect problems of that time. Jewish descendents still living in Transjordanian towns were prospering, and did not have many ties with Jerusalem or the temple. They continued to use some local unsanctioned shrines and altars, and many had adopted local pagan customs. The incident in Josh 22 may have been intended as a call of conscience for them to come back to their more authentic Jewish roots.

The final speech of Joshua in Josh 23–24 is worth reading in its entirety. Joshua spins out grim scenarios of intermarriage and idolatry, and calls on all Israelites to rededicate themselves to the LORD. The worry and warning behind Joshua's words fit in well with the worry and warnings of Moses throughout Num 32.

Section Twenty-Nine

NUMBERS 33:1–56

Introduction

Modern readers may be overwhelmed by the sheer weight of the many place names in this chapter. The perhaps overzealous claim in Num 33:2 that Moses wrote down these names, and the few clear references to well-known events in Exodus or Numbers, adds to the documentary style. On the other hand, many of the place names are unknown to experts, and discrepancies with other traditions are not completely resolved by this list. Levine notes, for example, that broad references to wildernesses (33:11, 15, 36) don't fit in well with the greater number of references to specific sites, known or unknown to us. Levine's comfort (2:511–25) in assembling archaeological and geographical evidence is far beyond my own training and teaching experience.

In effect, the details of the itinerary as a whole are basically anecdotal. Levine admits that the historical value of the chapter remains unclear or inconclusive. I would like to remind readers that we must keep in mind that historical accuracy is a recent, modern concern. How fair or logical is our desire for accuracy when studying competitive highly artistic and theological oral traditions about ancestors rescued by God and detained for decades within a regimen of short journeys and encampments in a wilderness area? After all, there is no agreement after all these years as to the exact location of Mt. Sinai, yet we accept the Sinai covenant as integral to both Judaism and Christianity.

Num 33 follows the particular tradition that the Mt. Sinai covenant took place fairly far south in the Sinai Peninsula, and then the people

Section Twenty-Nine

worked their way northeast to Elath (near the mouth of what we call the Gulf of Aqaba). Then they went far northwest to Kadesh, which is a good distance to the southeast of the Dead Sea. As was mentioned earlier in this book, there are differences in the various traditions that cannot be resolved. The Priestly traditions held that much of the long decades of wandering in the wilderness took place before their arrival at Kadesh, while the JE traditions had the long decades in conjunction with Kadesh. Both JE and P held to the idea that after Kadesh the people detoured as far to the east and north as needed to avoid battles with Edom and Moab, the peoples to the south and east of the Dead Sea. Then the Israelites turned to the west to arrive at the Plains of Moab, across the Jordan from Jericho.

In the account in Num 33 we find a new tradition: the people proceeded directly from Kadesh through sections of Edom and Moab. The place name Punon in 33:42 is a site in Edom, and Dibon-gad in 33:46 is a major site in Moab. Other sites mentioned in 33:41–48 fall along the direct trail from Punon to Dibon-gad to the Plains of Moab. There is some testimony from Moses within Deut 2:2–8, 18 that supports the notion that the Israelites went through Edom and Moab, rather than around their borders to the east.

Num 33:3–4 anchors the great journey firmly to the day after the first Passover, as the people walked by places where the firstborn of Egypt were being buried. The reference to the gods of Egypt is in line with Exod 12:12. The remark about passing through the sea (33:8) is too brief to help us in our study of the great events of Exod 14.

Aaron's death in Num 33:38–39 builds on 20:22–29, but adds new information that the death occurred in the fortieth year of the journey, with Aaron having reached the age of 123.

33:40 is a very brief allusion to the events of 21:1–3, but the place names are not repeated at this point.

In the final scene (33:50–56) the focus is on the immediate future. God has Moses remind everyone that when they conquer Canaanite lands to the west of the Jordan they must *deport* or *drive out* (*yrsh*) the inhabitants. The special verb form used in 33:52, 55 actually means *to dispossess*; the basic verb means *to possess*, and is used twice in 33:53. A rare related noun was used in Balaam's fourth oracle (24:18), *Edom will become a possession*. The reason for *driving out* or *deporting* the Canaanites is that otherwise they will be *barbs* (*sk*, used only here) and *thorns* (*zninim*; only other use is in Josh 23:13). The Canaanites will *cause trouble*. This verb, *zrr*, (*to trouble*), can also mean *to attack*. But the Canaanites can cause trouble in many ways beyond military skirmishes.

A passage close to this one is found in Deut 7. There Moses also warns everyone to remove all Canaanite shrines and to avoid idolatry or intermarriage. Harsh language is used about *destroying* and *devouring* the enemy, but milder verbs are included. Deut 7:1 speaks of *occupying* or *possessing* (*yrsh*) the land, and Deut 7:17 uses the special verb form to mean *deport* or *dispossess*. God is described as *clearing away* (*nshl*) the Canaanites in Deut 7:1, 22. The milder verbs just mentioned do not cancel the commands of Deut 7, but they do add to the realism of the context. The authors of Deut 7 knew that the Canaanites were in fact not destroyed or deported. Deut 7:3-6, 16, 25-26 admit that Israelites did not live up to their calling when they took over the land. In Deut 7:4, 26 stern punishments from God are guaranteed for adopting Canaanite beliefs or practices.

Num 33:56 adds a harsh note to the advice from God in 33:50-55. If the Canaanites are not driven out, then God will *change his plans* (*dmh*) from fighting the Canaanites to fighting his own people! The mention of *thorns* in Josh 23:13 is part of a warning in Josh 23:11-13 that also has the LORD allowing the destruction of the chosen people themselves if they follow Canaanite beliefs.

Questions

122. Aside from the geographic names, and the brief review of the sweep of events in Exodus and Numbers, what lessons are to be learned in Num 33?

123. Why would God be so testy in Num 33:50-56? Similar harsh examples can be found throughout Deut 7 and Josh 23.

Section Thirty

NUMBERS 34:1-29

Introduction

Following on the itinerary from Egypt to the Plains of Moab, we find in Num 34 a detailed outline of the borders of Canaan, which God now promises his people, and a list of the tribal chieftains who will be in charge of allotting individual parcels of land. Levine's ability to systematize place names and lists of clan chieftains and elders is impressive (2:529–43).

The southern border is described as an arc descending from the southern tip of the Dead Sea westward to Kadesh and coming back up to the Wadi of Egypt, a point on the Mediterranean parallel to the southern tip of the Dead Sea. The western border is the Mediterranean itself, going all the way north to Mt. Hor, above Byblos and far above Tyre and Sidon. This is not the same Mt. Hor where Aaron died (Num 33:37–39); that site must have been near Kadesh.

The northern border stretches in a wavy line from the Mediterranean to the east as far as Hazar-enan, above and well past Damascus. Then the border drops southward to a point a bit past the parallel with the bottom of the Sea of Galilee, then turning westward and returning to that point on the Sea of Galilee. Finally, the Jordan constitutes the traditional eastern border from the Sea of Galilee down to the Dead Sea.

The upper half of this map, sometimes called Greater Canaan, goes north and east far beyond the borders of the traditional shape of the Holy Land or modern Israel and Palestine. It includes much of what is now Lebanon, a good bit of the southern half of Syria, and some of Jordan. The tribal divisions or regions usually shown on biblical maps do not extend into most of this upper half of Greater Canaan.

Another biblical partial outline of the Promised Land can be found in Josh 15:2-4, where the southern boundary for the tribe of Judah is the same as that found in Num 34:3-5. Levine argues that Num 34 borrows from this paragraph in Josh 15.

The Mediterranean border mentions Mt. Hor far to the north, but ignores the hostile Philistine regions along the southwest coast, and the major Phoenician cities of Tyre, Sidon, and Byblos, all south of Mt. Hor. Levine argues that this image of a very large Promised Land is most likely a post-exilic tradition well known to the Priestly editors of this part of Numbers.

Other biblical references to the extent of the Promised Land offer less detail. Ezek 47:15-20 comes fairly close to what we find in Num 34. Gen 15:18 broadly alludes to the extent of King David's great influence to the north and east beyond Damascus. Some of David's achievements in Aram (Syria) can be found in 2 Sam 8:5-12. The Gen 15:18 phrase is found in Deut 1:7; Josh 1:4; 2 Kgs 24:7. The author of 2 Kgs 24:7 calls the area a former tributary to Egypt. Josh 11:17; 12:7; 13:2-6 have references to the north and east of Damascus. Judg 3:1-3 and Josh 13:5 mention Lebo-hamath, a city straight north of Damascus. The Transjordanian Jewish settlements prospered during David's time and for a considerable time after that.

Jewish rulers after David had less military or political influence in these far flung regions.

Levine notes that the Num 34 list of borders corresponds with the Egyptian territorial administrative system right after a major military defeat at Kedesh on the Orontes, in 1270 BCE. The battle site was northeast of Lake Huleh, which is on the Jordan, north of the Sea of Galilee. So the Priestly tradition shows God granting Greater Canaan, once under Egypt's control, to the Israelites. Perhaps this scene was meant to boost morale in the early post-exilic period, when rebuilding Judea was a difficult task.

Num 34:13-15 makes fairly neutral reference to the tribes of Reuben and Gad and the half tribe of Manasseh having their lands to the east of the Jordan. That leaves nine and a half tribes, counting the descendents of Joseph (Ephraim and the other half segment of Manasseh), to divide the Promised Land. In Pentateuch traditions the tribe of Levi does not get an allotment, but towns will be provided for them, as we will see in Num 35.

Eleazar and Joshua will supervise the allotment process. Caleb, the chieftain for Judah, is mentioned first, just as the southern border of Judah was mentioned first in 34:3.

Levine notes that there are several lists of chieftains and clans throughout Numbers. The lists in Num 1, 13, and 26 begin with the tribe of Reuben, the eldest son of Jacob. The lists found in Num 2, 7, 10 and 34 begin with Judah, the tribe of David and the core tribe of Judea (Judah), the southern kingdom, which outlasted the northern kingdom of Israel by centuries. David's conquest of Jerusalem, and the centralizing of worship at the temple there, would be integral to the later Priestly theological traditions, of course.

The first four lists, in Num 1, 2, 7, 10 contain the same names, set as they are in the early wilderness period. The next list, in Num 13, was of the time when the spies or scouts were sent to learn about Canaan. According to Priestly traditions this took place at Kadesh, near the end of the forty years of wandering. In this chronology these chieftains were of the next generation, not the men of the early wilderness period who had died off over the years.

Joshua was Moses' assistant by this time, and he and Caleb, the scout for Judah, were the only ones spared when God sent the plague on the other scouts (14:36–38). Because of that plague, the list of chieftains in Num 34 consists of new people, except for Caleb. We have no other information about the nine new chieftains, although the linguistic roots and spelling of their names seem to be authentic. Priestly editors have assembled all these lists with some care.

Questions

124. What impressions do you get when reading 34:1–15?
125. Does it make sense to list the current tribal chieftains in 34:16–29?

Section Thirty-One

NUMBERS 35:1–34

Introduction

The final two chapters of Numbers tie up a few loose ends of the narrative, but also introduce new topics. Num 35 can be divided as follows (Levine, 2:547–48):

Num 35:1–5	Allotment of towns for Levites and their families
Num 35:6–8	Further details, including mention of *cities of refuge*
Num 35:9–15	Those who slay without intent may use the cities of refuge
Num 35:16–29	Examples for distinguishing murder from manslaughter
Num 35:30–34	Strict regulations to prevent exemptions in either case

A very brief outline of the difference between murder and manslaughter, and of someone being granted or denied asylum in these cases, is found in Exod 21:12–14. That mention is extremely brief; by comparison the passages to be mentioned in Deut 19, Josh 20, and Num 35 are much more substantive. Levine handles this complex legal topic well (2:547–71).

In Jewish tradition blood was considered a life force, a medium within which the soul thrives (to use a more modern term). Solemn sayings by God in Gen 4:10–12 about the blood of Abel, and in Gen 9:4–6 about God requiring a reckoning for the shedding of human blood, use the same image. The balance of life and death among all beings was disrupted by murders and wrongful deaths. Thus we find laws in Exod 21:28–32 about punishing the owner of a habitually violent ox that gores a human to death. The ceremony in Deut 21:1–9 calls for the civic ritual slaying of a calf to atone for a murdered corpse found in open country, a case in which there is very little chance of finding the one responsible. The blood of the animal served as a substitute for that of the murderer, and the elders of the nearest town paid the costs and performed the civic ceremony. All cases of murder and manslaughter involve the community and affect its relationship to God.

The three Transjordanian towns of refuge are named in Deut 4:41–44, and the topic of taking refuge is discussed at some length in Deut 19:1–12. Deut 19 allows for three towns of refuge in Canaan and perhaps three more if the nation grows in size (apparently not being the three in Transjordan). In Josh 20 the topic is also discussed and the three towns in Canaan are named (Kedesh, Shechem, Hebron) along with the three for Transjordan (Bezer, Ramoth, Golan). Several towns are needed so that the one seeking refuge does not have to travel too far, since he may well be in danger on the way.

Readers need to remember at this point that the tribe of Levi had been set aside for priestly (and subsidiary service) duties and so was not given any tribal territory for large-scale farming or herding. In addition to donations of food from sacrifices and shares of other temple activities and funds, the nation was asked to provide many towns for the Levites to use. The Levitical towns may have been smallish in size, but they came with large enough common tracts immediately surrounding them to provide for gardens and grazing ground for small numbers of family farm animals. In Num 34 we read of forty-eight towns for them, provided in proportion by the various tribes. These houses with their assigned gardens and small pastures for farm animals were not deeded to individual Levites to be used for collateral or resale; they were properties still held in common by the donor tribes.

Levine notes that the word for *town* or *city* (*yir*), used about two dozen times in Num 35, should be thought of primarily as a space or place, without regard to the number of people who live there. In our own culture, following Western rather than Middle Eastern thought patterns, we think of a town or city mainly as a social and political system, and we often use different words (village, town, city, metropolis) to note the relative size of the population as well. Given that only one word is used in the Hebrew of Num 35, we could consistently use a word such as *town* throughout the entire chapter.

In 35:6 the author jumps ahead a bit to mention that six of these Levitical towns will also serve as official places of *refuge*. The word *refuge* (*miqlat*) is used only in the description of these special towns. Levine assumes that ancient Near Eastern shrines or pilgrimage centers were the original sites for this custom of asylum or sanctuary. A person present at a shrine or temple could be under the protection of its god, at least for a time. This may be why in Jewish custom the towns of refuge were among the Levitical towns. Levine suggests that because of the linking sentence about towns of refuge in 35:6, the first section of the chapter, vv. 1–8, might be a later addition to Num 35 as a whole. Now it serves as an introduction to a larger topic.

In many cases the area for refuge may have been a special quarter or subdistrict within that town, rather than the entire town. Something like this subdistrict is found in 2 Sam 12:27, which speaks of Rabbah's *water city*, meaning the town of Rabbah's main spring or cistern system. See also 2 Kgs 10:25, where one part of a Baal temple is called a *citadel* (*yir*).

In Josh 20:4 anyone coming for refuge or asylum must explain his case in a preliminary hearing with the elders of the town of refuge before being accepted by them. The main hearing or trial is to take place before the *congregation* at a later date. In Deut 19:11–12 a murderer who misuses the system of refuge may be extradited from the town of refuge by petition of the elders of the town where the murder took place.

Levine suggests that those seeking refuge probably lived in shelters provided by the Levites, and that they may have had to earn their keep on work details—something in the manner of indentured farmhands.

The ensuing discussion in Num 35:16–29 of intentional murders and unintentional cases of manslaughter is complicated, but not impossible to fathom. In Num 35 the verb *rzh* (*to slay*) is used often, but two different words must be used in English translations. The reason for this is that the Hebrew verb changed its meaning over the centuries, gradually including the dimension of motive, which was not present in the verb in earlier times. The NRSV uses *slayer* or *murderer* as needed for clarity. Levine uses *slayer* (or the phrase *one who commits homicide*) and [*accused*] *murderer* as needed. In 35:27, 30 the same verb is used for the *execution* of a murderer. The NRSV uses *is killed* in v. 27, and *be put to death* in v. 30.

The same verb was used for the Fifth Commandment (Exod 20:13), where many commentators prefer to retain *you shall not kill* rather than word it as *you shall not murder*.

The other verb used several times in Num 35 is *strike* (*nch*), which carries the same range of meanings as we have for the word in English. It also has to be translated in various ways in this chapter for the sake of clarity.

Taking the NRSV translation as accurate and adequate for our study of Num 35, we can follow the logic of the discussion. In 35:11 Levine takes the command to *select* (*qrh*) places of refuge to mean *provide places that are easily accessible*. He bases this on Gen 27:20, where Jacob lied to Isaac and said that God had made the game animal easily accessible in the hunt. The text actually says that *God made it come* [*hqrh*] *to me*.

Towns of refuge could be used by a *slayer*, someone (Israelite or resident alien) who killed a person *without intent*. The noun here, *intent* (*shggh*), is from the verb *shgg*, meaning *to do something inadvertently*. It was used in the regulations for atonement rites in Num 15:22–25. 35:22–24 attempts to explain how such an event might have happened. The one who killed in the heat of the moment without intent was not an enemy in the usual sense, and did not wait in ambush. He may have dropped something like a large stone without looking first to see that no one was in the way. In Deut 19:5 another example is used, of someone chopping a tree with an axe, and the axe blade breaks from the handle as it is swung and the blade kills someone nearby.

The slayer seeking refuge is fleeing from the *avenger* (*goel*) or the *avenger of blood*. A *goel*, the closest male relative of a husband in a family crisis, could have several different responsibilities. These included securing property or making loans, marrying a childless widowed sister-in-law, or avenging a wrongful death. In any case, the *goel* himself may not enter a town of refuge to avenge a case.

In clear cases of murder with intent, such as we find in 35:16–21, the avenger is appointed as the official executioner (35:19, 21). In cases of slaying without intent, the *congregation* from the town where the death occurred judges between the slayer and the avenger at the main hearing, and may "rescue" the slayer by their decision. Still, after the main hearing the slayer must return to the city of refuge until the time of amnesty at the death of the current high priest. Should the slayer leave the city of refuge for any reason prior to the time of amnesty, he is fair game should the avenger find him beyond the city limits. At the time of amnesty the slayer can return home in safety; the avenger's duty is effectively cancelled.

The accounts of these cases in Deut 19, Josh 20, and Num 35 are somewhat jumbled. This happens at times where everyone knows the topic well, forgetting that later readers will need more clarity. We know that the *avenger* (*goel*) needs to be authorized to pursue and execute, but in these passages the avenger appears quite early in the accounts, with little explanation of how long it took for him to be authorized. In Deut 19:6 the avenger is described as one *in hot anger* who might catch and kill the slayer *although a death sentence was not deserved*. In Josh 20:5 the elders of the town of refuge must not give up the slayer to the *avenger in pursuit*.

Also missing are more details about when and where the main hearings were held. Apparently they were convened at neutral places, excluding the town of refuge and the town where the death occurred. It seems that a convicted murderer could have then been executed by the avenger on the spot, but one convicted of manslaughter was returned under security back to the town of refuge.

A related set of regulations is added in Num 35:30–34. Two witnesses are needed to prove any murder; one witness will not suffice. *Ransom* or *compensation* (*koper*, from *kpr*, the verb in *Yom Kippur*, the *Day of Atonement*) may not be offered or accepted in murder cases, nor may civil damages be paid to allow a slayer living in a city of refuge to return home before the time of amnesty. These rules help to keep the land holy; murders must be avenged whenever possible, and cases of unintentional slaying must be tried and resolved properly. A holy God can abide living only in a holy land, where justice is paramount.

An interesting case is found in 2 Sam 14:1–17. As part of a staged scene to convince King David to spare Absalom, a woman appealed to David to spare one of her two sons, who had killed the other son in an argument. This appeal would only make sense if she were arguing that the killing was not premeditated in any way. Kings functioned as judges, so David's handling of this appeal was appropriate. While the story in 2 Sam 14 has other purposes, it is a good example of the heart-wrenching decisions an entire society has to make in these cases.

Questions

126. What do you learn about the Levites in 35:1–8?
127. What is the logic of the regulations in 35:9–15?
128. What moral or legal principles are behind 35:16–21?
129. What is the logic of the regulations in 35:22–29?
130. What is the purpose of 35:34–35?

Conclusion

Society could not let a proven murderer go unpunished, nor let someone who had slain unintentionally go free without some period of restraint (asylum). Towns of refuge could provide a buffer against automatic clan blood vengeance, and give an angry clan an honorable way to back down from a strong mindset for retaliation.

The use of towns of asylum might have come about after shrines were closed (Deut 12–16). As we have noted, Josh 20 lays out practical rules for residing in a town of asylum. See also Deut 17:8–13 for special appeals to Jerusalem in quite complex legal cases, including bloodshed.

Jewish law consistently prohibits the right of any person to take the law into his own hands out of a feeling of personal injury. We cannot become self-appointed avengers. There was an appropriate public role for authorized avengers in ancient tribal societies with no police or jails, but that era is long gone.

I think it fitting to end with the quote regarding the Fifth Commandment by Terence Fretheim. He argues that the traditional translation *You shall not kill*

> serves the community of faith best, forcing continual reflection on the meaning of the commandment and reminding all that in the taking of human life for any reason *one acts in God's stead*, in the face of which there should be a lengthy pause filled with careful soul-searching and the absence of vengefulness and arrogance. As a result, taking a life should be very rare indeed. (233)

Section Thirty-Two

NUMBERS 36:1–13

Introduction

This appendix is related to the scene in Num 27:1–11, where Moses replied to a request by the five daughters of Zelophehad, a man of the Machir clan who had died having no sons. They requested a change in inheritance law so that they, as unmarried women, could inherit their father's land in their own right. The request may be anticipatory to us as readers; earlier chapters in Numbers had not focused much on specific conquered territories, since the people were still on their journey to the Plains of Moab. Some Transjordanian territorial conquests are mentioned in Num 21, and in the census in Num 26 Zelophehad's daughters are mentioned by name (26:33). Moses approved their request, and 27:8–11 contains a series of inheritance provisos that includes this very case.

Further along in Numbers we have chapter 32, where the tribes of Reuben and Gad and the clan of Machir bargained for the right to settle in Transjordan. In chapter 34 we read where the borders of Greater Canaan were defined and tribal leaders were appointed to distribute the land west of the Jordan after it was conquered.

Num 36 can be divided into three paragraphs and a closing remark (Levine, 2:575):

Num 36:1–4	Question arises of tribal rights to conserve all its territory
Num 36:5–9	Moses agrees; women should marry men of their own tribe

Section Thirty-Two

Num 36:10–12	The five daughters set example by obeying this decision
Num 36:13	Concluding sentence covering 22:1—36:12

Commentators note that few women in ancient Near Eastern cultures had many property or inheritance rights, but there were variations through the region over time. In ancient Jewish custom property usually was handed down through patriarchal lines. In that system if a woman married across tribal lines, her sons would inherit property for their father's tribe, not for their mother's. If she became a widow with no sons, other male relatives of the deceased husband would inherit her holdings.

One Old Testament custom, levirate marriage, offered a partial solution in some of these cases. A brother of the deceased man could marry the widow and perhaps provide her with a son in his brother's name. This custom was possible when polygamy was allowed. In a later period (represented by Num 27 and 36) it was replaced by marriage to male cousins on the father's side. Various redemption and adoption schemes were also developed. No one of these solutions became absolutely mandatory in all cases.

The bold request of these five daughters in Num 27 was based on an individualistic notion of preserving the father's name within the clan. The objection raised in Num 36 is based on preserving tribal property. Levine (2:575–79) considers Num 36 as secondary, a spin-off from Num 27. He notes that anyone would have seen right away the conflict between the permission given to the daughters in Num 27 and the question of alienating tribal property.

The reference to the Jubilee Year (36:4) was based on the fact that Jubilee laws had to do with loans and mortgages, but did not cover inheritance law. The property lost to another tribe by marriage might never be regained.

So now the leaders propose to Moses that the daughters be required to marry within their own clan and tribe. The principle in 36:7 is that no tribal properties should be *transferred* (*sbb*) to any other tribe. The verb *sbb* means *to revolve* or *encircle*; here it means no property should be *turned over* to any other tribe. In 36:9 each tribe is to *retain* (*dbq*) its original boundaries. The verb *dbq* can mean *to physically adhere* or *cling*, and its use here is a bit melodramatic. It is the key word used in Gen 2:24 to describe marriage. In Num 36:8 the verb *yrsh* (*possess*) is used twice.

A woman may *possess* an inheritance, but in the bigger scheme of things the tribe must always *possess* the same piece of land.

Question

131. Describe the tone of the negotiations in 36:1–12.

Conclusion

The story of these five daughters comes up again in Josh 17:1–6. Daniel Hawk notes that in the Hebrew of Josh 17:1–2 father and son terms abound. *Firstborn* (*bcr*) is used twice, *father* once, and *son* or *sons* nine times; the paragraph ends with with an over-precise reference to all these as *male descendants* (*hazzekarim*) (the NRSV simplifies these two verses). All these references to males, especially the last, indicate a patriarchal slant, perhaps highlighting or critiquing the initiative of the daughters' request in the next four verses of Josh 17.

The Josh 17 text about the daughters' request is difficult to follow. Hawk calls the details "a mess—textually, socially, and geographically." The reason for the remark is that the daughters seem to be asking for property in Canaan, west of the Jordan, rather than within the Machir clan territory in Transjordan. Hawk argues that 17:2a refers to Manassite land in Canaan, while 17:6b speaks of the Transjordanian properties of the same tribe. Apparently the daughters' part of the *ten shares* or *portions* (17:5) is west of the Jordan, even though their clan settled in Transjordan. Hawk notes that some of the boundary and town information in Josh 17:7–13 is puzzling, and he concludes that Manassite borders in Canaan must have been "permeable," often contended by native Canaanites.

Levine notes that the names of two of the daughters, Hoglah and Noah, are known by archaeologists as names of ancient districts or towns in Samaria, part of Canaan. Levine agrees with Hawk about the Joshua text, and suggests that this account of the daughter's case was originally used, as in Joshua, to justify Manassite rights in Canaan, and that it later was reused by Priestly editors to add support to claims of the Machir clan to Transjordanian land.

Levine notes that the many references to these five daughters have come to have a double function. Their request to Moses has its own merit as a case that may have helped change inheritance law, and it was also used in the complex traditions of how the various clans of the tribe of Manassah came to settle in areas on both sides of the Jordan, something that did not happen with any other tribe.

Author's Retrospective of Numbers

Given the kaleidoscopic or crazy-quilt assembly of Priestly topics, JE graphic stories of murmurings, and the high notes of destiny spoken by Balaam, it is worth rescanning all the chapters of Numbers to form some final retrospectives. Three informal questions will be inserted where needed within this overview. For those questions I've added the instruction **Stop and answer**, since each reader will make different choices. My own answers follow immediately in each case, so these three questions and answers will not be included at the end of the book.

The Priestly chapters of Numbers could be outlined as follows:

1	Census; Levites not counted, but their work is described
2	Order of camping and marching
3	Distinction of priests from Levites; Levites' clans, duties, and their substitution for firstborn
4	More on Levites' clans, numbers, and duties
5	Some rules on injustices, and trial by ordeal for suspect wife
6	Nazirite customs; Aaron's benediction
7	Tribal leaders make donations for tabernacle
8	Blessing and commissioning of Levites
9	Passover reestablished; provision for travelers to have Passover following month; pillar of cloud controls camping and migrating
10	Mention of system of using trumpets (10:1–10)
15	Rules for sacrifices and purifications; case of man collecting firewood
17	Story of Aaron's rod blooming
18	Review of duties of priests and Levites, arrangements for their support

19	Red heifer ceremony provides holy water for eliminating impurity associated with contact with the dead
26	New census; older generation died over the forty years
27	Case of daughters' request for inheritance rights
28–29	Regulations for all public ceremonies of the liturgical year
30	Regulations about vows made by women
31	Major battle against Midian; Moses intervenes in aftermath; officers make special donations to tabernacle
32	Major decisions about Transjordanian settlements
33	Stages of camping over the forty years
34	Map of borders of Greater Canaan; names of new tribal leaders
35	Levitical towns, towns of refuge, rules on murder and manslaughter
36	The daughters of Num 27 must marry within their tribe

Question: Identify one or two of these Priestly chapters from which you can draw lessons for today. You might want to also list one or two chapters that still seem odd or upsetting. **Stop and answer.**

For my answer, I can point to Num 6, about Nazirite customs. It makes me think of individuals seeking deeper religious answers within a belief system that allows and supports such searching.

I also appreciate the effort in Num 35 to develop laws and penalties for cases of manslaughter. Any society or faith must hash these things out and meet new challenges to its system of justice.

A chapter that still upsets me is Num 31, where Moses calls for adherence to a harsh code of holy war. I'm not distracted by judging the ancient rules, or by the editors' doctrinal reasons for having Moses defend the custom. I am more saddened by the harsh war codes trumped up throughout history by many people of many religions, including my own.

The JE graphic history components form a significant part of the book, along with the oracles of Balaam, which are from an independent source. The JE chapters include:

10	First move after Sinai; Moses' father-in-law guides (10:11–36)
11	Brief murmuring story in 11:1–3; major murmuring story about wanting meat; Moses appoints seventy elders, two more act independently; God sends a glut of quails, and many people die
12	Miriam and Aaron rebel, God disciplines them
13	Scouts spy out land, issue fearful report; Caleb challenges everyone
14	People refuse to move forward; God issues the punishment of forty years of wandering; people then engage in battle without God's approval, and they lose
16	Major revolt of Korah and others; earth swallows their families, and flames kill those using censers; the people are angry about all this and God again sends a plague, averted in part by Aaron using incense in atonement
20	Murmuring at Meribah; Edomites refuse passage; Aaron dies
21	Another murmuring story, ending with use of bronze serpent; some Transjordanian conquests mentioned
[22–25	Oracles of Balaam (independent passage)]
26	The great incident of idolatry at Baal Peor

If one were to simply add up all the Priestly chapters, not counting by verses, the total is twenty-four, plus the opening part of chapter 10. The other chapters add up to eleven, plus the larger part of chapter 10. We should keep the Balaam chapters separate from the JE stories of rebellion and punishment. In this rough sorting Priestly materials dominate about two-thirds of the book.

Another way to divide the Priestly material might be worthwhile. Some of the chapters, such as 1–4, 7—10:10, 17, 26, and 31–34, describe events directly associated with the wilderness period. These include censuses, orders of march, details about priests and Levites, Passover regulations, details about the pillar of cloud and the use of trumpets, Aaron's rod, the Midianite war and officers' donations, the decisions about Transjordanian settlements, the map of Greater Canaan, etc.

The other Priestly chapters, 5, 15, 18, 19, 27–30, and 35–36, could be counted as a more timeless level of laws and liturgical regulations. These include the trial by ordeal of the suspect wife, rules for sacrifices and purifications, rules for support of priests and Levites, the red heifer ceremony, the inheritance rules of chapters 27 and 36, the details of the liturgical year, vows made by women, and the logic of towns of refuge and distinctions between murder and manslaughter. While some of these chapters are set within the wilderness framework, they do look forward to Israelite society of all ages more than to the wilderness story itself.

If we were to take the first group of Priestly chapters, those more directly associated with the wilderness period, and combine them with the JE and Balaam chapters listed above, then about two-thirds of the book would be firmly anchored in the wilderness framework. These two subdivisions, the first group of Priestly chapters and the combination of JE and Balaam chapters, are nearly equal in length.

However we divide the Priestly chapters, they do present a picture of great organization, with Moses giving laws and making decisions under divine guidance. Tribal custom and leadership is consistently confirmed, matters of worship take precedence over almost any other topic, and many laws and social systems are retrojected back to the time of Moses. The people survived the forty years by being obedient in the main, following the leadership of Moses. The old generation passed away, but their children stood at the Plains of Moab with a massive amount of blueprints for their future.

By contrast, the JE stories show a people of chaos, quick to lose trust in Moses and Aaron or even in God, fed up with relying on manna, angry about water shortages, fighting over who should lead or who should be ordained to what level of ritual service. They suffer death sentences in large numbers from an angry God, repent for brief periods, and then do sinful acts of stubbornness all over again. The idolatry at Baal Peor provides a fittingly incomprehensible end to this astounding profile.

Commentators find the overall relationship between the chosen people and God at this point to be a dysfunctional one. Handcuffed to each other in a truly mutual covenant, the cycle of sin, punishment and mercy seems endless, even if it only spans forty years.

On the other hand, the high destiny reliably foreseen by Balaam, even though he is not Jewish, looks to a hopeful future, but not to the gritty events of the JE traditions. Balaam sees a serene Israel, protected by a loving God, taking its place in Canaan with security and prosperity. How much irony can we see in Balaam's praises? He speaks of *upright people, not denounced by God*. He says that God *sees no trouble in Israel,* that *every nation that blesses Israel will also be blessed*, and that a great leader, a *star*, will rule over regions surrounding the chosen land far and wide. In the first paragraph after Balaam's final words (25:1-9), twenty-four thousand Israelites and some of their leading people died at God's command for idolatry at Baal-Peor. The irony continues.

Question: Identify one or two of these JE chapters from which you can draw lessons for today. You might want to also list one or two chapters that still seem odd or upsetting. **Stop and Answer**.

For my answer, I find Num 13-14 very interesting. I can appreciate the indecision of the scouts and the dread of the people after the fear-filled report. God's disappointment, Moses' spirited mediation, and the final fiasco of going to battle without approval all contribute to the realistic emotional panorama of frustration and indecision.

Some troubling scenes for me include Num 11 and 21, where God firmly plans to use quails and serpents to wreak his punishments. These chapters challenge me to keep thinking of God's just relationship to an entire people.

Question: What passage from the Balaam oracles seemed most helpful to you as a reader? **Stop and answer**.

For my answer, I focus on the first oracle (23:9-10). The reference to a people living alone, a people called to be upright, can remind us of our own calling. But God does not want his people (then or now) living on a reservation; he wants their covenant example to be an effective force for good for everyone. He can even use a Balaam to make his point known in public.

As I work my way through this study guide for Numbers, my mind and heart keeps coming back to the scene in 16:46-50. After the earthquake consumed the rebel leaders, and the fiery death of the 250 men with censers, the people were angry at Moses and Aaron. As the inevitable plague came down from above, Moses had Aaron take a smoking censer and run to the place among the people where he might atone for this rebellion by swinging the censer in reverence to God. Aaron was able to stop the plague, which was advancing in some sort of a visible line across the camp. The death toll before Aaron succeeded was 14,700 people.

The image of this elderly man obeying what might have been a wild guess or a desperate suggestion by Moses, then running and swinging the censer, should be made into an icon.

Retrospective

Called by God to help his brother in Exod 5 and beyond, Aaron was also the inept leader who contributed in great part to the golden calf disaster in Exod 32, and to the sinful dispute in association with his sister in Num 12. Yet at other murmuring scenes in Numbers he is faithful, and assists Moses in confronting the people or in begging God for mercy. At this point in Num 16 he and Moses succeed in atoning and getting the plague stopped, but Aaron must have realized that winning this battle was not the same as winning the war, to use a modern phrase. How much hope did Aaron have that his people had finally learned their lesson, or that God would now calm down completely?

A few short chapters after this scene, we come to the death of Miriam and the crisis at Meribah, where Moses and Aaron were told that they would not be able to cross over the Jordan themselves, as a punishment for their own inconstancy. Then we read of Edomite hostility (not punished by God), and finally the brief, stark story of Aaron's death at Mt. Hor (20:22–29). Aaron ascends the mountain, accompanied only by his son Eleazar and Moses. They remove Aaron's priestly robes and insignia from him before he dies (to avoid ritual contamination of the vestments) and put them on Eleazar. There are no words recorded in this scene.

So Aaron never sees the happy ending. His priestly service and leadership role did not protect him from himself and his own sinfulness. The people he served were often in the same boat, racked by their own sins. Hostile nations did not always fall down at their approach. At the end we read of Aaron's son becoming the high priest, but there is no record of Aaron's feelings. Was he proud of his son Eleazar, his brother Moses, and his sister Miriam, and of their great adventures in God's service? Or was he just worn out and confused? After all, he died at the age of 123 (Num 33:39). Moses died a few months later at the age of 120 (Deut 31:2; 34:7).

My questions about Aaron's feelings at the plague scene in Num 16:46–50 and my questions about how he felt just before his death make the same point. Aaron represents the whole nation (just as Moses does). The people of Numbers are guided by a God who has an unending supply of detailed plans for them, but who feels that he must consistently punish infidelity. Blessed and admired by the seer Balaam, they are a chaotic, sinful people at the same time. They must have had more questions than answers, but looking for a golden calf or better food or a way to have the same power that Moses had only made things worse.

The book of Numbers keeps its focus on the entire nation, on all the tribes, on their need for laws and rituals, on their high calling and on their raging insecurities and lack of trust in God. Aaron's swinging of the censer is just one stopgap act of atonement, one pause within a nightmare of belief and unbelief.

The more we Jews and Christians learn about Israel's history, often envisioned as going back to the time of Moses, the more we also learn about our own heavenly Father. The verses from Balaam in 23:19–20 ring true for all of Abraham's children.

> God is not a human being, that he should lie,
> or a mortal, that he should change his mind.
> Has he promised, and will he not do it?
> Has he spoken, and will he not fulfill it?
> See, I received a command to bless;
> he has blessed, and I cannot revoke it.

ANSWERS

Section One: Numbers 1:1–54

1. The Exodus traditions describe a mixed multitude of peasants or serfs—men, women, and children—working out their relationship with Moses, and with God, and preoccupied with their physical survival. The design and construction of the tabernacle at the end of the book of Exodus provided a stable procedure for their worship, but did not solve all of their everyday woes.

    The later Priestly traditions in these chapters of Numbers portray a cohesive system of tribes and clans quite capable of selecting and supporting large numbers of warriors as needed. The main impression here is one of military preparedness.

2. Having an exact census of each tribe could lead to better ways of sharing in land grants and common tasks, perhaps including taxation (as needed by later kings, especially David and Solomon). Since the Levites were to be set aside for the practicalities of tabernacle ceremonies, all the other tribes will have to provide more warriors in the long run to protect the nation. On the other hand, the Levites would not be allotted tracts of land like the other tribes.

    In several biblical passages the taking of a census is considered sinful; one example is 2 Sam 24. This may reflect old tribal logic that there were tactical advantages to having others think that your tribe was larger than it actually was, or that a central government would seek lower taxes based on supposed lower numbers.

3. Most of the clans of this tribe will function as the support staff for all tabernacle activities, and all will camp closest to it during the journeys through the wilderness. While all the Israelites will escort the tabernacle and worship according to the established customs,

Answers

the Levites will have special ritual roles assisting the priests. The references to the death of outsiders (1:51) and wrath (1:53) describe God's desire that no one be harmed by inadvertent intrusion into his holy presence.

1:48–53 is a bit general. It seems to refer to all the duties of the Levites but not to priestly actions in detail. This passage serves as a platform for the distinctions between priestly and Levitical duties in the coming chapters.

Section Two: Numbers 2:1–34

4. The authors are imagining a very ideal disposition of the tribes around the tabernacle, both when it is set up and when it is being transported. When the people are journeying, six tribes in sequence precede the Levites, who cart or carry all of the holy structures or vessels, and six tribes in sequence bring up the rear.

   When the tabernacle is pitched, the twelve tribes form an outer square, three tribes abreast to a side. The tribe of Judah is at the center of the eastern side, facing the main entrance into the tabernacle courtyard. Note that Judah and Ephraim, the center tribe on the western side, stand for the two nations after the time of Solomon, the southern state of Judea and the northern state of Israel. The Reubenites, the center tribe on the southern side, considered themselves the descendents of the oldest son of Jacob. Perhaps this central southern position honors them for this seniority.

   Num 2:17 makes a simple reference to the priests and Levites being closest to the tabernacle when it is pitched, thus forming an inner square. Further details about their camping system will come in the next chapter.

   These maps of positions and the order of march show the importance of the tabernacle, and of the need to protect it from harm. But surely the logistics of moving and camping are being simplified here. There is no description of anyone aiding the elderly or infants, of parents rounding up uncooperative children or flocks, nor of the complex steps in packing and unpacking tents and other possessions.

Section Three: Numbers 3:1–51

5. The cascade of first-person phrases (*I hereby accept . . . the Levites shall be mine . . . all the firstborn are mine . . . when I killed . . . I consecrated for my own . . . they shall be mine . . . I am the LORD*) is in the royal style, the language of great kings and pharaohs. The first phrase is even more forceful in Hebrew: *and I, behold, I have accepted* (see also 8:14–19, done in the same style).

6. In Num 3 the division of status and duties between the priests (Aaron's clan of the tribe of Levi) and their assistants (the men of the other clans in that tribe) is simply described as God's plan from the beginning. The authors focus instead on the census of the other three clans, their different duties, and where they were to camp in the inner square near the tabernacle. The priests' clan camped on the eastern side, facing the entrance to the temple and backed by the tribe of Judah on the outer square. In this chapter there is no description of priestly duties, nor is there a census of them mentioned.

    In 3:11–13, 40–51 there is the additional explanation that the three clans of Levites now represent and stand in for all the firstborn of the entire nation. Thus they belong to God in a special way. When a census of all the nation's firstborn showed a surplus of 273 (more than the total number of the men in the three clans), the additional firstborn were redeemed by a special assessment paid to the priests.

    Levine notes that the concern for such an exact census and extra fees implies that such a census should be taken on some regular basis in the future.

Section Four: Numbers 4:1–48

7. Given the focus on the details of moving the entire tabernacle complex, with all it ceremonial objects, one could say that the priests and their assistants are sharing one great task. Clearly the priests have the exclusive right to handle the most holy objects. In 4:5–14 the priests alone wrap up the ark, altar, and all the sacred vessels and utensils, and install the carrying poles as needed. Then and only then (4:15) do the assistants come near to do the actual carrying of the covered and wrapped objects. Any assistant who looked at or

touched one of the objects before it was covered, or who took it by some part other than the carrying poles, would risk divine wrath (4:15, 20). Aaron and his sons must personally oversee all the work of the assistants, even though their duties as assistants have already been itemized extensively (4:17–19, 27–28, 32–33).

Some of the priests (here Eleazar) had to guard and carry the special oils and incense; this does not seem to have been delegated to assistants (4:16).

The dismantling process obviously stands for the same level of attention needed for setting the tabernacle back up at the end of each stage of the journey, and ancient readers would have been aware of most of the other duties specifically reserved to the priests.

All of these duties and cautions are described as the direct will of God; there is no hint that ceremonies could have grown in complexity through human initiative over the years.

8. The design of the tabernacle and of later versions of the temple in Jerusalem allowed the laity to see some of the outdoor activities, especially the fires of animal sacrifices, but the necessarily smaller inner worship spaces were for the priests as representatives of all the people. Attending the sacrifices and being involved in special moments during the liturgical year, such as Passover or *Yom Kippur*, were truly communal experiences of worship. In addition the lengthy descriptions of the inner rooms, furnishings, and sacred objects of the tabernacle found in Exod 25–31 and 35–40 were for everyone's information and education, as were other passages in the Torah describing each feast day of the year. With everyone having this information, people would be able to challenge any later additions or questionable variations. Ezekiel's critique of later unwarranted temple practices is a striking example of this possibility (see Ezek 8).

These ancient ideas about authentic worship are intrinsic to Jewish faith (and have been adapted and woven into synagogue life), and should not likely of themselves generate a harmful clericalism.

Section Five: Numbers 5:1–31

9. Here the idea of defiling must mean disrupting some ideal state that should include everyone without exception, everyone eligible for common worship. The priests felt that ideally there should be no serious bodily flaws or blemishes among any of the chosen people, priests, or worshippers; in the same way the animals, incense, oils, and even the firewood for rituals had to be of first quality and physically sound (e.g., no larvae in the firewood). Moving the body of a dead person and attending to the details of burial was another troubling situation, even though a very small percentage of the people would have had that duty at any one time. Perhaps the physical diseases or the presence of a corpse represented evil forces or the effects of sin in our world. As classifications or degrees of worthiness for community worship grew in complexity, moralistic terms such as *unclean* or *defiling* became jargon. Neutral terms indicating exemption from or ineligibility for assembly may be more helpful to modern readers. Perhaps we could call such people *on leave* rather than *unclean*.

    We need to be aware of the communal nature of Old Testament thinking. In designing ceremonies, assembling laws, and reforming wrong ideas the priests and prophets thought about the whole nation, since the whole nation was in one covenant with God. Barring lepers or people who have just buried a loved one from communal worship was not considered a superstition or a prejudice; it was simply the best way to perform communal adoration.

    In the century or so before 70 CE some prejudices (even if pious) crept into this way of thinking. Some handicapped individuals, mutes or those blind or crippled from birth, were thought to be an ongoing sign of the moral unworthiness of the entire people to merit the coming of a Messiah. Criminals, prostitutes, and tax collectors suffered the same stigma. In one of the Gospels, the disciples asked Jesus about a blind man. They said, "Who sinned, this man or his parents?"

    Most American Christians are at the other end of the pendulum—focusing on their individual relationship with God. There is nothing wrong with this focus, but it does not serve us well unless

10. In this passage great emphasis is put on the sinful nature of these injustices. Betraying others is also betraying God. The sin must be publicly or ritually confessed, a ram must be sacrificed in atonement, and 20 percent added to the amount to be repaid. If the injured party has since died, leaving (in rare cases) no heirs, restitution is to be made as usual to any one of the priests, standing in for God and the chosen people. It might seem odd to us that the restitution would finally benefit one priest who was in no way involved, but that priest would be present only by the chance of the work schedules, and in this instance giving the restitution to him represents the best way to atone to God.

11. This passage in Numbers is quite complex. We can think about how such a ceremony ever came to be designed and used, or we can ask why the Priestly editors wanted to put it here.

    Let's start with the husband. He may be upset because his wife has a habit of flirting or being overly fond of a neighbor. Perhaps the husband thinks he has found out early on that his wife is pregnant, but is unsure if he himself is the father. Lacking any proof as to possible wrongdoing on his wife's part, he decides to use this ceremony of oath and ordeal. Ancient Jewish commentary focused on the possibility of flirting. Some suggested delaying the ceremony long enough so that if the wife were pregnant the child would be born safely. Other sages allowed for the ceremony to take place right away.

    Levine squarely faces the topic of miscarriage or abortion. The oath taken by the wife invokes potential disasters upon her own body, should she be guilty. The editors of Numbers describe those disasters with blunt if broad language. Even the blessing in 5:28 does not of itself guarantee that a current fetus would not be miscarried. The account assumes that the husband and the priest have the right to ask the wife to swear to all this. On one level (following Levine) it seems that God is being asked to allow for a miscarriage, or to allow for possible permanent damage to the wife's reproductive system. In Lev 20:10 a couple caught in adultery would have been stoned.

it is balanced by communal prayers and concerns. As Christians we are in that same covenant, as one worldwide believing people.

Answers

The wife may be asked to take this oath, but there would be no point in forcing her to do so. She might be quite willing to proclaim her innocence, or to protect her property rights at the least. Another option would have been to have a quiet divorce, with loss of any further support from her husband.

Levine cites the Babylonian Code of Hammurabi, which provided a river ordeal for some suspected adulteresses. If a wife was accused just by her husband, she simply took an oath. If she were accused by a third party (presumably in a credible fashion) then she had to leap into a major river. Levine notes that the river ordeal was much more dangerous than the drinking of bitter water.

12. Num 5 is not the only place in the Old Testament where God is depicted as sending warnings about specific judgments. Many of the prophets and patriarchs received dreams and visions. The pagan sailors cast lots to find out that Jonah was the one fleeing from his god. Within that story God did admit to sending the storm and the whale. In the book of Esther the enemy Haman cast lots to find the right or lucky day to persecute the Jewish people. In early times the high priest carried two stones within his robes (the *urim* and *thummim*), which apparently functioned as lots for discerning divine decisions. When Deborah ordered Barak to lead an important battle, he was reluctant to do so unless Deborah took an equal risk. But then he did obey her command. So there was an understanding that God could make his will known in specific cases.

This ceremony is entirely controlled by what is holy and miraculous. The couple comes to the outer court, bearing a simple sacrifice (the barley); some sacrifice was needed in any ritual. The earthenware cup was also a simple instrument. The water was pure of itself, not toxic; the bit of dust from the courtyard floor was not toxic, nor was the ink from the written oath. Perhaps it represented the entire shrine, or the spirit of penance that was part of the ceremony. The disheveling (untying, unbraiding) of the wife's hair may have indicated her status as a suppliant, rather than act as a sign of certain guilt. In other rituals, loosened hair was part of mourning gestures.

Things followed in order: the oath was first, then the grain offering, and then the drinking of the water. It was necessary for the water to have a bitter taste. Adding the ink from the written document reminds us of the power in the Bible of curses and of blessings when sanctioned by God. One need only look at Lev 26 for this. Another clear example is found in Zech 5:1–4.

So the entire ceremony was built upon God's care for justice and holiness. The husband and wife come as worshippers, even if the wife has the burden of the oath ahead of her. All the solemn titles for the water, the added dirt and ink, the loosened hair, the dramatic words (esp. Num 5:21–22), remind them of the risk of taking such an oath. By the same token, if the wife survives the ordeal and is protected from harm, she has to be considered truly innocent and clean by her husband. As Levine notes, the curses and the water have all the power they need—religious power, the power of God's aversion to sin.

As a postscript, I think we should realize that the idea of unlimited power of curses and blessings, the value of the casting of lots, the interpreting of dreams, and the protection offered by a bronze serpent or an ark holding testimonies to the covenant, can all be reduced to an interest in influencing or even controlling those powers. In short, a trust in the miraculous could degenerate into a trust in magic. Ancient Israel saw the flaws in pagan magic early on, but it took them some time to see that it can creep into any religious system. As the centuries went by, Israel became more sensitive to the problem. So now they have no charms or special stones, spells, curses, bronze serpents, arks, dream charts, or the like. And, unlike the silly archeologists in *Lost Ark* movies, no one would use them if they returned to the light of day tomorrow.

13. In the final verse of this procedure the husband is *free* or *immune* (*nqh*) from iniquity. The reference may not be to a sin of false accusation or cruel jealousy, but to the larger corporate sin of not challenging the potential infidelity of his wife! Readers are often irritated by the juxtaposition of the final reference to a guilty wife, without any balancing refrain from 5:28 about an innocent wife.

Levine reminds us that this ceremony was a supplement on divorce law in Leviticus and elsewhere. Priestly editors were filling in a gap, the problem of suspected adultery without witnesses. They were protecting marriage, but mainly by considering the rights of husbands. Their views on marriage were strongly influenced by other ancient Near Eastern cultures.

Section Six: Numbers 6:1–21

14. In these opening five verses we learn some rules for Nazirites—they are to let their hair grow throughout the period of dedication and must avoid all grape products. We learn that individual men and women may take a Nazirite vow but there are no hints as to how old the ones taking vows should or could be, nor of how isolated they need be during this time. Could they do their normal jobs and chores? Nor do we learn why anyone would want to take such a vow.

    The long hair and prohibition from wine may be symbols of nomadic simplicity or opposition to city living, since nomads never tended vines of any sort. The care of vines is a long-term, labor-intensive routine.

    Jeremiah 35 speaks of a small clan called Rechabites, Israelites who lived in tents and never tended vines or drank wine. They moved into Jerusalem only for protection during those current troubles. Jeremiah praised this group for their dedication to the old nomadic ways, and prayed for God's blessings on them.

15. While contact with a corpse rendered anyone temporarily ineligible for worship at the tabernacle, the rules for Nazirites seem extreme. They were to stay away from attending burials of immediate family, an obligation otherwise laid only on the high priest himself. Further, the idea that the vow days completed to date would need to be repeated seems extremely strict. Even though only a small percentage of Nazirites may ever have experienced the misfortune to have to repeat time, the rule applies to every Nazirite, without exception and without explanation. One could conclude that the status of a Nazirite was quite high within the community. We could think of the respect among Christians for devout Quaker or Amish communities.

16. The many sacrifices, and the head shaving and burning of hair, bring the now completed vow period to a dramatic close. One might think of a graduation or retirement reception rather than an ordination. We can assume that some of the peace offering may have provided a feast for family and friends, and that a cup of wine or other special dish using grapes or raisins might have been especially enjoyed by the now honored Nazirite graduate. The ceremonies seem to be

much more than prescribed worship by one individual. His or her status as a Nazirite must have been valued by the community, so the closing ceremonies were meant to foster community celebration. The exhortation for well-off Nazirites to go beyond these already significant ceremonial expenditures supports this impression.

Section Seven: Numbers 6:22—8:4

17. The blessing is majestic in style. The LORD is mentioned in each verse, and the two verb phrases in each verse enrich the basic two-fold image of spiritual favor and actual gift.

    In the Hebrew, each verse has a few more words in it (going from three to five to seven), and even the count of consonants is ascending (from fifteen to twenty to twenty-five).

    Here is an attempt to portray the Hebrew word count pattern in English. Words connected by a hyphen represent a single prefixed or suffixed word in Hebrew; the conjunction *and* is also a prefix, which I will leave out here for clarity.

    > YHWH bless-you, keep-you;
    > YHWH shine his-face to-you, grace-you;
    > YHWH lift his-face to-you, give to-you peace.

    We can say that this blessing "works" because we trust that God wants to do these things, and we take comfort whenever we hear these words from a holy person, be that a rabbi, priest, grandparent, parent, or friend. This passage is often used in Christian funerals.

18. The main point of the lists in Num 7 is that each and every tribe contributed an equal amount of goods and animals for these ceremonies. One way to drive this home is to list all the equal details for each tribe, no matter how repetitious this may seem to us. One might think of teachers and parents surviving graduation ceremonies, where each student's name is read and each student is given a diploma, no matter how long that takes.

    In 7:4–5, 11 we are reminded that God instructed Moses to accept the gifts. In 8:1–2 God instructed Aaron to light the seven lamps of the stand. These might seem to be obvious steps, for which Moses and Aaron would not need further commands or, to use a current term, micromanaging. Perhaps these verses simply add to the solemn style so favored by the priests.

In Exod 30:11–16 mention is made of an annual half-shekel tax on each adult Israelite for maintaining the tabernacle. This became the ordinary support for the temple over the centuries, rather than the tribal tributes mentioned here. The temple tax system functioned until 70 CE, when the temple was destroyed.

19. In giving the totals of all the gifts, and in adding a postscript about the lamp stand, the focus is clearly on the cult, the rituals and sacrifices that will form the yearly cycle of community worship. The ongoing private revelations to Moses are mentioned just in the one verse.

Levine notes in Lev 1:1–2 another instance of God giving Moses instructions at the tent of meeting. By contrast, in Lev 16 the many rituals prescribed for Aaron in the holy of holies do not envision any opportunities for conversation between God and Moses. Levine suggests that as time went on the cultic practices prevailed in Priestly thinking, and the idea of God speaking to Moses with or without Aaron, or of God speaking to any more prophets, seemed less likely. The later generations of Priestly authors and editors relied on the rituals of atonement, purification, and adoration. They trusted that God, though silent, was very present in their lives.

Section Eight: Numbers 8:5–26

20. The cleansing and shaving procedures are quite thorough, and the bringing of some animal and grain sacrifices is a *sine qua non* for any important tabernacle or temple ceremony. We should not think of the thorough cleansing of these men as a sign of their personal wickedness, but more as a way to honor God. The laying on of hands by the people is most likely a sign of designation or separation rather than a sacramental or consecrating action in itself. In some way Aaron then gestures to show that these Levites have become a presentation offering, at least by analogy.

21. When the Levites place their hands on the heads of the two bulls, it shows that they are designating or separating the animals for their role in the ritual. Then Aaron offers the first for a sin offering to

seek atonement (or protection) for the Levites, and the second, the whole-burnt offering, is the first rite of adoration in which the new Levites are involved. 8:13 basically repeats 8:11, and 8:15 indicates that the ceremony has been completed. The elements of the ceremony seem fairly simple or plain, but 8:14 reminds us that the Levites, as a presentation offering, now belong to God himself, again at least by analogy.

22. God's proclaiming of his new ownership of the Levites, in place of his ownership of all of Israel's firstborn, human and animal, and his reference to striking down Egypt's firstborn at the time of the exodus, are thundering assertions by an absolute monarch, even if we do not understand why he finds this ownership and history of his rule so important. Next, God regifts (to use a recent term) these Levites to the priests to assist at rituals, thus protecting ordinary Israelites from coming too close to what is holy and dangerous. This regifting is without qualification; the priests, Levites, and the rest of the chosen people are simply to follow all these divine commands. 8:20–23 highlights the obedience God expects and receives at this ceremony.

Section Nine: Numbers 9:1—10:28

23. The request in 9:6–7 is unusual; we would not expect any of Moses' people to disagree with the ineligibility rules regarding contact with a corpse. Taboos about grave, bone, and corpse are deep seated in many biblical books.

    Further, Passover, while a major holy day, is not the single feast that defines active Jewish identity in and of itself. Over several centuries it eventually became the most family-oriented annual sharing in the faith, and perhaps this request reflects that popularity. In 9:8 the note that Moses had to ask God for the answer is a literary device that often indicates that later laws are being added to older narratives.

24. In 9:9–14 God's provision for an alternate date for those few ineligible for the regular Passover, or for those on long journeys at the time, might exemplify his flexibility, and the growing importance of

Answers

this feast as time went by. There are no accounts of other holy days needing alternate dates.

25. The basis of Jewish spirituality and worship is uniformity in practice rather than uniformity in carefully defined doctrines. So resident aliens and their families (the men having been circumcised) were welcome, but not obligated, to share in these formative monotheistic (or at least henotheistic) liturgies, especially when they were held in homes. There was much less leeway about temple attendance. Even in New Testament times some Gentiles freely attended synagogues in Israel and lived by much of the Jewish moral code.

26. By its wooden and repetitious style, 9:15–23 praises the absolute obedience on the part of everyone, including Moses, to God's sovereign and unexplained will. The flame and cloud are used directly by God to exercise (or even enhance) his authority. We assume that the various breakings of camp and journeys were for everyone's protection as well as for their spiritual good. The reference in 9:23 to Moses' co-leadership does not apply to this immediate paragraph about the flame and cloud.

27. The odd part of this passage is not that trumpets were used in the wilderness period, but that the authors make such importance of them. Priests are supposed to be the trumpeters, and this is called a *perpetual institution* or *ordnance (huqat olam)* for all generations. Trumpets sounded in wartime would cause the people *to be remembered before the LORD your God* and to be *saved* by him. Trumpets played on holy days and at sacrifices shall *serve as a reminder on your behalf before [the LORD] your God*. The verb *to be remembered* and the noun *reminder* are from the same root, *zcr*. This is one of the most important words in biblical Hebrew, and is used extensively to explain how God interacts with us, and we with him. The rousing ending *I am the LORD your God* makes the rules about trumpets sound almost as important as the Ten Commandments!

The trumpets are also a good image of our corporate relationship to God. An individual can pray or beg for help in an emergency without such instruments. But a large crowd needs the loud blares of trumpets just to know what everyone is supposed to be doing. So too with the pillar of fire and cloud spoken of in the previous answer. The multitudes did not follow mystical promptings as they went across the desert for decades; they followed the gifts of light and smoke and sound that were available to everyone.

Section Ten: Numbers 10:29—11:35

28. This friendly request from Moses reminds us of the scene in Exod 18, where his father-in-law was very supportive and gave practical advice to help Moses appoint minor judges as assistants. Here in Num 10 Moses values his father-in-law's knowledge of the wilderness, and wants him to be a guide and scout. Two points are being made in all this. Some non-Israelites, such as this Midianite family or clan, were not hostile. They were helpful at times, and could even become allies or "naturalized citizens," to use a modern term. We will come back to other cases in which other Midianites are foes of Israel.

    Secondly, the stories show that God can work through whomever he wishes. Moses and Aaron do not have all the answers; they are not perfect in every way. We can say the same about the chosen people, and about ourselves.

29. The first two verses, 10:33–34, describe the first move of the whole camp after Sinai. The pillar of cloud and fire indicate the LORD's presence, and there is no mention of anyone else witnessing this group on their wandering pilgrimage or migration.

    The two ancient poetic anthems used by Moses in 10:35–36 are clearly prayers used in time of war, when the ark was near the battle lines rather than safely in repose in the camp.

    Editors had no trouble combining the two passages; all the verses add to the solemnity. Levine suggests that, by position, the first two verses make the battle anthems less striking, and more like liturgical hymns.

30. The complaints must be very sinful in nature, deliberate attacks on the covenant promise to rely on one God alone. If the crying out of the people to Moses is at all mindful of the covenant, then his prayer for them can be effective and move God to forgiveness. We wonder about the sincerity of people who complain not once or twice but ten times. But we should remember that perhaps a parallel

Answers

is being drawn with the Egyptians, who would not give in during ten plagues. Highlighting the complaints also highlights the number of times God sent down stern punishments. He and his people are locked into a relationship that seems unworkable at times.

31. The details in 11:1–2 are skeletal at best. In 11:4–10 the complaining is clearly identified as contempt for the manna, and nostalgia for the plentiful diet they had in Egypt. The very itemizing of vegetables and fish and the description of processing manna into something less tangy, like polenta or tofu (this is a wild guess on my part), contribute to the believable emotions of the scene. God is again angry at this sinful spurning of their covenant fidelity to him.

    One other difference between the two accounts is that Moses was asked to intercede in 11:2, whereas in 11:10 Moses is a witness, but he speaks to God first about his own discouragement and weariness as leader and spokesman.

32. Moses feels overwhelmed with the burden of leadership. Many other biblical passages underline his worries about this. Clearly he wants more support from God, or less blame to be laid upon him by the people. He cannot imagine how to provide alternatives to the manna, even if God gave them permission for a break from it. Levine argues from the Hebrew grammar, especially in 11:15, that Moses is respectful of God during this entire speech, but the heartfelt agony of many of the dramatic phrases should impress any reader and remind us of what it must have been like for Moses to have the buck constantly stopping with him.

33. We can assume that in addition to judging small cases these elders would field some of the complaints or disputes among the people. Perhaps they could serve as a council of advisers for Moses. They have no more ability than Moses to provide any alternative for the manna, and that topic is not mentioned here. Given that their spiritual power was derived from that of Moses, we should assume that their purpose is to assist him and the people.

34. This speech starts out with details of the vast amount of meat that will be coming soon. The *weeping* or *wailing* (*bch*) of 11:4, 10 is also mentioned in 11:18, 20. God is fully determined to carry out this punishment; he announces it beforehand, but is not negotiating.

Answers

In many of the speeches to Pharaoh in the early chapters of Exodus, a similar absolute style is found. Look at Exod 9:13–19 or 10:4–6 as examples.

35. Moses may still be caught up in his own anxieties, as seen in 11:11–15. The two verses may also indicate that he does not know that the meat is going to be part of a punishment rather than a blessing.

    God's reply is cryptic, focusing on his own power but not mentioning his intentions. The *word that will come true* is likely the grim image of 11:20.

36. In this story we do not know why Eldad and Medad remained behind, even though we assume they were among the seventy chosen. The anxiety of some of Moses' followers about these two men is unexplained; perhaps the followers were being protective of Moses. His amusement about their prophesying or preaching is capable of two interpretations. He may have welcomed it, or he may have felt that their work would be to no avail, just as his own.

37. We can only assume that the people were anchored in their sinful violation of the covenant, despite the efforts of Moses and the newly empowered elders and despite the sudden supply of quail. Look back at question 34. The chosen people here are no more cooperative than were Pharaoh and the ruling classes of Egypt at the time of the plagues.

Section Eleven: Numbers 12:1–16

38. The disapproval of this marriage seems to have been just a stepping stone or straw man to lead to the more important struggle by Aaron and Miriam for equal status with Moses. The emotional dissatisfaction over the manna in Num 11 was more clearly outlined than the problem with this marriage.

    Aaron and Miriam either resent Moses' absolute authority or feel that they should have equal responsibility or merit for their roles. The dispute is serious, and God moves immediately to chastise them and to reconfirm Moses' unique role.

Answers

39. God's speech to Aaron and Miriam is not an example of pastoral counseling. The two of them are simply reminded of the inestimably unique role of Moses, and of God's great displeasure at anyone questioning this arrangement. The most important seers or prophets or messengers God may choose will not come close to having the influence with God that Moses has as leader, judge, and lawgiver.

    The speech is dramatic; at the end of 12:8 there is a double phrase, "Why then were you not afraid to speak *against* my servant, *against* Moses?"

40. The only logical reason why Aaron does not get a similar skin discoloration is because of his priestly duties, not because of his lesser guilt. Any priest with a skin blemish could not perform ceremonies. This was the custom until 70 CE.

    We can say that the punishment fits the crime. The skin discoloration and the seven days in quarantine sent a message to everyone who might have been party to the original discontent. Grousing about Moses is grousing about God, their covenant partner. Aaron and Miriam most likely had followers, such as those who complained in the various murmuring stories heretofore. Aaron and Miriam may represent many in the community; thus the whole camp must wait the seven days for her atonement.

    We are again reminded that the years of wandering took their emotional toll on everyone, even Moses' siblings. Non-Israelite peoples were not the only enemies on the scene. The Israelites who murmured at so many points were bringing equally devastating damage to themselves and to their covenant.

Section Twelve: Numbers 13:1—14:45

41. Favorable (perhaps idealistic) traditions about the Israelite tribal system pervade biblical accounts up to the time of King David. This team of scouts will have to report back on important military details. Moses must have taken care to choose a respected, competent representative from each tribe to promote unity among them all. However he made his choices, there seemed to be no divisiveness in the outcome. Later, of course, Caleb and Joshua proved to be of stronger faith than the other ten.

Answers

42. The style is detailed, but neutral. The instructions from Moses lead us to believe that he and his people had no other information beforehand. The account mentions the city of Hebron, and the names of three Amalekite leaders or cities, without any further explanation. The mention of the grape cluster and other fruit seems to be a good sign.

43. As the scouts continue to describe what they saw, their words become much less neutral in style. They think the Canaanites are strong, living in large, well-fortified towns. Anakites are mentioned, as well as several other ethnic groups who dwelt in the desert, mountain, and coastal regions. Some of these groups were in fact opponents of David in later eras.

    By 13:30 the people are upset; Caleb intervenes to argue for a quick invasion. The scouts are convinced that the people dwelling there could easily defend themselves. The final verse mentions Nephilim and Anakites of gigantic stature. The image of grasshoppers indicates the low morale of most of the scouts at this point.

    The comment from P in 13:32 identifies the report as a sinfully unfair and unfavorable one. The remark that the land *devours its inhabitants* seems odd. I mentioned in the Introduction that the sense could be related to a genre of curses, but perhaps it points to limited natural resources for the natives or for invaders. Given all the other images of the strength, prosperity and invulnerability of Canaan, this one saying could be seen as advancing Priestly concerns about their lack of trust in God.

44. In this passage the bonds between the people on the one hand, and God and Moses on the other, have fallen like a house of cards. The people are ready to walk away, retrace their steps, and go crawling back to Egyptian rule. Moses and Aaron remain loyal to God, and Caleb and Joshua plead for the people to trust God, and not to rebel against him, not to cut and run. According to Caleb and Joshua the land is fertile and the Canaanites will be easy prey; they are people who have lost the protection of their own gods. These claims had no effect on the people. God intervenes immediately at this complete breakdown in trust and courage.

45. God rightly feels betrayed, and even when he forgives in v. 20 he plans for this generation to live out their lives on this wilderness

journey, and for the next generation to actually enter the Promised Land. This rebellious older generation will expiate for their sins by a lifetime of reliance on God, Moses, and manna.

46. Moses pulls out all the stops, as he had in Exod 32–34. He invokes public relations in the pagan world, and the quote of God himself from Exod 34 about being slow to anger and forgiving. Moses indicates that God's forgiveness of the recent murmurings is part of his greatness, and begs for him to be great one more time.

    He paints a picture, a worst-case scenario, of Egyptians and other non-believers already knowing how the covenant between God and his people has had its ups and downs. If God slays his own people now, everyone would take it as a sign of God's inability to complete the exodus task (Num 14:16). Moses is sure no one would understand God's feeling of betrayal; no one would pay the slightest attention to his right to avenge a broken covenant, a covenant freely chosen to the death. Instead, everyone would immediately conclude that God's only real power was to be able to slay his own. Even the verb for *slaughter* (*shht*) in 14:16 is mostly used for animals. The logic of 14:13–16 is a public relations argument, pure and simple.

    Then Moses puts his best card on the table, the great saying of Exod 34:6–7 (also in brief in Exod 20:5–6). Moses does not only recall the saying about God's patience; he takes patience as the best way for God to use his power. In Num 14:17 Moses says *and now let the power [ch] of my lord be great, as you have spoken when you said . . .* This is the same *power* (*ch*) mentioned in 14:13 (translated as *might* in NRSV), the power to bring them out of Egypt. This is a new public relations argument; God could thus be seen by all the world as one who forgives abundantly.

47. Here God issues stern decrees of punishment for sin, not inviting Moses into any dialog. In 14:28 God admits that he will pay them back for things they had said, perhaps a reference to 14:3. The mention of the little ones being called *booty* in 14:31 also refers back to 14:3. Joshua is mentioned in 14:30, whereas he had not been mentioned with Caleb in 14:24.

    The ones who will not get to the Promised Land are the ones twenty years or older as of the census. This precision is a sure indicator of Priestly detail. So is equating the forty days for the scouting mission and the forty years of exile to cover the age span of the older generation. The death of the ten unworthy scouts is by God's hand, in a typically blunt Priestly style.

The whole passage of 14:26–38 is much more damning than the original scene in 14:20–25. To talk of people who will not enter the Promised Land, and then to advise them to go up by the safer Red Sea route (14:25), is not as stark as thrice mentioning dead bodies falling in the wilderness or showing God striking down the unworthy scouts, except for Caleb and Joshua, who *remained alive* (14:38).

48. As the people react too late to Joshua and Caleb's plea of 14:7–9, they can be seen by Moses (and by us) as attempting to evade the expiation due for their rebelliousness.

    Through the whole two chapters the people and the scouts in question have shared their anxieties and their erratic responses toward their leaders and their God. Whatever the actual history of early Israelite probes into Canaan, the delays and failures are now portrayed as matters of sin, forgiveness, and expiation. Even a scouting mission such as this was a test of faith.

Section Thirteen: Numbers 15:1–41

49. The stock phrase about pleasing odors may add some more solemnity to an already solemn passage. The use of the phrase does indicate that it is God's will that such sacrifices take place. Any human initiative in designing or modifying rites is left out of the picture.

    It is probable that most of the resident aliens were not Jewish, but they were permitted to participate at these ceremonies if they wished. They were not allowed to publicly celebrate any polytheistic ceremonies of their own.

50. The first two classes of failings—by the nation and by individuals—seem to involve either obligations omitted or actions committed in sincere ignorance, perhaps fine points (or confusing points) of civil law or religious ritual. At some point an observer would have had to come forth to point out the specific fine point or matter of ignorance. The passage provides for atoning sacrifices, and assures that God will forgive in such cases.

The last class—individuals who intentionally violate a well-known commandment—are to be shunned for the good of the community.

15:30–31 does not treat of national acts of intentional disobedience, even though we have seen several stories of the people rebelling against God and against Moses during the years of wandering.

51. The Priestly writer clearly takes this as a worst case—a hard violation of a major covenant clause by someone who had been through the great events in Exodus. The stoning by the entire community demonstrates that the man had offended or disgraced the entire community; his hard violation put the community on the spot—they had to defend their covenant bond with God. As is often the case in Priestly traditions, the punishment is depicted as God's direct will, so it serves as an object lesson for future generations.

52. We could consider the regulations about grain offerings, drink offerings, and the first seasonal offering of dough before baking bread to be refinements or expansions of older customs. Levine suggests that the treatment of unintentional failings was, at least in part, another example for adding the grain and drink offerings (15:24).

    The mention of the gatherer of firewood is an example of an individual sinning intentionally (15:30) about the most important part of ritual—the Sabbath. So too the focus on the custom of using blue piping or cord adds a final ritual to a chapter devoted to many of them. The caveat of not following the lust of one's heart and eyes contrasts to the willfulness of the gatherer of the firewood.

    On the other hand, readers troubled by the death penalty for the man gathering firewood will likely find the sudden switch from the act of stoning the man to divine instructions for everyone to use blue cord to be bizarre. How could God be so imperturbable? Sudden jolts such as this remind us to be patient and not to ridicule ancient editors who looked at the world differently. In their thinking, having God relay all these major and minute regulations to Moses is for the good of the entire world in the long run, and the Sabbath is an essential part of how we can know God through respect for the created world.

Answers

Section Fourteen: Numbers 16:1—17:13

53. In these few verses we read about a man named Korah, from the leading Levitical clan, three Reubenites, and 250 other respected men of Israel. We might assume that they came from all the tribes, but that is not made clear. Their complaint is that Moses and Aaron are exalting themselves above everyone else. It is not clear whether this had to do with everyday leadership or religious leadership, although the complainers mention God twice and affirm that God is present to all (by virtue of his presence in the tabernacle). The reason for Moses' falling or lying down is not explained. Readers should assume that this confrontation is the start of a serious incident.

54. The test will be for Korah and all his *company* (*adat*). This is the same word used often by P for the *congregation* or *community* of all Israel, but here Korah's company must be just a fraction of the whole. In 16:7b, 8, 10 Moses speaks of *you Levites* (*you sons of Levi*) and in 16:9–10 he focuses on the Levites as assistants to the priests in the ministries of the tabernacle. They are not satisfied to be assistants; they want to be full priests. Moses seems to ignore the Reubenites and any other non-Levites at this point.

    We might wonder about 16:5–7. At this point, does Moses know that Aaron will be the only survivor of all those who will bring censers to the tent?

55. Dathan and Abiram want an end to the wandering! They blame Moses for not providing better leadership, better food, and actual fields and vineyards for them to settle. Moses is accused of lording it over them, in the manner of an absolute ruler who would even consider putting out their eyes as rebels.

    In reply (to God) Moses denies any embezzling or intent to harm anyone. He would like the wandering to end soon, just like everyone else.

56. Only in 16:16 does the phrase *you and your company* refer to a fraction of all Israel. The point of the question, however, is to note that as God is angry at this fraction in 16:16, so he is equally angry at all Israel in 16:20 (except for Moses and Aaron). After the prayer of

Moses and Aaron in 16:22, God is willing (16:24) to spare all those who immediately back away from the rebels.

57. As in 16:5-6, so here in 16:26, 28-30, we could ask whether Moses knows what will happen next. It would seem so; otherwise the warning in 16:26 would be superfluous, unless we took it as simply him obeying the command of 16:24. The test will be whether the earth will swallow these people alive or not. Pardon my humor in calling this an "open and shut" case.

    But Moses is doing more than simply being an announcer or emcee. He is explaining that these punishments in 16:28-29 are God's will, not his own. In 16:30 Moses affirms again that when the rebels blamed him for the fact that the wandering was not yet finished and that no one had yet settled down, they had in fact *despised the LORD*.

58. While many people apparently backed away for safety in 16:27, the report in 16:34 shows us that they had been close enough to see the earth swallow the rebels, and that they were not completely confident in God's good intentions toward them as non-rebels. Their unease will be seen again in 16:41-42.

59. In recounting many of their ancient miraculous legends such as the flood in Genesis, the plagues in Egypt, the escape at the Red Sea, and the people who died when God sent them great flocks of quail in Num 11, biblical authors downplay much of the debris, much of what we might call the collateral damage. They also ignore any question of even the impression that God was being unfair or unjust. The only correct stance for us is to try to understand what the writers were doing, not what they were ignoring.

    In talking of the reuse of the metal the writers are still fixed on the need for priests and Levites to perform their duties with total loyalty to all the divinely inspired liturgical regulations. Any deviation that could offend God would also disgrace the entire people. The Priestly authors were aware, of course, of the centuries of superstition and clandestine polytheism that Israel experienced, and even times of public expression of their divided loyalties about the LORD.

This is all the more reason to highlight the ideal relationships, the ideal way to honor the one creator and covenant partner, the one reason for being Jewish.

The image of the recast and reworked metal has its own logic. There are memorials in our country made of metal from the buildings destroyed on 9/11, and they are meaningful for us.

60. The *murmuring* (NRSV *rebelling*) of 16:41 is just as sinful as the previous cases, and God again takes personal offense, even if the murmuring was directed at Moses and Aaron.

    But the events now are told at breathtaking speed. God appears in the cloud right away. The contagious plague begins before Moses can give Aaron any instructions. Aaron must carry the censer *quickly* (the same Aaron who was eighty-three years old when he and Moses first met Pharaoh in Exod 7:7). He *ran* to the moving borderline between those already stricken and those not yet stricken. Despite his success in stopping the plague, the toll of the dead was 14,700.

    This nightmare is told in ten verses, start to finish. There are no quotes from the people, aside from their initial accusation, *You have killed the people of the LORD*.

61. Yes, even though the image of one staff miraculously producing almonds, while the other twelve staffs just stayed the same, is much more peaceful than the extravagant showdowns involving earthquake, fire, and pestilence. In 17:5 God wants to stop the continual *murmurings*, and in 17:10 God notes that those who complain against him in spite of this blessing of Aaron's staff *will also die*.

62. The panic and stress in 17:12–13 probably looks back more to chapter 16 with its greater catastrophes. It may be that 17:1–11 was a separate tradition about Aaron simply inserted here by Priestly editors. It is anticlimactic by comparison to chapter 16.

    The people seem demoralized and despondent, but who wouldn't be after such events? God wants everyone to obey him, and to have this long period of camping, moving, receiving laws by the hundreds, and worshipping to be a long period of spiritual growth for everyone. Perhaps that's a tall order.

Section Fifteen: Numbers 18:1–32

63. One might be encouraged that God gave such clear rules, or that he approved of this system of holy days and sacrifices, and the unity that these ceremonies can and did foster among the chosen people.

    Some of the style is monarchical—warnings against offenses, against Levites trying to do the work of priests, or non-Levites trying to come too close to the sacred areas. The stern mentions of *death* and *wrath* in 18:3, 5, 7 are equally dour, raising the question of the image of a touchy or finicky God.

    But we must not confuse style with substance. God is locked into a covenant freely made with free partners. He designed every inch of the tabernacle, and all its purposes. He needs the mercy seat over the ark within the privacy of the holy of holies, the inner room, within the cloud of glory, to protect us from overwhelming contact with him. So we should think of a generous, loving God, even if his ruling style is given to much detail.

64. God seems to be generous and concerned for the support of these priests and their families. They receive meat from many types of sacrifices and other foodstuffs—grain, flour, bread, oil, firstfruits. At other times fees or larger donations may have been distributed or divided among them.

    The purpose of all this is service; they are to support the religious needs of an entire nation by having this one clan inherit priestly obligations. Individuals do not discern a calling to this priesthood—it comes at birth. This clan receives no tribal lands; their service was not compatible with farming or shepherding. But supporting a people in their religious needs is not as easy as it sounds. In the role of a priest one cannot simply send up sacrificial fires and clouds of incense. One must also be a teacher and administrator and, at times, a prophet, critic, or reformer, as needs change.

65. The Levites' tithe to the priests is commanded by God without explanation. In one way, the Levites are being classified as if they belong to other tribes. They have the same obligation of tithes (but not sacrifices) as everyone else. Most commentators note that the priests alone benefit from the Levites' tithe, even if this Levitical donation is a small part of the picture. So this special tax from those

already serving the priests can be said to enhance, or at least acknowledge, the commanding role of the priests in Israel's system of worship.

Section Sixteen: Numbers 19:1–22

66. The reddish color of the young cow (or perhaps a bull) might represent its blood or life force, or it might just be a rare color among the ordinary cattle. Reducing the entire animal to ashes could certainly represent the fact of death. Levine notes that the ashes or dust of humans or animals demonstrates the ultimate biodegradable condition of their mortal being. Sprinkling blood toward the tabernacle might indicate the purpose of the ceremony—to protect the tabernacle from impurity. The unblemished young animal, not bred or yoked for labor, is fit for sacrifice, since only the best should be used in sacrifice. The washing of garments and staying away till evening are simple images of purification and quarantine.

    In ancient folk medicine, one of the methods used was to have like counter like. A substance or symbol or process was used that was thought to be something like the illness in question. Here the ashes of death could be mixed with water and tossed against the uncleanness of death. The purpose was not to restore life, but to restore the barrier or boundary between the living and the dead.

67. One could think of invisible radiation of a gas like radon, or of germs endangering people and open vessels within a house. Outdoors, touching might be the only way to be endangered. The quarantines work as they always do, isolating those already exposed to something so that the community has time to defend itself. The defending comes by faithfully using the special holy water on the third and seventh day. No alternate remedy is considered. Everyone can and should use the mix of water and ashes provided by God's revelation. Should anyone choose not to use it, that person will be held personally responsible for violating the common good.

    While we can think of disease or try to imagine the spiritual equivalent of radon gas, the law is basically religious. We should not simply write it off as a taboo or a silly ancient custom. There is a giant barrier or boundary between the living and the dead, and God's presence in the tabernacle or temple is for the living. In obedience to his will, this sacramental mix of ashes and water is to be used in honor of that barrier.

Section Seventeen: Numbers 20:1–22

68. In JE in Exodus a dispute about water took place near Mt. Horeb (Mt. Sinai). In Num 20 Priestly traditions make the complaints more pointed, and Moses is told to speak to the rock.

    Levine points out that there is a purpose for the two similar accounts of God providing water from rock. The Exod 17 scene is at the beginning of their great journey, before the covenant of Exod 19–24. The Num 20 scene is near the end of the journey. The first one is followed by a battle with Amalekites (Exod 17:8–16), and the second by a battle with Negeb Canaanites (Num 21:1–3). In both cases God clearly supported his people in victories, even though they had whined sinfully.

69. The people start by mentioning that they would rather have died with their kindred. This may point back to Num 17:12–13, which seems to point back to the turmoil of Num 16. How could anyone have wished to have been blasted by the fire that wiped out the 250 men, or to have been swallowed up by the earth, or stricken by the plague that took 14,700 lives?

    Num 20:5 repeats much of 20:4, for dramatic effect, adding the mention of Egypt, and the dearth of figs, vines, and pomegranates. One can easily see how Num 20:5 is a play on Deut 8:7–10, where the riches of the Holy Land are depicted as boundless.

    In recent murmuring scenes God sent various punishments. Here God seems to think only of providing the water, as demanded. Moses' ironic or taunting question in 20:10 might remind one of the irony and anger in God's words in 11:18–20, where he promised to provide meat in great quantities.

70. Perhaps the ironic or argumentative question in 20:10 was prideful and counterproductive, or was meant to accompany other words from God that Moses did not deliver. Another guess is that *striking* the rock was a poor substitute for *commanding* the rock with God's words alone. Some suggest that Moses was supposed to strike

the rock *once*, so striking it *twice* showed a lack of resolve or trust. *Showing the holiness of God* to others takes deep faith and humility.

Of course, these are all guesses. In Deut 3:23–29 Moses describes being told by God that he would not enter the Holy Land, but that account does not mention the incident at Meribah at all. In Deut 3:26 Moses says *the LORD was angry with me on your account*, without any further explanation.

71. Moses is polite throughout. He explains the history of his people in a few verses, and asks for safe passage, with clear promises not to forage or raid or use any grasslands or water without paying. At the first rebuff, Moses repeats the main points, calling the request *a small matter*. The king of Edom simply says no again, without any attempt to go into greater detail or to seek greater reassurances.

    None of the Israelites seem inclined to enter battle here. There is no fervent call to arms as we saw with Caleb in 13:30, or with Caleb and Joshua in 14:7–9. Instead, the people simply move eastward to circumvent the whole territory.

72. Aaron's death may have been witnessed only by Moses and Eleazar, Aaron's son, while the people waited at the foot of this mountain. Eleazar receives and dons Aaron's vestments and inherits the high priesthood before Aaron dies. The two of them, Moses and Eleazar, return to the camp, with Eleazar in his new role. The vestments were an essential in the ordination accounts in Exod 29:1–37 and Lev 8, so putting them on Eleazar makes sense. The thirty days of mourning for Aaron will also be matched by a like period for Moses at his death. Further, before Moses' death he will be succeeded by Joshua.

    In the scene in Num 20 there are no quotations except for God's instructions, no prayer texts, and no fond farewells between two brothers or between father and son. The account is very matter-of-fact, with the main concern on the succession by Eleazar.

Section Eighteen: Numbers 21:1–35

73. As in several of the previous murmurings and punishments readers have to supply elements of understanding. We need to imagine the dysfunctional frame of mind that could drive people to complain about the food once again, after all the previous punishments. We

need to think of their complaint as a direct sin against God that merits such punishments. We have to get past magical notions and see God responding in mercy; looking at the bronze serpent must be a form of prayer, and God spares their lives accordingly. The image of a snake counteracts the venom of the many snakes by the folk medicine principle of like curing like. We saw this same logic in the burning of the red heifer for the special ashes.

Still the death of many by snakebite is troubling. Even if Moses had a team of metalworkers and craftsmen, building the bronze image must have taken some time—at least a day. What about those who died while waiting for the image to be completed? This is the same problem as we faced at the story of an aged Aaron, straining to get to use the censer between the living and the dead. We need to think of Israel in its corporate relationship with God, and not as thousands of rugged individual pioneers. The forty years in the wilderness was not like a Western wagon train trudging through Utah or Wyoming on its way to Oregon.

74. In some cases enemies were destroyed, but in several places it says that the Israelites occupied captured towns and settled down. There is no emphasis on the details of the settlements—how many people stayed in each town or village. The journey story simply keeps on moving to the next event, as though all of the Israelites were still on the way toward the Promised Land.

Section Nineteen: Numbers 22:1–41

75. The belief in the power of cursing might seem unusual, although that was not the case thousands of years ago. What does not make much sense is why Balaam talks only to the LORD, and not to Moabite deities. Balaam is quite confident that he can get in touch with the God of the Israelites, and he follows orders easily when told not to go to Balak. The style of the story is so matter-of-fact that it almost comes to an end in 22:14.

76. One could say that the plot thickens in this paragraph. The key is the contrast in 22:18–19. After clearly repeating the command Balaam, not being Jewish, had received from *the LORD my God*, he gives himself (or God) one more chance to deal with this King Balak. This

one more chance is not logically necessary, but it happens anyway, and God prepares Balaam to say only what he will be told to say.

77. Balaam loses his cool in 22:23–30. He was *enraged* at the donkey and struck it several times. When the animal lay down (22:27) it may have been a deliberate choice, rather than a collapse from the stress of the situation and the beatings. Balaam seems to be totally blind to the possibility of any religious force controlling the moving and the talking of the donkey! In 22:29 he accuses the donkey of *making a fool of him* (*yll*). This is the same harsh verb used in Exod 10:2, where God speaks of *making fools* of the Egyptians. The episode ends with the donkey remonstrating, *Have I been in the habit of treating you this way?* Levine fine-tunes this statement to, *Have I ever before sought to gain an advantage by behaving toward you in such a manner?* All Balaam can say is no.

The whole story is a spoof of Balaam. The donkey's personal remarks and questions in 22:28, 30 make sense, but Balaam's replies make him the bigger jackass. In context, his dealings with the donkey are truly inane.

78. The angel's presence was revealed to Balaam; he did not figure it out on his own. At that point he admits to sinning against or displeasing the angel of the LORD, and offers to return home right away. We are not given any insight into what sin Balaam might have committed; we only know about his ignorance and his anger at the donkey. At this point the angel simply instructs Balaam to continue on the journey, with the same instruction, to say only what he will be told to say.

79. The king seems totally preoccupied with his project of getting curses for his enemies. He busies himself with preparations, and pays no attention whatever to Balaam's honest and accurate remark in 22:38.

Section Twenty: Numbers 23:1–30

80. Apparently a diviner has to be able to see those he is supposed to curse. Balaam orders the various whole-burnt sacrifices, and while we are not told why, it is a fair guess, based on Near Eastern

Answers

customs, that they are to honor the LORD and to call his attention to this event. Should the offerings be accepted and the honored god come near, then the one seeking to bless or curse might have a better chance of receiving divine instructions.

Moving away to a nearby quiet place gave Balaam a chance to search for God's presence. Then he is given the exact words of the oracle, just before he is to pronounce it.

81. Balaam explains his situation in the opening two verses. He has been hired to seek a curse, but feels that the LORD will not allow him to curse under any circumstances. In the last two verses Balaam focuses on the chosen people—how they live alone, are great in number or in the size of their camps, and are upright or courageous. He may admire their human powers more than their religious virtues, and he may be oversimplifying how long they can continue to live alone, but he does seem to be truly impressed by them, rather than just being a mouthpiece for their protecting God.

82. Balak seems to be taken aback by the blessing he has just heard; he acts as though Balaam had never mentioned the constraints upon him. The move to another high place to see part of the Israelite people was an attempt to get some kind of second opinion from Balaam or whatever divine forces he could summon. The most unusual statement from Balak is the question, *What has the LORD said?* It indicates that he paid some attention to Balaam's previous statement in 23:8 about the LORD not denouncing his own people.

83. The second oracle is somewhat longer than the first. Balak is directly addressed in 23:18. Balaam mentions himself only in 23:20. The second oracle focuses on how protected and powerful these people are. They have unqualified approval from their God, and will be able to win offensive or defensive battles. The poem is God-centered and rousing in its praise of God's unity with these people. Balaam stays more in the background, and does not speak of wanting his end to be like theirs, but his words paint a majestic picture of a people destined for success.

84. Balak seems to be getting irrational at this point. He wants an end to curses and blessings (23:25), but then he moves Balaam to a third location, although his hope that it *will please God that you may*

curse them for me there has no logical basis. He may be paying some attention to Balaam's statements about God, but he cannot accept failure for his project.

Section Twenty-One: Numbers 24:1–25

85. From this site Balaam can see all of Israel encamped below. He was empowered in the third oracle with fewer preliminaries. The mention of the *spirit of God* coming upon him is a forceful claim, in the style of the way prophets were empowered. It may indicate that Balaam is entrusted with more responsibilities here.

86. The opening lines seem much more elaborate, as Balaam indicates how he hears the words, and sees the visions, and swoons or falls down. Some verses are quite flowery in style (24:5–7a). Taking 24:8 as a general statement of how Israel will conquer its enemies, the mention of outdoing a known king (Agag of the Amalekites, conquered by Saul) makes 24:7–8 an indicator of future victories, whereas the first two oracles paid more attention to events contemporaneous with Balaam.

87. Balak takes out his frustrations on Balaam, sarcastically blaming the LORD for saving Balak from having to pay Balaam handsome fees.
    Balaam repeats his standard defense that he was only able to say what the LORD enabled him to say. But then he goes on to make a prediction that the Moabites will suffer at the hands of some future leader of these people. Most would suppose, since this prediction was foreboding and unsolicited, that Balaam delivered this in anger.

88. After an elaborate introduction akin to that of the third oracle, Balaam describes a future period of devastation for Moab, Edom, and the region at the hands of the Israelites under a great leader. Even though his prediction could be for something centuries ahead, it offers no comfort for Balak and any others who heard it.

89. The ideal profile of 23:9b, 10b is stirring. How blessed to be an independent people, without need of alliances! Balaam wishes to have such an end for himself. 23:19 is moving, and 23:21 exclaims that *the LORD their God is with them, acclaimed as a king among them.*

24:5–6 paints another idyllic scene of their camping in the wilderness, but the harsh realities of war and victory in 24:7b–8 are also seen as part of God's long-range plans. Finally, the star, the ruler from Jacob's line, will bring greater victories at some distant point (24:17–19).

The irony of all this should not be lost on us. These people who have rebelled numerous times, raging on about shortages of water, too much of manna and not enough leeks, or about who should share in Moses' leadership or Aaron's priesthood, have in no way merited these blessings so majestically outlined by a prominent pagan diviner.

Section Twenty-Two: Numbers 25:1–18

90. In these five verses we are not completely sure that Israelite men are marrying these Moabite women under normal circumstances, nor do we have much idea why they got so enmeshed in serving one or more of the Moabite deities.

    We are not told how many chiefs were guilty of this, nor of the total number of guilty subjects of these chiefs. There are no details of whether or not the executions took place as ordered. The authors may have assumed that their readers could fill in the missing details or read between the lines, as we say. After all, this is not the first description in Numbers of infidelity, rebellion, idolatry, or massive punishments.

91. Zimri and his Midianite partner Cosbi must represent the open attitudes toward intermarriage and the polytheistic practices held by many more people. The whole congregation of Israel had a messy history in these matters, even if they seemed united in their weeping at the moment.

    The couple were from high ranking families, and must have felt safe or justified in acting out their religious devotions in public. They seem to have ignored whatever executions or deaths from plague had already occurred, and also ignored the weeping taking place in the camp. At this point Moses is silent, and so is everyone else. Phineas takes the initiative on his own.

Zimri's impudence in particular stands for the decades of covenant violations by the majority of his fellow Israelites.

92. We may find these stories grim, thinking of this one couple, or the 24,000, or the others who were executed as individuals. But for the Priestly writers all relationships with God are corporate, and God's own wrath against the worship of other gods is intrinsic not only to the covenants freely accepted by all of Israel at Sinai, but intrinsic to God's nature as sole creator. It's all part of God's ongoing struggle against sin and evil. So in this account we might not enjoy the praises laid upon Phineas, but there they are. His action was accepted as atonement for others.

93. The accusations in 25:17–18 are that the Midianites used trickery and deceived the Israelites into worshipping one or more of their gods. Moses will say the same in 31:16. But in the JE account in 25:1–5 the one clear point is that Israel deserves all the blame—they took the Moabite women, they accepted the invitations to worship idols, they yoked themselves to these polytheistic beliefs, and they received the death sentences from God.

Likewise, Zimri *brought* Cosbi *into his family* (25:6). The Hebrew idiom may not refer to a full marriage, but in any case Zimri acts of his own accord, and Phineas will execute him for this. The executions of the leaders and the massive deaths from the plague make more sense if we consider the Israelites responsible for their actions, and not naïve newcomers being bewitched by shrewd and beautiful opponents of *Yahweh*.

Section Twenty-Three: Numbers 26:1–65

94. 26:2 calls for counting able-bodied soldiers, but 26:52–56 suddenly switches to the subject of land distribution. In much of the chapter clans are named, but only the tribal numerical totals are given. The second part of 26:4, at least in the NRSV, seems to refer to the Israelites of the first generation out of Egypt, while the context points to the new, second generation. The mention of the rebellious Reubenites and Levites in 26:8–11 is a side issue, not part of the main theme.

These small points may not seem important, but scholars do note matters like this as they look for patterns in comparing many different biblical texts. It can serve as a reminder for us that biblical authors and editors wrote or assembled traditions centuries after the events they describe, and that their artistry and their theological insights were much different than our own.

95. The image of all the tribes and clans being counted at this crucial point in their journey provides a sense of continuity with the previous generation. Despite all the fights with God resulting in the plagues, fires and raging earthquakes, and all the extra years wearing out the lifespan of the generation not allowed to enter Canaan, somehow the next generation is now ready to move on to its destiny, with God's help.

Modern readers may be uncomfortable with the notion of God and Moses planning for wars of conquest. Perhaps other warring groups from then to now have had the same overconfidence in their ability to find divine powers on their side, but they do not have to read their own ancestors' claims so baldly stated in a sacred book. We need not judge the nationalism of three thousand years ago; we need to judge our own.

Section Twenty-Four: Numbers 27:1–23

96. Working from 27:3, one could lose property permanently because of serious crimes; heirs would lose any claim to the property.

That is not the case here, of course. The daughters of Zelophehad, of the clan of Hepher, would not normally be listed among the *names* in 26:53, 55, since only men had inheritance rights. The permission to inherit in their own names, which they receive in this chapter, will be seriously modified later on in Num 36. Given the quick change in the law between Num 27 and Num 36, Levine takes the ruling in Num 27 to be a stopgap notice in the traditions to justify Manasseh tribal claims to its areas west of the Jordan.

Their plea was that their father's name not *be taken away [gry] from his clan because he had no son*. At this point the daughters may be focusing on their father as an individual more than as a member of a clan. In fact, in clan law the property would have been easily transferred to other male relatives and there would have been little concern for the ending of the line of one man's name. The important thing would be for clan or tribe not to lose any property in the long run.

97. The next few verses, 27:5–11, transform this permission for the daughters into new case law, to use our modern term. If a man dies without sons, *you shall pass on* [*ybr*] *his inheritance to his daughter(s)*. The use of *ybr* to mean *pass on* is so rare that it underscores how new this case is. In the following verses, 27:9–11, the ordinary word *give* is used instead.

    The chain of inheritance, after sons and daughters, goes to brothers of the deceased, then to the brothers of the father of the deceased, or to the next nearest male kin. This same chain can be found in Lev 25:47–49 regarding redemption of property of a relative in bankruptcy.

    We should not overemphasize the rights given to these women. Num 36 shows the weight of tribal tradition about controlling overall title to all tribal lands. There is no focus at this point on marriage laws, arranged marriages, etc. In Num 36:10–12 all five daughters will marry close cousins on their father's side; custom will prevail.

98. Moses seems humble, not argumentative. In Deut 3:23–28 Moses asked for a second chance to be forgiven so that he could cross over, but God declined to do so. On the other hand, in Num 27:15–17 Moses immediately prays for a successor to lead the people. He seems to be thinking of the greater welfare of all the people rather than his own situation.

99. The instructions are matter-of-fact, something like the recipe style of divine regulations for liturgy or law. God has high praise for Joshua, but there is no dynasty being established here. Joshua is not a son of Moses; he will in fact be succeeded by tribal leaders or judges. Joshua will not be the direct ancestor of future monarchs.

    Moses is to lay his hand upon Joshua and *commission* (*zwh*) him before Eleazar and all the congregation. The laying on of hands often symbolizes the transfer of authority or jurisdiction. The gesture is an important part of some Christian ordination ceremonies, as well as in some current rites for installing rabbis.

Joshua is to be made to *stand before* everyone; the Levites were also made to *stand before* Aaron at their ordination in 8:13.

Joshua's many high qualities could lead us to ask why Moses did not take the initiative to nominate him in 27:16–17 rather than ask God to appoint *someone*.

Section Twenty-Five: Numbers 28:1—29:40

100. The style is royal, regal, almost egocentric. There is no explanation of why whole-burnt offerings are pleasing to God. In various ancient Jewish commentaries, priests admitted that their work of sacrificing and burning animals was quite difficult at times, especially when surrounded by heavy smoke and harsh odors. They joked that God's concept of a pleasing odor must be quite different from their own.

101. Carefully marking the new moon of each lunar month helped keep all the people aware of the exact dates for annual ceremonies. It could also have been a way of thanking God for another month of life and protection.

102. Leaven was considered a dangerous substance, even though it was needed for fermentation and baking. Using new stocks of leaven each year was considered less dangerous than simply multiplying the older cultures. The leaven had to be replaced by everyone at the same time, in order to keep the land and the nation in right order. It is an example of corporate discipline for everyone.

    Passover regulations are featured in Exodus and elsewhere, so there was no need to explain those details here.

103. At this point in Numbers the feast is reduced to a mention of what is to be presented to God in adoration. The joy of the harvest and the firstfruits themselves are barely mentioned.

104. The regulations for *Rosh Hashanna* simply call for a doubling of the usual new moon sacrifices. It may be that the start of this month derives it significance more from the coming celebrations of *Yom Kippur* and *Succoth* than from the abstract notion of yearly cosmic cycles.

Answers

105. Taking into account Lev 16; 23:26–32, *Yom Kippur* indicates a very corporate sharing of our sense of sin and disobedience against God. The fasting and offerings of animals in atonement highlight inner dispositions we all need. Modern synagogal *Yom Kippur* services dramatically accentuate the same dispositions.

106. One could be turned off by the cascade of whole-burnt offerings, even though they have not been used since 70 CE, nor will they be reinstituted at any point in the future. Just looking at the lists of animals, it is hard for us to imagine that the week was something much like a state fair and Thanksgiving or harvest festival all rolled into one joyous reunion of families and friends.

Section Twenty-Six: Numbers 30:1–16

107. Women clearly had the right to make religious vows, even though a father or husband was supposed to confirm or disapprove when he was informed. Widows and divorced women did not need any approvals because of their marginal status in family or clan structures. We should also keep in mind that some of the actions promised in these vows would have cost money or goods in kind. Freewill offerings or various sacrifices or alms for the poor were likely to be promised. As we saw earlier, an ascetical vow such as the Nazirite custom could complicate family relationships and involve indirect costs. Nazirites had to provide a special feast at the end of their time of devotion.

    The father or husband probably had the power to confirm or nullify the vows of women because of expenses connected with the vows. The father or husband was obligated to promptly express his decision in each case.

108. The mention of *forgiving* the woman, or of the husband *bearing guilt* by the default of not speaking up promptly, are indications of the seriousness of such vows. Promises to God, freely made, were not simply individual acts of piety. They were meant to enrich the community in some way, and, more importantly, they were considered to be public acts of worship. Failing to honor a vow to God was demeaning to God. This concern to honor vows makes perfect sense

among a people who felt they had received so much in unmerited promises and covenants generously made by God.

Section Twenty-Seven: Numbers 31:1–54

109. The basic story of the battle in Num 31 is very matter-of-fact. There is no explanation of past hostilities, except for the passing reference to Balaam in 31:8. There is also no reference to the 24,000 slain Israelites (25:9) until that plague is mentioned in 31:16.

110. 31:9–12 sounds like the normal aftermath of a great battle between two peoples—dependents are taken captive, booty gathered, and villages burnt that will no longer be needed.

111. Moses alone invokes the harshest of the range of holy war customs, putting the blame on the adult Midianite women for the incident at Peor, even as he admits that the plague sent at that time against the Israelites were merited by themselves. Sparing unmarried daughters was not a humane or merciful gesture; they were forced to marry as they came of age. The young boys were written off as a mere extension of the vanquished Midianite forces.

    There is no concern whatsoever in 31:15–17 to describe or assess the executions or any emotional aftermath of the executions of tens of thousands. The feelings of Israelites or of the 32,000 surviving Midianite daughters are ignored.

    Most modern readers will consider the account (and Moses) as cold-blooded. Levine sees it as an example of the intense hatred for Midianites of later times.

112. The ritual purifications (for Israelites and Midianite survivors) for being in contact with the dead in battle or at the following executions are the sole focus of these verses. The sudden shift to such ritual technicalities cannot help but add to the cold-blooded tone of 31:13–18.

113. In this passage we see the equal division of spoils (including surviving captives or their monetary equivalent) between the soldiers themselves and the rest of the nation. The soldiers are to donate one five-hundredth to Eleazar, for the priests and the support of

Answers

the sanctuary. The rest of the nation is to donate one fiftieth of their share to the Levites (perhaps there were a large number of Levites, or they had greater needs). The enumeration and division of the spoils, including the fractions set aside for priests, Levites and sanctuary support not only cast no doubt on the validity of the battle or on the rightness of the subsequent executions, but in fact assure us of divine approval for all of this.

114. The final passage of Num 31 tells of the very significant free-will offering of the gold booty acquired by all the military commanders. The donation may represent all the gold they gained in this battle, and it seems that all of it was offered to Moses and Eleazar for sanctuary support. This was not another example of the mandated division of spoils and specified donations in the prior section of the chapter. It was an independent gesture in this one case. Nevertheless, it enhances the notion of divine involvement in the entire battle, and gives God praise and honor for protecting the lives of all the Israelite soldiers to the last man.

115. The hostilities of later Midianites were countered by Gideon, of the tribe of Manasseh, in Judg 6–8. The details in Num 25; 31 could well contain exaggerations, even if Deuteronomy lays down stern rules about the treatment of people in wartime. For that matter, the holy war policies in Deuteronomy may represent a puritanical or narrow idealized religious lifestyle that was rarely put into practice. Archaeologists have all the proof they will ever need of widespread Jewish idolatry and syncretism over the centuries down to the end of the Persian Era. No Israelites villages were ever smashed to smithereens for allowing polytheism; many polytheistic shrines went undamaged despite royal reform movements. The ideal scenes in Deuteronomy and elsewhere may indicate the shame of later editors looking back at all the idolatry of the past.

But painting pictures of God sending down violent plagues and epidemics, or of holy wars, where a ruler or priest or a Moses sent by God sets good example by destroying sinful Israelites or hostile Gentiles or a Pharaoh and his vast empire, may not be as effective as simply reporting the polytheism that actually took place.

The stories of the murmurings, the golden calf, and the second covenant in Exod 33–34 can teach us more than a story that describes mass executions of God's enemies, no matter how enticing their polytheistic beliefs or how hostile their intentions toward a ragged band of newcomers protected by a generous but little-known God.

Section Twenty-Eight: Numbers 32:1–42

116. There is a certain amount of clear information provided to readers here. The two tribes have many cattle, and valuable districts east of the Jordan have already been captured. The tribal leaders come to Moses, Eleazar, and the rest of the nation's leaders with their request, and it is couched in polite terms. We have no idea about how many cattle the other tribes own in comparison, but one could imagine that the fewer the tribes that cross the Jordan, the more land would be available for herding and grazing for all concerned.

    Readers might consider the request a reasonable compromise, if they assume that taking over Canaan would be an easy task with God's help. After all, the battle with the Midianites in Num 31 took place without any Israelite casualties at all.

117. Moses throws cold water on the entire request. He focuses on the battles to come, and on the total dedication and obedience needed by every tribe to fight for God's promises—promises made to an entire people. For Moses the request was not a reasonable compromise; it was a sinful act of treason, cowardice, and mistrust of God and his covenant. It could mean disaster for everyone, as great a disaster as the sentence of forty years of wandering in Num 14.

    We could say that Moses was being fair by expressing his thoughts clearly; but it is hard for us to judge the motives of the two tribes. Calling them a brood of sinners who don't care if they discourage and abandon everyone else might be rushing to judgment.

118. The two tribes seem cooperative and sincere in volunteering the needed military service, although they might have seen the practical or political need to meet some of Moses' main objections. In 32:19 they do repeat their strong desire to settle east of the Jordan in the long run.

119. In Moses' response, with the tribes' reply to it, the tone seems more positive, although Moses sternly repeats several conditions and warnings. The tribal leaders of Reuben and Gad respond politely, mentioning their obligations and not putting quite as much emphasis on returning to their territory.

120. The public announcement of the deal struck with Moses seems to pick up the anxieties that Moses had in 32:6–15, and the strong desire the two tribes had to settle to the east of the Jordan. 32:30 puts things in a new light; failure to share the military burden will result in the two tribes having to come with everyone else across the Jordan. While in the Introduction to this chapter I noted that it might have been difficult to enforce this proviso, other commentators take Moses at his word and think that he could have enforced his will if it came to that. 32:30 reminds us that this allocation of territory east of the Jordan was an uneasy compromise right from the beginning.

121. The opening and closing passages focus on real estate. If we were to bracket the intervening verses, there are no traces of the uneasy compromise here at all. Moses gives the Reubenites, the Gadites, and the clan of Machir the towns and territories won by conquest east of the Jordan without comment. Archaeologists have no trouble marking dozens of ancient Israelite settlements east of the Jordan.

Section Twenty-Nine: Num 33:1–56

122. Num 33 can give one a sense of God's providence and protection during the great trek from Egypt to the Plains of Moab. The authors and editors were always looking to see God's work of salvation for everyone within history itself. We have not been reading of saints who merited all this providence; these were timid mice living in Egypt, rescued by God's power. They did not become saints in the wilderness. The incessant moves and encampments were designed to while away forty years to punish the founding generation for their inconstancy.

In Isa 14:24–27 the prophet focused on how God ended the Assyrian Empire. His praises of God can also apply to Num 33.

> The LORD of hosts has sworn: As I have designed, so shall it be; and as I have planned, so shall it come to pass…This is the plan that is planned concerning the whole earth; and this is the hand that is stretched out over all the nations. For the LORD of hosts has planned, and who will annul it? His hand is stretched out, and who will turn it back?

123. In many places in the Old Testament, especially throughout Exodus and Numbers, God is depicted as either very generous or very quick to punish. Modern readers have to contend with gruesome accounts of holy war, or battles in which the enemy is practically demolished while those on the LORD's side suffer few losses. The deportation of conquered populations, or the taking of some of their women for brides, is just as troubling. The various plagues and punishments from God upon the Israelites themselves evoke the same dismay for readers.

    Scholars rightly caution that many of these stories contain exaggerations intrinsic to this or that literary genre, and are driven in part by the theological viewpoints of the time of later editors. Insofar as much of the Pentateuch represents centuries of oral traditions, we must remember that oral traditions need thicker brush strokes; heroes have to be very heroic, sinners very sinful, covenant partners very faithful. The God of Israel has to work very hard to save his very stubborn people, and when he feels demeaned he blows his stack, as would any great king. Without the thicker brush strokes, oral traditions don't last for centuries as these did. So we read God's words in Num 33:55–56, . . . *if you do not drive out the inhabitants of the land . . . I will do to you as I thought to do to them.* We need to think about the dangers of polytheism behind God's words, and not think of God as a demanding and irascible tyrant.

Section Thirty: Numbers 34:1–29

124. This passage depicts God as drawing the map, even if it is much larger than the area the Israelites would later occupy. We need to remember that the Promised Land was essential to the national covenant at Sinai, and it may be harmless for later generations to yearn for the influence King David briefly had over Syria (Aram) as far as the Euphrates.

Historians often remind us of realities glossed over in biblical accounts. Canaan was what we would call the boondocks: a mainly hilly, semi-arid land fit for sheep and goats but not large cattle, and for vineyards and hardy orchard trees. The rich lowlands, more fit for growing grain, were well defended by the Philistines, while the Canaanites in the hills were never well united for their own defense. The conquest of the land took more than a century, despite the cascade of victories touted in Joshua and Judges. Most of the outside world ignored the transition, until King David began to make his mark on the international scene.

125. Much of Exodus and Numbers is given to detail, often overdrawn or idealistic. The details were spelled out by a protective God making long-range plans. The tribal system is central to most of the book of Numbers, and readers probably do not think much about how complex and time consuming would be the conquest of Canaan and the redistribution of its land.

An image I use is that assigning tribal leaders for allotting lands in Num 34 is something like hiring an interior decorator for a new home long before one buys land or gets a building permit.

Section Thirty-One: Numbers 35:1–34

126. Commentators are of the opinion that most priests had a higher standard of living than Levites, perhaps through social and leadership connections. In Num 35 we read of the forty-eight towns set aside for Levites, and we assume that with their gardens and farm animals they supplemented their income from service at the temple. We have no information as to how Levites were assigned to the different towns, but those living further away from the temple would have had to have their service schedules adjusted accordingly. The reference to six of these towns serving as towns of refuge may indicate that Levites supervised this system of protecting those fleeing from avengers.

127. The towns of refuge are meant to provide temporary asylum from an avenger until a proper hearing can be held before the congregation (representing the town where the death occurred). If the one who caused a death was found not guilty of murder, he still had

to return to the town of refuge and remain there till the point of amnesty, when the current high priest died. So one guilty of manslaughter had to explain his case convincingly, and spend some time away from the scene of the death. Perhaps these tactics and delays would give the avenger and his clan time to accept their loss with honor.

128. Here the editors reaffirm that a convicted murderer cannot be left unpunished. Anyone who inflicts lethal injuries using a weapon or tool made of metal, stone, or wood is assumed to have had clear intent to do harm. Likewise, hatred for someone to which others can attest, or lying in ambush, also give evidence of clear intent. If standing hatred or enmity can be proved, then causing a death by hands alone, without weapons or tools, is another form of murder and can be judged for that.

129. In 35:22–29 we return to the cases where a slayer may have acted rashly or negligently, with what we could call diminished intent. Judges at a hearing could absolve the slayer from murder. Even so the slayer is not free to return home till the time of amnesty. As a reminder that the slayer must not return home early, the avenger is given permission to execute him if he strays from the town of refuge. It is an odd picture of compromise; a slayer not guilty of murder is confined for an indefinite period, with punishment for murder waiting for him if he breaks from confinement. The compromise may have been the best that society could devise under the circumstances. Aside from the brief examples, Num 35 does not explain at length how judges can cut through false accusations or false denials. How can one tell whether someone acted only in the heat of a moment, or whether close relatives have lost all objectivity over the wrongful death of a loved one? No wonder mention is made in Deut 17:8–9 that very complex cases should be brought to Jerusalem for review and final decision.

130. The final verses remind all of us that any murder affects all of society. Failure to prevent the crime or its causes, or failure to prosecute the guilty, lessens the holiness of everyone in important ways. Cases of manslaughter must also be handled in fair and consistent ways; the anguish of loved ones cannot be ignored.

Section Thirty-Two: Numbers 36:1–13

131. The request by the leaders is polite and matter-of-fact in style. The decision is also easily made. The opening phrase of 36:6, *let them marry whom they think best*, might seem more broad than its context. The Hebrew says *become wives according to what is good in your eyes*. The same yielding phrase *according to what is good in your eyes* appears in Gen 18:6, where Abraham allows Sarah to treat Hagar *as she wishes*, with unhappy results.

    But in Num 36:6 the condition about marrying within the tribe is immediately added. The key word is *only* in the NRSV; Levine uses *so long as*. These are translations of the Hebrew word *ak*, which forcefully introduces the restriction: *only it must be into a clan of their father's tribe that they are married*.

    The daughters immediately obey the new regulation, without any question. But this is the Priestly style throughout the Pentateuch; in their traditions divine laws are always obeyed promptly and entirely.

BIBLIOGRAPHY

Boyce, Richard Nelson. *Leviticus and Numbers.* Westminster Bible Companion. Louisville: Westminster John Knox, 2008.
Brueggemann, Walter. *Theology of the Old Testament: Testimony, Dispute, Advocacy.* Minneapolis: Fortress, 1997.
Fretheim, Terence E. *Exodus.* Interpretation. Louisville: John Knox, 1991.
Hawk, L. Daniel. *Joshua.* Berit Olam. Collegeville, MN: Liturgical, 2000.
Levine, Baruch A. *Numbers 1–20.* Anchor Bible 4A. New York: Doubleday, 1993.
———. *Numbers 21–36.* Anchor Bible 4B. New York: Doubleday, 2000.
Miller, William T. *The Book of Exodus: Question by Question.* Mahwah, NJ: Paulist, 2009.
———. *The Book of Genesis: Question by Question.* Mahwah, NJ: Paulist, 2006.
Propp, William H. C. *Exodus 1–18.* Anchor Bible 2A. New York: Doubleday, 1999.
———. *Exodus 19–40.* Anchor Bible 2B. New York: Doubleday, 2006.
Raphael, Chaim. *Festival Days: A History of Jewish Celebrations.* New York: Grove Weidenfeld, 1991.
Sanders, E. P. *Judaism: Practice and Belief, 63 BCE–66 CE.* Philadelphia: Trinity, 1992.
Sherwood, Stephen K. *Leviticus, Numbers, Deuteronomy.* Berit Olam. Collegeville, MN: Liturgical, 2002.
Vermes, Geza. *Scripture and Tradition in Judaism.* 2nd ed. Studia post-Biblica 4. Leiden: Brill, 1973.

www.ingramcontent.com/pod-product-compliance
Lightning Source LLC
Chambersburg PA
CBHW071941240426
43669CB00048B/2550